THE DIFFUSION OF RELIGIONS

A Sociological Perspective

Robert L. Montgomery

University Press of America, Inc.
Lanham • New York • London

Copyright © 1996 by
University Press of America,® Inc.
4720 Boston Way
Lanham, Maryland 20706

3 Henrietta Street
London, WC2E 8LU England

All rights reserved
Printed in the United States of America
British Cataloging in Publication Information Available

Library of Congress Cataloging-in-Publication Data

Montgomery, Robert L.
The diffusion of religions : a sociological perspective / Robert L. Montgomery.
p. cm.
1. Religion and sociology. 2. Religions. 3. Culture diffusion. I. Title. BL160.M635 1996   306.6'917--dc20   96-15351 CIP

ISBN 0-7618-0344-0 (cloth: alk. ppr.)
ISBN 0-7618-0345-9 (pbk: alk. ppr.)

∞™ The paper used in this publication meets the minimum requirements of American National Standard for information Sciences—Permanence of Paper for Printed Library Materials, ANSI Z39.48—1984

For my Wife, Polly
my supportive family,

and the Aboriginal People of Taiwan

Contents

Preface	ix
Acknowledgments	xi
Introduction	xiii
A "Demarcationist" Approach	xiii
The Field of Study	xv
Pointers and Gaps in the Studies	xvi
Following the Social Scientific Method	xix
My Respects to Missiologists	xx
A Return to Demarcation as an Aid to Interchange	xxi
1. The Concept of Diffusion in Relation to Religion	1
A Stubborn Concept with a Low Profile	1
The Concept of Diffusion and Its Associates	3
Results from the Study of Diffusion	5
Diffusion and Religion	7
Three Diffusing Religions	13
Variations in the Dependent Variable	14
Conclusion	16
2. A Theoretical Perspective and Methodology	19
Theoretical Considerations	19
Background Variables	
from the Two Sides of Diffusion	19
Macro Level Variables	23
Micro Level Variables	26
Summary Statement	31
The Methodology	32

3. Buddhism 37

    A New Moral Order for a New Set of Rulers 37
    Buddhism of the Old School - Theravada 39
    Mahayana or Elaborated Buddhism 42
    Variations Compared 47
    Discussion 49
    Conclusion 53

4. Christianity Before 1500 57

    Diffusion and Variations in the Mediterranean Basin 57
    Diffusion and Variations to the North 63
    Diffusion and Variations to the South and East 71
    Discussion 74
    Conclusion 76

5. Islam 79

    The Rise of Islam Among the Arabs 79
    The Initial Diffusion of Islam Under the Omayyads 81
    The Dissolution of Arab Power Under the Abbasids 84
    Diffusion to the Turks and Central Asia 87
    Diffusion to the East 88
    Diffusion to Africa 91
    Diffusion to North America 92
    Discussion 93
    Conclusion 96

6. Christianity After 1500, Part I The Societies in Asia 99

    Diffusion to the Middle East 100
    Diffusion to South Asia 101
    Diffusion to Southeast Asia 105
    Diffusion to East Asia 110
    Discussion 117

7. Christianity After 1500, Part II The Societies in Oceana, Africa, and the Americas — 121

- Diffusion to Oceana (including Australia) — 121
- Diffusion to Africa, South of the Sahara — 126
- Diffusion to the Americas — 135
- Discussion — 142
- Conclusion — 147

8. Conclusions and Some Directions for Study — 149

- The Nature of the Findings — 149
- My Unhidden Agenda — 152
- Arguments from the Data — 155
- Additional Support from Recent Case Studies — 160
- Religion and Domination — 161
- Religion and Identity Formation — 166
- Some Directions for Study — 168

Appendix - A Theological Perspective With Missiological Implications — 173

- The Demarcation — 173
- The Three Religions and Human Yearnings — 175
- Seeing God at Work — 177
- Domination and Resistance — 178
- New Identities — 184
- The Sociology of the Knowledge of God — 187
- The Message and the Method — 189

References — 195

Name Index — 209

Subject Index — 215

Preface

The selection of a research topic in the social sciences usually has a normative basis and the normative basis for writing this book comes from my experience as a missionary to Taiwan, where my wife and I served for the Presbyterian Church from 1956 to 1972. Few missionaries have the privilege of working among such responsive people as the aboriginal people of Taiwan. My particular responsibility was among the Amis people, who lived primarily on the east coast of the island, although many moved to the cities in the north and on the western plain.

Unlike the area in which I lived as a child (north Jiangsu Province in China), which was homogeneous ethnically, Taiwan had three major Chinese language groups and some ten aboriginal cultural-linguistic groups. The aboriginal people of Taiwan made me think of my own tribal origins in Europe and of the time when Christianity was first brought to my ancestors. I was also reminded of the aboriginal people of North America, whom my more recent forebears had encountered (often on an unfriendly basis) and who have had a rather different response to the Christian Message from the aboriginal people of Taiwan, as well as from my own tribal ancestors. Also, I could not forget my childhood experiences in China where we were often called "foreign devils," for good historical reasons, and where on the whole, there had not been a large-scale reception of the Christian Message as among the Taiwan aboriginals.

While in Taiwan, I also began to notice patterns of response in various other countries of Asia. In Korea, for example, there was a very positive response to Christianity, but not in the neighboring country of Japan. Also, various minority groups in Southeast Asia had responded as positively as the aboriginals of Taiwan. Adding to my curiosity has been the fact that since we returned from Taiwan in 1972, the response to Christianity on the China mainland has changed remarkably. When visiting China in 1988, we saw the crowded churches and the church in which I was baptized has become much larger than when missionaries were there.

My desire for answers drove me back to school where I entered a program in social scientific studies of religion at Emory University, completing my doctorate in 1976. Beginning before my formal studies, but especially in the two decades since, I have been putting together the theoretical approach presented in this book.

In the Introduction, I will give the background for my approach, including some of the assumptions behind it and the intellectual context in which I am working. In the first chapter I discuss the dependent variable (what I am trying to explain) and in the second chapter, the independent variables (the causal factors I am considering) and the method I will use to examine the data. The following chapters are reviews of historical data with a final chapter to express some conclusions and possible future directions for study.

As can be seen from the language I have just used, this book will seek to employ a sociological approach. However, I add an Appendix with some theological and missiological reflections.

My hope is that this book will add to the conversations among social scientists, missiologists, and others, especially those with field experience. These conversations will make it possible to adjust and elaborate the theoretical perspective of the book. My additional hope is that this book will be a stimulus to the development of a sociology of missions within the sociology of religion and that missiologists will find this subfield a useful augmentation to their interdisciplinary field.

Robert L. Montgomery

Acknowledgments

I want to acknowledge first the aboriginal people of Taiwan for awakening my curiosity about the subject of this book and for their great encouragement in my work among them. I also want to acknowledge the specific encouragement of the Rev. C. M. Kao, then Principal of Yu Shan Theological Institute, a school for training ministers for the aboriginal churches, who later became Executive Secretary of the Taiwan Presbyterian Church.

I also appreciate my home church (then Presbyterian Church U.S. and now the reunited Presbyterian Church U.S.A.) for supporting me during the first part of my graduate program at Emory University. After completing my studies in 1976, I became an "independent scholar" (unattached to academia), but my various work-places encouraged me in my studies. These were the Research Division of the Presbyterian Church U.S.A., the Federation of Protestant Welfare Agencies of New York City and the First Chinese Presbyterian Church of New York City, the last two jobs being concurrent much of the time.

Beginning in 1987, I served as a chaplain at the Seamen's Church Institute of New York and New Jersey, where I enjoyed using my Chinese language and, even occasionally, my Amis language. The Seamen's Church Institute provided numerous opportunities to continue my study interests. Since my retirement in the fall of 1994, I have been able to concentrate on my studies.

Finally, I want to acknowledge the interested support of my family and friends, some of the latter being in the sociology of religion field. I especially want to acknowledge the help of my wife, Polly H. Montgomery in doing much detailed work to prepare the text for publishing.

Introduction

A "Demarcationist" Approach

Since this is a study of religions, about which most people have strong views, it is important to state how I intend to approach the subject matter. I am what Donald Wiebe (1994) has called a "demarcationist." For me, this means that it is useful to distinguish as clearly as possible between a social scientific approach and a normative approach. I am obviously not a positivist in philosophy (are there any left?), but I believe in the value of a consciously applied positivistic methodology. Just because some people make a religion out of science should not cause the rest of us to reject it as a useful tool, albeit with built-in limitations, for gaining knowledge.

I do not hide the fact that I have been trained in theology and, in fact, have served as a Christian missionary and am a Presbyterian minister. However, I believe that social scientists on the one hand and theologians and other scholars in the humanities on the other hand need to be protected from each other! That is, the social sciences and theology represent distinct fields of knowledge, having distinctive methodologies, and these differences need to be respected and guarded.

I realize that maintaining the distinction is not a simple matter and that the humanities in general, to which theology belongs, share much of the same subject matter with the social sciences, namely human behavior. Truth is one and as humans we seek to unite our knowledge, but our perception will always be partial and there are different disciplines to guide our approaches to knowledge. In this regard, I believe that it is both possible and helpful to develop a consciousness of movement back and forth between normative and non-normative approaches. It is useful, therefore, to specify this movement in order that we may communicate knowledge between disciplines, particularly, that people may know how to evaluate what is communicated. The fact is, my theology (a central part of my normatively based views) supports the attempt to preserve the integrity of the scientific approach.

In short, I will be attempting to avoid a normative approach in my examination of the subject of the book. I do not deny, of course, a normative interest in the subject (as explained in the Preface.) A major practical difficulty is that the subject matter, human behavior, which the social sciences share with the humanities, is not so easy to examine in as controlled and systematic a fashion as the natural sciences examine nature. Nevertheless, my goal is to make this book a social scientific examination of the diffusion or spread of certain world religions.

As stated, my view is that a scientific approach is supported by certain theological views of human nature, the most important one being that human beings inevitably have a partial, distorted, or biased perspective. "Bias" is an everyday word in English, but has become a technical term in science, one of the main goals of the scientific method being to control for bias.

I say something more in the Appendix about the theological basis for demarcation between a scientific approach and other approaches, particularly those that are basically normative or based on beliefs. I have also set forth a background for my views regarding a theological basis for the social sciences some time ago in an article, "Bias in Interpreting Social Facts, Is It a Sin?" (Montgomery 1984) and I am seeking publication for a paper on "The Biblical Ethic and the Spirit of Science," which gives further background of my view of the theological support for the scientific approach. However, whatever may be accepted as a theological argument for the support (including protection) and use of the social sciences, the social sciences have no obligation towards theology, other than to include it in a sociology of knowledge. It is theology, and religion in general, that must come to terms with the social sciences, not the other way around. In this sense, theology (and philosophy) must be a more comprehensive discipline than science and include all knowledge in its vision, whereas the social sciences must limit themselves to what can be demonstrated empirically.

The Field of Study

It was important for me to see what light the social sciences, apart from any theological views, could bring to understanding the wide variations in responses to outside religions. In the field, I started reading in anthropology, but in academia I shifted to sociology as more consciously reaching for explanation (theory) than anthropology. However, I retain my appreciation for anthropology and regard the fields as largely overlapping. Over the years, I have put together the theoretical approach that will be presented, which I regard as open-ended. I have published preliminary articles (Montgomery 1986 and 1991) and also consider this book as exploratory. A major purpose for this book is to expose its views to critical review, revision, and elaboration. I am primarily addressing social scientists, in particular, sociologists of religion, but the subject should also be of interest to social scientists who are interested in socio-cultural change. Although not strictly a social scientific field, missiology, as an interdisciplinary field, incorporates (increasingly) the social sciences. Also, many missionaries and other field workers have more than a nodding acquaintance with the social sciences and I hope that they will react to the book.

I see the subject of this book as being in a sub-field of the sociology of religion, which may be termed "sociology of missions." This is a relatively neglected area within the sociology of religion, in spite of the effort of David Heise (1967) and others to stimulate its development. Since "mission" is a religious term such as "church," it may be that the "sociology of missions" is not an appropriate term. "Sociology of the diffusion of religions" is a little awkward, but has the advantage of using the term "diffusion," which dates from the 19th century in the social sciences. Perhaps the subject of this book will find a place in the studies of conversion or of globalization. In the end, the use of the term "sociology of missions" is not that important. My basic concern is that the spread or diffusion of religions might receive the attention of social scientists and that those already interested in the spread of religions, such as missiologists and field workers might add the sociological perspective in their use of the social sciences. Some missiologists have made much use of anthropology (are anthropologists), but the sociological perspective has been less used.

Pointers and Gaps in the Studies

As will be seen in the first chapter, diffusion studies have an important place in the social sciences and there has been a convergence of various research traditions, as Everett Rogers has shown (1962, 1971 with F. Floyd Shoemaker, 1983, 1995). (See also Katz, Hamilton, and Levin 1963 and Perry 1992). However, religion and even ideology have received little attention in sociological studies of diffusion. On the other hand, religious studies, even those concentrating on missions, have made little use of the concept of diffusion.

Social and religious movements have received much attention, but social scientists have rarely considered how or why these movements may be part of the diffusion of a religion or ideology. Globalization is now attracting great interest without much attention being given to how the diffusion of religions has been part of the process. Roland Robertson and Chirico (1985), Robertson (1985, 1987), and Peter Beyer (1994) have analyzed the relationship between religion and the developing global system, but the diffusion of religions in particular has not been part of that analysis.

Mission work is given attention in several articles in *World Order and Religion*, edited by Wade Clark Roof (1991), especially in the articles by A.F. Walls, Lamin Sanneh, and Michael A. Burdick and Phillip E. Hammond, but this is quite rare in sociological literature and the first two writers are missiologists. Jon Miller's (1994) study of a missionary society is certainly an important contribution to a sociology of missions, but its focus is on the sending side rather than the receiving side of missions, the latter being the focus of this book.

An important book for the sociology of missions is David Martin's (1990) study of the spread of the Pentecostal version of Christianity, especially in Latin America. He places this development in a worldwide and historical context. However, what needs to be done and has not been done extensively is to examine the spread of all the versions of Christianity, as well as of other religions on a comparative basis.

Introduction							xvii

A work that is clearly in the field of sociology of missions and looks at the receiving end of diffusion is that of Rodney Stark (1995) on early Christianity. In fact, he (1995,229) has been working "during the past few years...to reconstruct the rise of Christianity," focusing most recently on the role of women. I believe this is the kind of research which is very much needed on the diffusion of Christianity and other religions, but not only on the time of their origins. Study is also needed of the numerous variations in responses from beginnings to the present.

Of course, sociologists of religion have made careful studies of church membership changes, primarily in North America, a classic being *Understanding Church Growth and Decline: 1950-1978* (Hoge and Roozen 1979.) A sociology of missions must take account of these studies because many variables will apply in cross-national studies, but missions is a special type of religious growth involving acceptance (or rejection) of religions introduced from outside the group or society. Therefore, cross-national or at least intergroup relations will be of central concern.

Because of religious pluralism in modern societies, the examination of the various world religions (as opposed to simply religious movements and cults) from a sociological perspective is receiving increasing attention. Richard Wayne Lee (1992) considered "Christianity and Other Religions: Interreligious Relations in a Shrinking World." The International Sociological Association published papers from its 1993 Conference, *"Religions Sans Frontieres?" Present and Future Trends of Migration, Culture, and Communication* (Cipriani 1993).

Of special importance for the study of religions around the world, including their missions, is the fact that studies of religious involvement may now be extended to numerous countries (Campbell and Curtis 1994). N.J. Demerath (1994), in an address before the Religious Research Association, discussed "a current project to investigate religion, politics, and the state in more than a dozen countries." Lester R. Kurtz (1995) has written *Gods in the Global Village, The World's Religions in Sociological Perspective* in which his special concern is to address the problems of multiculturalism and religious and social conflict.

"Comparative religion" from a sociological perspective clearly has application to a sociology of missions. Also, how missions are faring in religiously pluralistic societies is an important question for study. However, mission activity and response to it is one aspect of religions that needs special attention. As important as understanding, tolerance, and interreligious dialogue are in the contemporary world and as unpleasant as mission activity (often called "proselytism") may be to many, mission activity has been and will continue to be an important activity for major religious bodies, not just fringe groups. Either way (main bodies or fringe groups) it would deserve study, but the fact is, mission activity remains a highly organized and well funded activity and, apart from the size of the activity, the size of the impact is considerable. It is the latter that is the focus of this book..

The field of anthropology has contributed considerably more to the social scientific study of missions than has sociology or its sub-field, sociology of religion. An important contribution was made by Margaret Mead's (1975) *New Lives for Old*. An excellent recent example of this contribution is found in *Conversion to Christianity*, edited by Robert W. Hefner (1993). I found Hefner's discussion of world religions very helpful and I used the cases presented in this book as a check against my broad historical reviews. Although the traditions of study are different in anthropology and sociology, a sociology of missions must make great use of the results of anthropological studies. The overlap will be large, but nevertheless a sociological approach will often contain a thrust towards theoretical explanation that is not found to the same extent in anthropological studies.

As noted above, the major attention in mission studies has been on the mission effort rather than the response to that effort. This is not only because of the size and drama of the mission activity, but because the recent missionary outreach came primarily from the West where so many studies have been carried out. Relatively little attention has been given to the perception and reception of the targets of mission, of whom some were strongly resistant, some receptive (sometimes after periods of resistance), and some mixed in their reception and resistance. As noted above, a major purpose of this book is to contribute to the shift of attention from mission activity to those affected by this effort. The work of Lamin Sanneh (1991a, 1991b, 1993), a missiologist, and David Martin (1990), a sociologist, are evidence that a shift may be underway. David Barrett's (1982) monumental *World Chris-

tian Encyclopedia has also helped to draw attention to what has happened in the lands to which Christian missionaries were sent.

Following the Social Scientific Model

Perhaps the most difficult distinction that I seek to make in the book is between the social sciences and history, the distinction between the social sciences and theology being rather clear. Probably, in principle, there need be no distinction between an historical and a social scientific study. The data that I use are historical data from secondary sources, and historians and area specialists will be free to criticize and evaluate them. The line between the social sciences and historical studies is often quite vague and in some cases may not even exist. However, the use of historical data for the social sciences is always problematical. Controls over the data are more difficult to apply than over currently collected data and are therefore more simulated than actual. Basically, the social sciences are driven by theory rather than by description, which to historians may often seem pretentious and premature. However, in spite of the difficulties, there is a strong tradition of social scientific studies of historical data. The works of Frederick Teggart (1916, 1918, 1925, [1939] 1969), as well as the better known Max Weber (for example, *The Protestant Ethic and the Spirit of Capitalism*, [1904-05] 1976) provide good examples of the use of historical data for the development of theory.

Although my study is exploratory, I will follow a social scientific model for examining data. In social scientific fashion, I will begin by setting forth as clearly as possible what I am attempting to demonstrate and how I intend to do it. Historians, in addition to undertaking thorough descriptions (much more thorough than mine), also undertake explanations for change over time. These explanations are most likely to involve multiple factors and consist of extended lists of reasons, usually set forth in a concluding discussion. The social scientific approach tends to be parsimonious, in which a few of the most important factors affecting general classes of events are isolated (Babbie 1986, 54). Furthermore, the expectations (the theoretical relationships) regarding these factors are often stated first (the hypothesis) and then tested in some fashion. Although my approach is somewhat formal, I am not claiming that I am "testing an hypothesis," but rather exploring the usefulness of a particular perspective. Perhaps that is all that can be done with such a wide range of historical data. The "class of events" I am looking at will be discussed in the first chapter, along with the conceptual tools to be used. The second chapter presents the theoretical statement and a brief description of the straightforward method to be used in looking at the data.

My Respects to Missiologists

Finally, it is important to say something about the field of missiology. Missiology is essentially a theological field and I am glad to attempt to wear the missiological hat when needed, although in this book I am consciously *not* doing so, except in the Appendix. This does not mean that I do not wish to communicate with missiologists and I hope that this book may be of use to them.

I am deeply indebted to missiologists. Many in this interdisciplinary field are historians and I have employed their studies, particularly those of Kenneth Scott Latourette (1937, 1938, 1939, 1943, 1944, 1945, 1953, 1956) and Lamin Sanneh (1991a, 1991b), both of Yale Divinity School, but from different eras, Lamin Sanneh being currently the Professor of Missions and World Christianity. Also, the data from David Barrett's (1982) *World Christian Encyclopedia* were extremely useful to me.

Jan A.B. Jongoneel (1995) has written in his *A Missiological Encyclopedia* of the attempt to approach the study of missions scientifically. Although not clearly identified as a special field by others, Jongoneel, with his European perspective, distinguishes a "sociology of missions." For Jongoneel, James S. Dennis (1842-1914) may be considered the founding father of the sociology of missions. In the nineteenth and early twentieth century, many theologians saw a connection between missions and social progress and saw sociology as a discipline to clarify the connection. Archibald G. Baker (1934) wrote *Christian Missions and a New World Culture* in which he employed social-psychology to examine the effects of Christianity where it had been introduced. In general, however, missiologists have not made great use of sociology or interacted on an extensive scale with sociologists.

On the other hand, of the social sciences, missiologists have made the greatest use of anthropology, a number becoming anthropologists and making substantial contributions to the field. The journal, *Practical Anthropology*, succeeded by *Missiology*, established a tradition of relating the social sciences, especially anthropology, to missions. Linguistics, of course, with its highly scientific methodology, has been extremely important in missions and missionary scholars have also contributed greatly to the field.

Religious conversion has been studied extensively from the psychological perspective since at least William James (1902), but the other social sciences have given it less attention. H. Newton Malony and Samuel Southard (1992) edited a *Handbook of Religious Conversion* in which Lewis R. Rambo, William Sims Bainbridge, and Alan R. Tippett, wrote on the psychology, the sociology, and the cultural anthropology of conversion respectively. Tippett's (1992) article has the most direct contribution to a sociology of missions because it deals with the change brought about when an outside religion is introduced to a social group.

A Return to "Demarcation" as a Aid to Interchange

The interchange between social scientists and missiologists (many of them being represented in the same person) appears to be increasing and there are members of both groups who are interested in increasing the interchange. I would argue that the interchange is facilitated if the distinction between disciplines can be maintained. When the distinction is not maintained, there is difficulty in communication, particularly evaluation by social scientists of the work of missiologists. For example, Peter Takayama (1984, 210), a sociologist of religion, in reviewing *Exploring Church Growth* (edited by Wilbert Shenk, 1983) stated:

> In general, this is a difficult book for social scientists of religion because, except for one or two chapters, theological, methodological, and sociological languages are fused. Nevertheless, several essays are fruitful for sociology.

Missiology needs to recognize and maintain the demarcation in disciplines because it incorporates and makes use of the social sciences, but places them in multiple theological contexts. At the same time, social scientists, who espouse a methodology in which normative considerations are suspended, need to be held to that goal. This is not always easy since social scientists are likely to be less conscious of their norms than missiologists.

There will probably always be social scientists who will consider any study by any person with professed religious convictions as too "tainted" to consider. Likewise, some people of faith will consider a social scientific study as secular or "godless" and therefore of little value. However, I hope that this book will be useful to those who are willing to apply a social scientific perspective, temporarily suspending their norms, whether those norms be anti-religious or religious. As far as I am concerned, positivism as a philosophy may well be dead in today's post-modernist world, but there is still room for positivistic methodology. Because some people make a religion out of science (water), it isn't necessary to throw out the scientific approach (the baby)!

Chapter 1

The Concept of Diffusion in Relation to Religion

A Stubborn Concept with a Low Profile

The concept of diffusion has stubbornly survived in the social sciences. It is as old as Herodotus, who compiled his histories in 450 B.C.E. and in many ways is based on a common-sense recognition of the mingling of cultures (Hodgen 1974, 28). However, its earliest social scientific use can be traced to Edward Tyler's (1865) treatment of culture change (Perry 1992, 487). Diffusion is not a complex notion and may be defined as "the spread of culture traits from group to group" (Horton and Hunt 1976, 445). Everett Rogers (1995, 5), who has done the most to summarize the results of studies of diffusion, defines it as "the process by which an innovation is communicated through certain channels over time among the members of a social system."

Some early schools of thought about diffusion did not endure. One was represented by the English anthropologists, G. E. Smith and W. J. Perry, who made Egypt the center for cultural origins which progressively diffused over the rest of the world (Perry 1992, 487). Another school came out of Germany and was represented especially by Fritz Graebner (1911), who "proposed that certain critical aspects of culture - toolmaking, for example - originated in a small number of isolated societies" or "culture circles" ("Kulturkreise") (Perry 1992, 487). One characteristic that has given the concept of diffusion staying power has been that it makes possible the discussion of social change without reference to evolution. The American anthropologist, Franz Boas (1896) opposed nineteenth century cultural evolutionism partly with the concept of diffusion. Both he and the many whom he influenced, including Alfred Kroeber (1923) and Robert Lowie (1937), demonstrated the diffusion of culture traits (Perry 1992, 487-488). Margaret T. Hodgen (1974, 28), an anthropologist, discussing the social scientific approach to history, states:

> At all events, diffusionism today is the modern version of an old problem of cultural similarities or correspondences. It has persisted in thought certainly from the Renaissance, and long before academic anthropology assumed its present organization and methodological structure. Latterly this solution has been considered as an alternative to another old paradigm of the process of cultural change, or that envisioned logically as natural, inevitable, continuous, developmental, or evolutionary.

A sociologist, Piotr Sztompka (1993, 110-111) writes that the concept of diffusion, in contrast to some evolutionism, stresses change through "reciprocal exchange and borrowing of organizational forms, cultural rules, lifestyles, etc." which "may significantly reshape the developmental route taken by each society." Furthermore, he (1993, 111) states

> The same diffusionist argument counters the idea of inexorable stages. Some stages may be omitted and some processes accelerated precisely because of the use made of the experiences of other societies, or through outright intrusion by other societies (conquest, colonization, domination).

Apart from using the concept of diffusion as a corrective, however, he does not specifically incorporate it into his theoretical construction of historical change, termed "social becoming" (1993, 213-232). Nevertheless, it appears that in principle, the concept of diffusion can be easily incorporated into his theory of social change that includes "agency," "history-making" and "the contingency of historical events." Whether that is the case or not, the concept of diffusion clearly has a place in the theoretical problem area of social change.

The use of the concept of diffusion by both Hodgen (1974) and Sztompka (1993) indicates that it is not only a check to an extreme form of evolutionism, but that the concept has a positive contribution to make in the current concern of both anthropology and sociology to study historical events as they are linked in processes. In this common concern, the two disciplines have become overlapping in their use of the concept of diffusion. What has happened, according to Perry (1992, 487-488), is that after providing a basis for empirical research in both anthropology (the "cultural diffusion" tradition) and sociology (the "diffusion of innovations" and the "collective behavior" traditions) there has been, since the late 1970s, a merging of research and theory related to diffusion. This merging is discussed in detail by Rogers (1983, 1995). Ronald Perry (1992, 488) summarizes:

> Currently, diffusion is seen as a mechanism for culture change that typically accounts for a large portion of any particular cultural inventory. The deterministic, linear diffusion hypothesis associated with early British anthropologists is discredited. Sociologists concerned with macro-social processes and societal change acknowledge and use the concept of diffusion in much the same way as anthropologists (Lauer 1973).

Thus, the concept of diffusion, in spite of its low profile, has both a venerable history in the social sciences and a continuing utility in both anthropology and sociology, especially as both disciplines wrestle with appropriate ways to examine and explain socio-cultural change.

The Concept of Diffusion and Its Associates

It has already been seen that the concept of diffusion, although not a friend of evolutionism, at least in its earlier form, has persistently, though not prominently, appeared in discussions of socio-cultural change. This places the concept at the core of the social sciences. As Sztompka (1993, xiii) writes, "The study of social change is at the core of sociology. Perhaps all sociology is about change." As already noted, this has meant that the social sciences have had an ongoing dialogue with history. This dialogue has sometimes been muted, even hostile, with clear distinctions being made in methodology and style, but recently a social scientific approach to history has received renewed attention and favor.

Some scholars have tried to bridge the gap between history and the social sciences. Frederick J. Teggart (1916, 1918, 1925, 1939), is much respected by social scientists for his important contributions to the understanding of social change. Robert A. Nisbet (1969) dedicates his book, *Social Change and History,* to Teggart, whose book, *Theory of History* (1925), Nisbet (1969, viii) calls "one of the profoundest and most original works of this century." The particular work of Teggart that has had an enduring effect is described by Hogden (1974, 38):

> Professor Teggart found his problem in a class of recurrent events well-known to historians as the barbarian invasions of the Roman Empire from 58 B.C. to A.D. 107. However, the procedure he adopted to account for this class of datable, historical instances of a similar and repeated human activity was not an educated guess, nor did his treatment of these similar dated events involve the usual composition of a narrative, based upon a selection among them, followed by inquiry into "causes"...Within the chosen decades, according to Teggart (1939, 236) "every barbarian uprising in Europe followed the outbreak of war either on the eastern frontiers of the Roman Empire or in the 'Western Regions' of the Chinese." Thus the primary result of this twofold classification of two supposedly unique events was the establishment of *correlations* in classes of dated events.

Historical studies such as Teggart's help to clarify how internal change may be the result of outside forces. On the basis of Teggart's work, Nisbet (1969, 280) emphasizes the importance of exogenous, as opposed to endogenous forces:

> It is impossible to deal with the entities so vast as Greece or Rome or Western Europe or the United States in terms of endogenous forces, that is, apart from the relationships of each of these to literally scores of other peoples, to intrusions stemming from political, military, economic forces, to such matters as trade routes, wars, invasions, migration, importation of alien values, and so on, it is the less likely that a plausible theory of change concerned with institutions can be constructed in the absence of explicit reference to such relationships, intrusions, and impacts.

Thus, the concept of diffusion within the large theoretical problem area of socio-cultural change over time is associated with many other concepts that point to outside influences in social change, for example, "culture contact," "borrowing," "innovation," "acculturation," "faddism," and "social movements." A central dependent variable in these concepts is "acceptance." Barnett (1953, 292) notes, "Diffusion, acculturation, and faddism are all therefore manifestations of the same phenomenon. They are varied patternings of the process of acceptance." He adds that conventionally diffusion is used for collective response and acceptance for individual response.

Although religion may not be the subject in many studies of historical social change, diffusion and related concepts mentioned above clearly support an examination of historical events as affected by intergroup relationships. How diffusion has been studied will be considered in more detail below.

Results from the Study of Diffusion

In reviewing the work of early twentieth-century American anthropologists, Perry (1992, 488) identifies "five broadly accepted and empirically supported claims regarding cultural diffusion."

> First, borrowed elements usually undergo some type of change or adaptation in the new host culture. Second, the act of borrowing hinges on the extent to which the element can be integrated into the belief system of the new culture. Third, elements that are incompatible with the new culture's prevailing normative structure or religious belief system are likely to be rejected. Fourth, acceptance of an element depends on its functional utility to the borrower. Finally, cultures or societies that have a history of past borrowing are more likely to borrow in the future.

As will be seen in the next chapter, I am particularly interested in *why* borrowed elements get borrowed in the first place and then after borrowing (acceptance) get changed or integrated, with little conscious change, into cultures. Also, I am interested in *why* new religions are perceived as incompatible on the one hand or as functional on the other. I see the characteristics or quality of intergroup relations as being important for answering such questions. My approach opposes making judgments about "compatibility" and "capability of integration."

Although clearly overlapping with anthropology, sociology used the concept of diffusion in considering how innovations spread, primarily within societies. In his discussion of social change, Alvin

Boskoff (1972, 232-238) traces the work of Robert MacIver (1942, 1947), Karl Mannheim (1940), Howard Odum (1947), and others in relating the relative success or failure of specific innovations to "(a) key features of the process of dissemination and (b) the characteristics and perceptions of a 'target' public or social category." After discussing "agents of diffusion" and "cultural facilitation of diffusion," Boskoff (1972, 235-238) outlines three types of "reception theories" that deal with (1) "Dynamic Assessment," (3) "Social Characteristics of Early Adopters," and (3) "Motivational Patterns."

"Dynamic assessment," developed by MacIver (1942) drawing on W.I. Thomas and F. Znanieki's concept of "definition of the situation," refers to an evaluation process that takes place in a large number of groups when there are "changes in one's experience with 'familiar' settings" (Boskoff 1972, 236). "Early adoption," according to Boskoff (1972, 236) is associated with "relatively high status (in terms of education, income, occupational responsibility) as a precondition of receptive attitudes toward innovation and thus increasing the probability of adoption during early stages of diffusion."

Various "motivational patterns" affecting diffusion were identified by Boskoff (1972, 237-238) from studies which included (1) reaction to dissatisfaction spurred by "culture conflict, marginality, conditions of rising expectations" or "emotional deprivation in early socialization;" (2) "identification with the future of the community" as contrasted with a more narrow concern with family and neighborhood; and (3) "achievement need" or "desire for merited social mobility."

The most complete discussion to date of the results of research of diffusion is given by Everett M. Rogers (1962, 1971 with F. Floyd Shoemaker, 1983, 1995) in a series of four books. By 1995, Rogers (1995, 42-43) had classified almost 4000 studies into eleven major diffusion traditions (with the following percentages): anthropology (4 percent), early sociology (less than 1 percent), rural sociology (22 percent), education (9 percent), public health and medical sociology (7 percent), communication (12 percent), marketing and management (15 percent), geography (4 percent), general sociology (8 percent), general economics (5 percent) and other traditions (14 percent). It had been noted that researchers in the various traditions "scarcely know of each other's existence" (Katz, Levin, and Hamilton 1963, 240), but what is rather surprising is that sociology of religion did not develop any tradition of diffusion research nor is either religion or ideology mentioned by Rogers as an object of research. It is true, however, that the anthropological tradition has given attention to the diffusion of religions to groups, usually small groups.

In addition to identifying diffusion research traditions, Rogers (1971, 70-76) also carried out the detailed work of classifying 6,811 generalizations found in the Michigan State University Diffusion Documents Center into eight types of diffusion research findings. His (1995, 88-94) latest study reported the same typology. Roger's (1983: 128-130) aim was to develop "theories of the middle range," to use a term from Merton (1968), and he organized some eight types of research or topics under which to group these theories. Perry (1992, 490) further groups these theories into three categories as having to do with "the innovation-decision process, innovation characteristics, and adopter characteristics and opinion leadership."

Regarding the effect of this research in the social science community, Rogers and Shoemaker (1971, 77) quote "two members of the diffusion research fraternity," Fliegel and Kivlin (1966) who complain: "Diffusion of innovation has the status of a bastard child with respect to the parent interests in social and cultural change: Too big to ignore but unlikely to be given full recognition." However, by 1995 Rogers (97) finds that diffusion research "has achieved a prominent position today." His (96-97) basic reason for this assessment is that "the results of diffusion research have been incorporated in basic textbooks in social psychology, communication, public relations, advertising, marketing, consumer behavior, rural sociology, and other fields" and "both practitioners (like change agents) and theoreticians regard the diffusion of innovations as a useful field of social science knowledge." In other words, diffusion research has proven itself as useful to numerous fields, most of them quite practical. My perspective is that it is time for religious studies to get involved. Some aspects of the research will not apply to religion, but some will. And research in the diffusion of religions may add to the understanding of the diffusion of other aspects of culture.

Diffusion and Religion

In focusing on the diffusion of religions it was helpful to consult the discussions of both the elements or components of diffusion as they have been researched and the gaps or difficulties in this research. In this regard, I found the discussions of Rogers (1962, 1971 with Shoemaker, 1983, 1995), of Katz, Levin, and Hamilton (1963), and finally of Perry (1992) very helpful.

The need to apply diffusion research to religion is clear. Because of the focus in applied research on particular innovations being diffused (usually "functional-technical innovations"), it has been noted that "we know much more about how fertilizers, weed sprays, and antibiotic drugs spread and much less about the diffusion of new ideas in political behavior or human learning" (Rogers and Shoemaker 1971, 79).

"Acceptance is the dependent variable in most studies of diffusion" (Katz, Levin, and Hamilton 1963, 240), as it is in my study, but a crucial problem in acceptance has been the question of time or process in acceptance. Anthropologists particularly have noted how religions have been changed in the process of reception so that the question can be raised as to whether they are the "same" item after diffusion has taken place (Katz, Levin, and Hamilton 1963, 241). By making religious identity the measure of acceptance, which can be applied to religions and ideologies in contrast to items of material culture, it is possible to short-circuit discussions of "true" religion. At the same time, change after acceptance is important and not random and I attempt to consider major variations that develop with diffusion.

The difference in rates and extent of diffusion between material and non-material (outer and inner) aspects of culture has been much debated. Ogburn's ([1922] 1966, 200-203) famous lag theory posited that "adaptive culture," which included religion, lagged in change after "material culture." On the other hand, groups have been known to make rapid and dramatic changes in religion which preceded significant changes in material culture (Margaret Mead 1956). Clearly aspects of culture do not change at the same rate, but in some circumstances religion may change more rapidly than material culture.

In general, I do not examine separately the stages in the innovation-decision process (knowledge, persuasion, decision, implementation, and confirmation from Perry 1992, 490), but do note the direction in which the decision process moves. For religions, the movement is often "upward" between groups and "downward" within groups. For example, perhaps unlike material items, religions often diffuse to marginal groups from outside the larger society, but to leaders within those groups, for example to leading women in the Roman Empire and elsewhere or to the leaders of ascendant, but previously backward nations. This is also where "adopter characteristics" enter into my analysis, although this is not a major focus.

A study by James H. Grayson (1985) of the diffusion (called "emplantation") of Buddhism and Christianity in Korea uses an anthropological approach to establish stages of diffusion (based on the diffusion of Buddhism to China). Although primarily descriptive of cultural change, Grayson (1985, 130-143) recognizes the importance of "political factors." What is significant for my theoretical perspective stated in the next chapter is Grayson's (1985, 142) recognition:

> Although core values of a society offer the greatest hindrance to the acceptance of new beliefs, dramatically altered political and cultural circumstances create conditions which tend toward easier acceptance of such new beliefs in spite of any contention with the core values.

It is for this reason that I will focus on intergroup relations rather than cultures.

The individual decision-maker has been the primary unit of analysis in the sociological research reviewed by Rogers (1995) rather than collectivities, such as communities or bureaucratic organizations. James Coleman's (1958) recommendation is employed by Rogers and Shoemaker (1971, 80) to call for attention to social structure and interpersonal variables: "It has been erroneously assumed that because individuals were the units of response, individuals also had to be the units of analysis." Anthropologists, of course, have typically focused on the group as an adopting unit (Katz, Levin, and Hamilton 1963, 245) and this will be my approach as set forth in the next chapter.

In comparing the diffusion of material and non-material aspects of culture, it is certainly plausible to suppose that the quality of relationships between groups would have less effect on the reception of material items, such as tools and weapons, than on the reception of a religion. This difference, in fact, may be observed in the relationships of Native Americans to Europeans in which material items were welcomed, while the religion of the Europeans was resisted. Leaders of many non-Western societies have also made this distinction between Western technology and Western values, the former being welcomed and the latter being resisted.

The definition of diffusion already given clearly incorporates all aspects of socio-cultural reality and religion may be considered as one of these aspects. However, in the "traditions of diffusion research" it is the anthropological tradition which has given attention to how the world religions have affected groups, particularly tribal or aboriginal groups. H. G. Barnett (1953), for example, in his study of innovation makes a number of references to the spread of Christianity and of the influence of "missionizing" in particular. In a rare study of the effects of intergroup relationships, Edward Spicer (1954) examined how different patterns of acculturation by Native Americans in the Southwest resulted from different kinds of treatment by the Spanish. He pointed out how Spanish colonization and missionization were much less intensive among the Cahitan peoples (Yaqui and Mayo) than on the Rio Grande among the Pueblos. Missionaries approached Yaqui settlements without military escort. "These conditions of contact, then, the competing village patterns, prestigeful innovators, and the techniques of substitution, gave rise to fusion of cultural elements rather than to resistance with compartmentalization under pressure" (Spicer 1954, 677). When it comes to the diffusion of religion, the nature of intergroup relations appears to be especially important. However, Spicer's study is over forty years old and his lead does not seem to have been followed.

A recent example of the historical and anthropological study of the diffusion of world religions is *Conversion to Christianity*, edited by Robert W. Hefner (1993). Although it does not specifically employ the concept of diffusion, in almost all of the cases presented, conversion involves diffusion. The book's discussion of world religions and its case studies of specific groups (their conversion or resistance to conversion) is so important that I used it as an additional check on my theory of how religions have diffused.

Clearly, then, religion may be included in studies of diffusion and, in fact, has been included in studies of diffusion, primarily in anthropology, but usually under one of its associated concepts, such as "acculturation" or "conversion." However, no tradition of diffusion studies of religion has developed in sociology. Of course, to "play the game" of the social sciences, any study of religion must "follow the rules." This means, to begin with, that any normative view of religion must be put aside. This includes, of course, both the views of adherents and those of non-adherents, the latter often not recognizing that their views of religion are just as normative as the views of adherents.

One of the reasons why the diffusion of religions has not received more attention may be that proselytizing or missionizing is viewed negatively, especially by intellectuals. At the same time, given the dedication to mission by religious people, it is somewhat surprising that no tradition of diffusion research developed for missions in the applied research field of sociology. David Heise's (1967) "Prefatory Findings in the Sociology of Missions" and Elihu Katz's (1967) response were not enough to initiate a sub-field in the sociology of religion. Although studies of "church growth" and "membership change" have been plentiful by sociologists of religion, these scholars have not given much attention to cross-national diffusion studies. This type of study is expensive, but also, apparently the contributions of the anthropology tradition were deemed sufficient by most church leaders and missiologists so that generally sociologists of religion have not been approached for aid in the study of missions.

In addition to the "cultural diffusion" tradition of anthropology and the "diffusion of innovations" tradition of sociology, according to Rogers and Shoemaker (1971, 91) and Perry (1992, 497), studies of collective behavior have also contributed to the understanding of diffusion. Religion has often played an important part in various sociocultural movements as have also, more recently, secular ideologies. In the social sciences, religion and ideology are closely linked and therefore the study of the diffusion of religions should include the diffusion of ideologies and vice versa.

Clearly, then, religion should be included in studies of diffusion, but religion is more complex than many of the diffusing cultural items that have been studied, particularly in the applied research tradition of sociology. It is not my purpose to focus on the diffusion of religious ideas or values, but on the diffusion of religions themselves. This does not mean only the diffusion of religious organization or even practices, although some form of organization and set of practices are always associated with a religion. I am considering the diffusion of religions as determined by the identification of adherents. This does not raise the question of the truth or orthodoxy of beliefs and practices, but only the religious self-identification of adherents and the description and comparison of various means of expressing religion.

It is important to recognize that the study does not consider diffusion in its broader meaning which includes diffusion by migration. As pointed by out by Chris C. Park (1994, 99-100) in his study of geography and religion, diffusion may take place by communication ("expansion diffusion") or by migration ("relocation diffusion"). He (1994, 100) further divides expansion diffusion between "contagious diffusion" (diffusion through direct contact) and "hierarchical diffusion" (adoption or reception from the top of the hierarchy down). Since I am primarily interested in diffusion across socio-cultural lines, it is expansion diffusion rather than relocation diffusion that will receive attention. Of course, individuals or groups of missionaries may relocate or migrate to new societies, but the kind of diffusion that I am considering is when a religion crosses a socio-cultural boundary between groups as in "expansion diffusion." I am not interested in diffusion by migration except as it may facilitate diffusion across sociocultural boundaries.

The unit of analysis in this study is not individuals, as in individual conversion, but social groups. Some groups may be as small as tribes or even a particular social category, such as the elite of a society, women, slaves, or "untouchables." Other groups may be large societies, which often incorporate many sub-groups, for example various minority ethnic groups. These sub-groups are often crucial for diffusion. All groups, whether small or large enough to form societies, are in multiple relationships with other groups and it is these relationships with other groups that will be given special attention.

In regard to these intergroup relationships, I am particularly interested in the relationships that are characterized by domination and resistance to domination. This is part of my "unhidden agenda" because it appears to me that domination and resistance to domination have had important effects on the diffusion of religions. Another part of my purpose is to compensate somewhat for the attention that has been given to culture by drawing attention to the importance of intergroup relationships. In general, the approach of this book is opposed to the intellectualist or mentalist approach (Hefner 1993, 22-25), sometimes characteristic of an approach that emphasizes culture, perhaps in a more narrow sense.

For people who are accustomed to the individualism of the modern era, particularly in the West, this attention to groups may appear to be unsuited to a current study of diffusion of religions. Perhaps this is the reason why the individual has been the primary unit of analysis in applied research studies of diffusion. It is true that one of the characteristics of modern societies has been the increasing isolation of the individual and the development of individualism with an emphasis on the importance of individual decision-making, particularly when it comes to religion. Religious culture, particularly in the West, has participated in, and undoubtedly contributed to, the development of individualism.

Although it may seem so to some, the study of groups and their relationships does not in itself reduce the importance of the individual, as, for example, in individual conversion. As a matter of fact, the theoretical statement will include both macro (intergroup relations) and micro (individual motivation) levels. Nevertheless, the approach of this book is sociological, which focuses on group forces and considers individualism itself as a product of group forces, as well as a characteristic of groups.

Three Diffusing Religions

A narrowing of the dependent variable is aided by the surprising fact that out of the world religions, only three have diffused (through the transmission of the religion by communication as opposed to simply by migration) to a large number and variety of socio-cultural groups and are still doing so. These three religions have crossed numerous boundaries between groups and become accepted as part of the social identities of new groups of people.

In the historical order in which they developed, the three religions that have diffused most extensively are Buddhism, Christianity, and Islam. The diffusion of Christianity is well known. The diffusion of Buddhism is sometimes thought to have been only in the past, but Finney (1991), among others, draws attention to the continuing diffusion of Buddhism. Islam is certainly diffusing to new groups, for example, among African-Americans.

Other religions, for example, Hinduism, from which Buddhism developed, and Judaism, which highly influenced Christianity and Islam, have had a great impact on many cultures, aside from the influence they exerted through their daughter religions. However, the diffusion of Judaism has been primarily through migration, many times forced. Hinduism found considerable acceptance in Southeast Asia and has been part of the spread of "Eastern" ideas to the West. However, although Hinduism has more adherents than Buddhism, unlike Buddhism, it is primarily located in South Asia and its modern diffusion is associated primarily with immigration from India. The cases of Judaism and Hinduism demonstrate that being a "world religion" with universalistic doctrines apparently is a necessary, but not a sufficient, reason for a religion to diffuse widely by crossing many socio-cultural boundaries.

Manichaeism, Confucianism, and the modern ideology of Marxism were also successfully introduced to societies from the outside to become part of social identities in new societies. However, since Buddhism, Christianity, and Islam have spread the most widely, this book will focus on their diffusion with the assumption that the patterns uncovered will have application to other religions and ideologies.

Variations in the Dependent Variable

To clarify the dependent variable (diffusion of religions), it is necessary to distinguish specific variations in diffusion. This is the initial step in operationalization; however, in this study, operationalization will be kept on a rather broad level. I will not be looking at the different stages of the diffusion process, but rather at the process as a whole in which groups choose "to adopt, reinvent (modify), or reject an innovation" (Perry 1992, 490) Accordingly, I distinguish three major variations in the responses to religions that are introduced from the outside: refusal, acceptance, and acceptance accompanied by major alterations in the new religions.

The distinction between the second and third response is not always clear. For example, a continuum may be seen between the second and third possible responses because any religion crossing a sociocultural frontier will take on new characteristics reflecting the culture of the receiving group. However, a distinction may be drawn (as I am doing) between receiving a religion from the outside more or less in the form in which it is presented on the one hand and, on the other hand, accepting a religion, but consciously creating a new form of that religion. In the latter case, distinctive expressions and organizations are developed which set apart the new version of the received religion from the version of the religion that was originally introduced.

It is also true, that some forms of rejection produce religious innovations in traditional religions, which may incorporate elements from the outside religion being introduced. Thus, some responses to outside pressures often result in a combination of acceptance and rejection. It may be difficult to determine in what direction the greatest continuity lies, whether with the traditional religion or the new religion. For example, was the religion of the Taipings of China a form of Christianity? According to Latourette (1956, 356), "to the last the leaders professed adherence to that faith [Christianity]," but it is not clear about the bulk of the followers. It could be said that the movement as a whole was not yet Christian on the basis of the self-identification of most participants.

Some forms of rejection involve clinging to a traditional religion more or less in its traditional form (perhaps reviving some old forms). Other forms of rejection involve making deliberate and sometimes numerous innovations in the traditional religion, as noted above. In the latter case of rejection, some of the innovations may be borrowed from the introduced religion; however, the adherents of the innovative religion do not identify themselves as belonging to the introduced religion. I will grant, then, that a continuum may be seen from complete rejection to complete acceptance and the continuum may be divided at different points (and looked at in different sectors). However, the greatest aid in the distinction between rejection and acceptance (complete or partial) is the self-identification of the adherents.

My primary indicator, therefore, of acceptance or rejection of a religion is the self-identification of adherents, whether others consider them "true" believers or not. With self-identification as the basis for judging religious affiliation, I have found it more useful to distinguish two kinds of acceptance than two kinds of rejection. Therefore, I make the third or really "the middle response" one of acceptance with conscious and deliberate changes. The new believers identify themselves as adherents of the introduced religion, but the changes they make set the new religion apart from the original religion and, in particular, contribute to the religious distinction of the receiving group from the sending group.

In some respects, the third type of response, acceptance with change, has "gotten me in trouble." The presentation of this book is deductive, following the social scientific model of research aimed at theory or explanation. Actually, my research has alternated between deductive and inductive approaches and in a basic sense is inductive or exploratory. I simply follow the deductive model to give focus to the exploration. In the historical study that this book has entailed I observed what appeared to be various patterns of change that have been introduced to religions after they were accepted, usually when that acceptance was under pressure. Furthermore, these patterns of change after acceptance have continuities with the patterns of both rejection and "full" acceptance because they were similarly affected by intergroup relations. For this reason, I extended my historical review to include at least some of the major variations that were introduced to the three religions after they were accepted. Clearly the third response (acceptance with change) has proven to be the most complex to examine.

Conclusion

Diffusion is an old and relatively simple concept that has had an overt or covert presence in social scientific studies of socio-cultural change from the beginning of the discipline. The concept of diffusion fits well with the renewed interest of social scientists in the study of history and the analysis of events.

Although religion has been part of the anthropological study of cultural change, religion has not received attention in the research associated with the study of the diffusion of innovations that was carried on largely in sociology. This primarily applied research has contributed to the development of a set of theoretical propositions related to the innovation-decision process, innovation characteristics, and adopter characteristics. However, the individual, not groups or relationships, has been the primary unit of analysis and there has been a lack of attention to change outside of the West and to historical data. Basically, the study of the diffusion of religions, and even of ideologies, has been neglected by sociologists so that a separate tradition of diffusion research that gives attention to religions and ideologies was not developed. Nevertheless, some insights from the various traditions of diffusion research may be applied to religions. In addition, insights may also be applied, as will be seen, from a broad range of studies in the large problem area of social change.

Three religions, Buddhism, Christianity, and Islam, have diffused widely across numerous socio-cultural boundaries so that these religions have become part of the social identities of people in new groups. In the process of diffusion they have encountered three distinguishable responses: rejection, acceptance, and acceptance with conscious and deliberate change.

As already noted, the independent variable of prime importance to me (to be discussed in the next chapter) is the characteristics or quality of intergroup relationships. It was after some years of alternating in thought between the data (some of which I observed, but most of which I learned through the writings of others) and theory, I came to believe that domination/subordination and intergroup hostility were key variables on the macro level and social identity a key variable on the micro level. I developed a theoretical perspective which I will set forth in the next chapter. For me, the simulation of the theoretical research model, as opposed simply to description, is a way of clarifying the argument and laying groundwork for studies in which more controls may be applied.

Chapter 2

A Theoretical Perspective and Methodology

Theoretical Considerations

Background Variables from the Two Sides of Diffusion

The major source of independent variables that I will be considering for their influence on diffusion of religions is the quality of the relationships between groups. However, before stating the theory for which I will be setting forth supporting historical data, I would like to recognize two other sources for independent variables affecting diffusion of religions.

These two sources exist independently of diffusion, as well as apart from the relationships between groups. One set belongs to the religions themselves, some of which are more diffusion prone than others. The other set belongs to the societies to which the religions diffuse, some societies having characteristics which cause them to be more receptive to outside religions than other societies. These two sources for independent variables roughly correspond to what the literature calls "innovation characteristics" and "adopter characteristics" (Perry 1992, 490). I call them "background variables" because they exist prior to groups coming into relationship and diffusion taking place. Also, they are not in the "forefront" of my consideration. However, this does not mean that they are not important in the diffusion process.

The qualitative difference between religions (or ideologies) and tools and their technologies (material and non-material aspects of culture) means that some of their attributes are not comparable. Of the list of "attributes of innovations" provided by Perry (1992, 490) (compatibility, complexity, observability, relative advantage, and trialability), perception of relative advantage is probably the most important for a religion or ideology in diffusing from one group to another. For me, compatibility is the most problematical because so often judgments concerning compatibility are rendered after the fact and are tantamount to the acceptance-rejection process itself. In fact, a problem with all of these innovation attributes is that the perception of the receivers is crucial to acceptance or rejection of innovations and I am interested in what influences that perception. However, to some extent, innovations (both those with a large intellectual content and those that are primarily technological and practical) have certain attributes that may make them diffusion-prone or not diffusion-prone. It is worth considering what these attributes might be for religions.

As already noted, not all religions, not even all world religions, have diffused widely, diffusion here meaning crossing socio-cultural boundaries, not simply diffusion by migration. The three religions being considered (Buddhism, Christianity, and Islam) are quite different from each other and yet they share certain attributes which undoubtedly have contributed to their ability to diffuse. In addition to being world religions, having beliefs and norms which apply to humanity generally, these three religions: (1) offer salvation to all individuals, giving these religions an egalitarianism; (2) have moral systems which include an emphasis on compassion; and (3) have a missionary goal to spread their messages.. It is undoubtedly possible to add other attributes and certainly to refine statements of these characteristics, comparing them with the characteristics of other world religions. However, apparently these characteristics are sufficient and perhaps necessary to make these three religions diffusion-prone.

Rather than attempting to discuss these and other religious innovation attributes, in this book I am interested in the question: Given these three religions with their diffusion-prone attributes, why did they succeed in diffusion in some cases and fail in others, with many cases that seem to be somewhere in between? That is, why do some groups

A Theoretical Perspective and Methodology

perceive these religions as being compatible and providing a relative advantage to them and other similar groups perceive these religions as not compatible and as being a relative disadvantage to them? I want to deal with this question apart from the characteristics of the religions themselves other than the basic ones listed.

"Adopter characteristics" may be considered as a second set of pre-existing variables affecting diffusion which belong to the receiving side of diffusion. However, in the literature "adopter categories are classifications of individuals based upon how readily they adopt an innovation" (Perry 1992, 490). My purpose is to focus on groups and their relationships and not on individuals. At the same time, I recognize that individuals and their perceptions are important and at least the initial stage of acceptance-rejection at the micro level of analysis will be considered.

The importance of distinguishing between individuals and groups in diffusion of religions may be seen in the fact that although governments and group leaders are often early adopters (Boskoff 1972, 233; Perry 1992, 490), the groups to which the leaders belong may be of low or marginal status. Looking at groups or societies as a whole, it may be seen that some groups or societies appear to be more prone than others in receiving religions introduced from the outside.

In an early attempt at incorporating social psychology in understanding missions, Archibald Baker (1934) discussed the disintegration and reintegration of societies and cultures. Clearly, pre-literate societies that are relatively small are more likely to disintegrate under pressure than are large societies with organized and complex institutions. The pre-literate societies are more easily disturbed in their moral orders - to use a term from Robert Wuthnow (1987, 145-185) - than are societies with literatures and that are relatively large and well organized.

Charles Forman (1983, 10) after a study of church growth (in this case, involving diffusion) in Madagascar states in his conclusion:

> We are left then, with one reason which does seem to explain church growth. Growth has come as a large-scale phenomenon among preliterate peoples with a nonliterary religion. At times it has come quickly, and at times it has come after a long period of unresponsiveness, but eventually it has come. Seldom has it come among any other types of people.

One of the useful results of Forman's study is that he shows how some of the favorite explanations used for church growth such as the missionary methods, number of missionaries, doctrine preached, and other variations in missionary activity were not helpful as explanations of successful diffusion. Missionary activity, of course, is a necessary precondition for diffusion, but it is not a sufficient explanation for success.

In short, some groups or societies have more resources than others to resist a breakdown in their moral orders and it is the breakdown or rapid change of moral orders that establishes conditions in which people are receptive to religious innovation, either from within or without. The distinction between receiving societies as to whether they are literate or preliterate is important as an indicator of the resources a society has for maintaining its culture and for resisting an outside religion. All three of the diffusing religions bring a literature with them and therefore may be attractive to a society which has no extensive literature. However, also important as internal resources are the size, organization, and physical location of the receiving societies. As we know, having a literature is correlated with these other characteristics and all of them are indicators of strength for resisting outside pressure.

Thus, the adopter characteristics of groups or societies, in particular their internal resources, provide an important set of background variables affecting the diffusion process, but it is the relationships between groups or societies that brings these resources into play so that they become a basis for resistance to diffusion or facilitation of diffusion. For one thing, even small and preliterate societies (with few of the resources of large societies) have varied considerably in their responses to the diffusing religions, with some resisting the outside religions rather successfully. Also, and perhaps most important, the diffusing religions have had and are having success in diffusing to societies with literatures and state organizations, for example, Buddhism to China and Christianity to Korea. Furthermore, variations of these religions - for example, the Pentecostal version of Christianity - are spreading in areas previously dominated by an older version (Martin 1990).

Recognizing the importance of the background variables (innovation characteristics or the characteristics of the religions and adopter characteristics or the characteristics of the receiving societies), my approach will be to hold these variables constant in order to focus on intergroup relationship variables. The social sciences allow or encourage this kind of "superficiality" in order to highlight other variables, in this case, intergroup relationship variables at the macro level and variables related to them at the micro level. At the same time, it will be possible to refer to the background variables, when, in fact, it appears that they may be important. At the very least, this procedure allows for further investigation that may bring background variables to a forward position.

Macro Level Variables

My theoretical statement has two levels, the macro and the micro levels. The intergroup relations themselves are on the macro level, but the perceptions of these relations and the motivations that direct responses are on the micro level. The macro level variables are in the prior position, as is typical in sociological explanation, but the micro level variables are important as "intervening variables" between the effect of intergroup relations and the acceptance or rejection of religions that are introduced from the outside. I am especially indebted to Wuthnow (1987) for his emphasis on macro level factors and to social identity theorists (Tajfel et al) for their work in linking macro and micro (social-psychological) levels of analysis. Other studies, which I found helpful and which link the macro and micro levels, are A.F.C Wallace's (1956, 1967) study of the Seneca Indians, David Martin's (1990) study of the spread of Pentecostalism, and Robert W. Hefner's (1993) Introduction for a series of case studies of conversion.

Wuthnow (1987) moves beyond the familiar theory of relative deprivation as the primary cause for social movements to one that is socially based. He emphasizes disturbances in the moral order of society as creating possibilities for innovative ideological interpretations to be presented (Wuthnow 1987, 154-156). In some cases the innovative ideological interpretation may be developed from the traditional ideology or religion or, as in cases of successful diffusion, it may be accepted from the outside. Some innovations are deliberate mixtures of traditional and outside religions. I am particularly interested initially in how outside pressure may prepare a society for the adoption of an "oppositional ideology" (Wuthnow 1987, 170) from another source. In other words, the oppositional ideology may be nativistic or it may be accepted from an outside source. In the latter case, diffusion takes place when the newly introduced ideology or religion provides a resource for resisting pressure from another source and maintaining or reconstructing the moral order.

However, in addition, I am also interested in how an "oppositional ideology" may develop within a religion after its acceptance in response to domination. Kurtz (1995, 22-23) refers to the gap that develops between "what Redfield (1957) calls the 'big tradition' (the 'official' beliefs as defined by elites) and the 'little tradition' (the version of a religion to which everyday people adhere)." Some dominating official groups in religions are able to contain "popular" religion, but others are not able to do so and religious movements break away from the established religion. I will try to note the different patterns of resistance to domination.

Martin (1990, 274) in his analysis of the spread of evangelical and then Pentecostal religion speaks of the "breakdown of overarching monopoly which occurred in seventeenth-century English culture on either side of the Atlantic" and then occurred in the present century in Latin America. Also, Anthony F.C. Wallace (1967, 141-156) in his study of the Seneca Indians recognized the impact of macro level changes that disturbed the "steady state" or "moving equilibrium" of a society and led to "increased individual stress," "cultural distortion," and then to a "period of revitalization" and a "new steady state."

The above views are consistent with the view of MacIver (1942) noted by Boskoff (1972, 236) regarding receptivity to diffusion: "He suggests that reception (and dynamic assessment) is a contingent process dependent on sudden but understandable changes in one's experience with 'familiar' settings." Usually, religion is an important part of the moral order, the overarching monopoly, the cultural steady state or the familiar setting of a society and disturbances at this macro level (whether from external pressure, internal dissolution, or a combination of these) open the way for change in religion, either by innovation or acceptance of a new religion from the outside. Although disturbances in the steady state may be from "natural causes," such as climatic or faunal change, most often they result from intergroup contacts that bring about subordination of one group to another (Wallace 1967, 144). The disturbances often provide an opportunity for a new leadership to arise. The need for a new moral order is perceived by this rising new elite who want the new order to support their new status and their efforts to unite a set of groups under them.

In a discussion of the conversion of Ireland, William Henry Scott (1967, 196-197) notes:

> Whatever the actual details may have been, however, two significant facts emerge from this picture of politics in fifth-century Ireland: (1) society was composed of heterogeneous groups of sufficiently different back-ground to be conscious of the fact, and (2) the conquering class was seeking to consolidate its power by resolving these differences. This is a situation which has more than once in the world's history provided a fertile seedbed for a new religion.

In the cases where a rising elite accept a new religion, the perceived threat is more from the old or rival leadership than from the group from which the new religion is coming.

Most analyses of religious change or innovation are interested in the disturbance or breakdown of the moral order that becomes a conducive condition for innovation and social change. However, because of my interest in diffusion, in addition to the breakdown (or threatened breakdown) of the moral order, I am interested in the *direction* from which the perceived threat to the moral order comes and how this perception may affect the introduction of a religion from the outside. It is for this reason that I focus on the quality of intergroup relations as a key factor in the diffusion of religions.

However, I do not consider only the relationships between the sending and receiving societies. There are two major sets of intergroup relationships affecting diffusion. The first set of relationships is between receiving groups and sending groups. The second set is between receiving groups and other surrounding or nearby groups. The quality of these relationships, particularly the extent to which the moral order of a group is perceived to be threatened by other groups, is of crucial importance in determining how groups respond to a religion being introduced from the outside.

In this study, groups to which religions spread may be quite small, consisting of a tribe or sub-tribe or the ruling elite of a society. On the other hand, some groups may consist of whole societies with numerous sub-groups having distinctive cultures. However, all groups exist in relationships with other groups and whether the term "group" or "society" is used, the macro level relationships are similar for the purposes of this study.

Micro Level Variables

Since intergroup relationships affect response to an outside religion through the perception of group members, it is useful to include a micro level analysis. The fact is, the social sciences move back and forth (up and down) between the group and individual levels. A good example of this is found in Martin's (1990, 284) statement regarding the re-integration of life that takes place in evangelical churches in the mega-cities:

> A new faith is able to implant new disciplines, re-order priorities, counter corruption and destructive machismo, and reverse the indifferent and injurious hierarchies of the outside world. Within the enclosed haven of faith a fraternity can be instituted under firm leadership, which provides for release, for mutuality and warmth, and for the practice of new roles. In this way millions of people are absorbed within a protective social capsule where they acquire new concepts of self and new models of initiative and voluntary organization.

A similar movement between the macro and micro levels is seen in the earlier treatments by Wallace (1956, 1967) of the revitalization movement among the Senecas.

Boskoff (1972, 237) has pointed to the importance of "motivational patterns" in diffusion. There is also an overlap here with "adopter characteristics," since many early adopters of innovations may have various motivations, such as desire for the betterment of the community, achievement, or social mobility.

A very deliberate linking of macro and micro levels has been used by the social identity theorists, which I have found very useful in considering the diffusion process. The social identity perspective made its first public appearance in an article by Henry Tajfel (1972) and was advanced primarily by European scholars, who have continued their studies following Tajfel's death in 1982. It was experimental research with "minimal groups" that provided the "data in search of a theory" (Hogg and Abrams 1988, x). Minimal groups are groups that are created artificially so that there are no systematic differences between them. It was repeatedly found that members of such groups favored anonymous in-group members over out-group members without an "objective" reason for doing so (Tajfel 1981, 233-238; Wagner, Lampen, Syllwasschy 1986, 15; Hogg and Abrams 1988, 48-51).

A Theoretical Perspective and Methodology

I found encouragement in using the social identity concept in conjunction with that of intergroup relations in Spicer's (1994) 1974 paper ("Anthropology in the Society of the 1990s") in which he stated:

> Anthropologists have been involved throughout their history at the edges of phenomena of ethnic group relations without recognizing until recently one of the essential features of the phenomena, namely, the sense of identity that grows out of common historical experience. They have tended to study trait differences without developing serious interest in the systems of interethnic relations of which the trait differences are often fringe phenomena. The various systems of interethnic relations involve power differentials as well as culture trait differences.

The social identity theorists make exactly this connection between intergroup relations (often characterized by power differentials) and social identities. The central concept of the social identity theorists is that the social identity of an individual is made up of a cluster of identities that are gained through membership in various groups. Tajfel (1981, 255) deliberately limited his definition of identity as this passage shows (consider the masculine as inclusive):

> For the purposes of this discussion, social identity will be understood as that part of an individual's self-concept which derives from his knowledge of his membership of a social group (or groups) together with the value and emotional significance attached to that membership. This limitation is deliberate, and it has two aims. The first is not to enter into endless and often sterile discussions as to what 'is' identity. The second is to enable us to use this limited concept in the discussions which follow. There is no doubt that the image or concept that an individual has of himself or herself is infinitely more complex, both in its contents and its derivations, than 'social identity' as defined and circumscribed here. ... 'Social identity' as defined here is thus best considered as a shorthand term used to describe (i) limited aspects of the concept of self which are (ii) relevant to certain limited aspects of social behavior.

This deliberately limited approach to the self concept becomes a powerful tool in dealing with social structures and intergroup relations. Dominic Abrams and Michael Hogg (1988, 1990, 1993) have performed a useful service in reviewing, summarizing, criticizing, and making advances in social identity theory. Hogg and Abrams (1988: 26) state:

> The social identity approach makes an important contribution to an understanding of the dynamics of large-scale group relations, intergroup conflict, collective action, social movements, and so forth (Tajfel and Turner 1979; Taylor and McKirnan 1984; and especially ch. 3 below). This macro-social emphasis is particularly important since it directly addresses the relationship between social processes and individual behavior - the dialectical relationship between society and the individual, mediated by social identity. In many respects it was to deal with this feature that the concept of social identity was originally fashioned by Tajfel (e.g. 1974).

Recently, "social identity theory" and "identity theory" have been criticized and compared (Hogg, Terry, White 1995, 255-269). It was concluded that social identity theory was more useful than the latter in examining intergroup relations, as opposed to interpersonal relations, and the influence of groups on "sociocognitive processes," which includes the influence of groups on perceptions of other groups. These emphases are consistent with my approach.

The social identity theorists are very interested in the power, status, and prestige relationships of large-scale categories (such as race, sex, nationality, religion, class, occupation, etc.), and have studied the relationships of dominant and subordinate groups, although as in diffusion theory, religion has not received much attention.

The part of social identity theory which is most helpful in understanding diffusion is the model for social change that has been developed for ways in which subordinate groups may seek to enhance themselves or improve their self-image. Given the fact that there are usually a number of different aspects to social identity drawn from memberships in various social categories or groups, Tajfel (1981, 255-256) noted several consequences of these memberships. It was the first consequence that particularly caught my eye:

> It can be assumed that an individual will tend to remain a member of a group and seek membership of new groups if these groups have some contribution to make to the positive aspects of his social identity; i.e. to those aspects of it from which he derives satisfaction. (Tajfel 1956, 256).

Since religion is a more changeable aspect of social identity than ethnicity or nationality or even social class, especially social caste, it struck me that people might change their religious identities, which is one aspect of their social identities, if the new religious identity would contribute positively to another aspect of their social group identities. This fit some of the cases that I had observed where there was religious diffusion in which a change in religion enhanced ethnic identity. At the same time, I had observed people clinging to their religious identities when they felt that to change these identities would injure or reduce the strength of their social group. Usually it was domination of one group by another which was the stimulus for change by the subordinate group, either by changing the traditional religion or accepting a new religion from the outside.

This perception of a potential positive contribution to a valued aspect of social identity fits well with what researchers of diffusion have called "dynamic assessment" of "relative advantage" (MacIver 1942; Boskoff 1972, 236-237; Perry 1992, 490). In the case of religion, one of its major functions has been to strengthen and support group identification and if a new religion is perceived as making such a contribution, conditions will be favorable for its reception.

Incorporating what Tajfel and other social identity theorists identified as to how the various subordinate groups seek to improve their image, Hogg and Abrams (1988, 54-61) developed a model showing three basic routes of change. The first route of change is through social mobility in which individuals seek to assimilate to dominant groups. This takes place when dominant groups emphasize equality and welcome the participation of subordinate groups. The second and third routes, however, are ways by which subordinate groups resist dominant groups by seeking new ways of comparison with dominant groups or by direct competition. For me, it is useful to combine the second and third routes because they are both ways of resistance and may be the basis for accepting a new outside religion, a new version of an outside religion, or a revived traditional religion. If the dominant group is associated with a traditional religion, then a new religion may strengthen a subordinate group in its resistance. If the dominant group is introducing a new religion, then a new version of that religion or a revived traditional religion may strengthen resistance. If, however, the dominant group is open to upward mobility from the subordinate group, then the subordinate group may accept religious change through upward mobility. All of these processes of change may be at work in a given society, especially if it is large and complex.

The desire to enhance some valued aspect of social identity seems to be a key motivation for making a change in another aspect of social identity (e.g. religious identity), but the basic motivation in relation to social identity has been much debated by social identity theorists. Abrams and Hogg (1993, 173-190) in their latest discussion of motivation suggested that although self-esteem is still important as a secondary or "derived motivation," the prime group motivation is "subjective uncertainty-reduction." This motivation, although it is in individuals as are all motivations, can only be realized by group belongingness and, as such, is a group motivation. Both the need for self-esteem and for subjective uncertainty-reduction fit well with why group members may either cling to their old religion or may change to a new religion that strengthens some aspect of their social identities. For my purposes it is not necessary to choose one of these motivations, but simply to recognize that both of them are powerful motivations and contribute to either religious change or resistance to change in religion. Most people want to preserve and if possible enhance certain groups of which they are members and a new or a reformulated religion may be an important means of doing so. At the same time, if a moral order has been disturbed, a new religion (developed from within or introduced from the outside) may help to reduce uncertainty through introduction of a new order. The theory of diffusion in this book is that intergroup relations are crucial in determining the direction from which a new religion may come.

Before concluding this discussion of theory, I would like to relate briefly the work of Hans Mol (1976) on identity to the present approach. The social identity theorists deliberately consider only the social aspects of identity so that they may examine the effects of intergroup relations on changes in those aspects of identity. Religious identity is clearly one of the aspects or parts of social identity, which, in fact, may be easier to change on the affiliation level (perhaps not on a deeper level) than other aspects of social identity. However, Mol deals with identity in a comprehensive way, which includes both personal and social identity, but which also makes it difficult to define (see pages 55-65). For Mol, identity becomes the central concept of his social scientific theory of religion, which may be defined as the sacralization of identity. His approach is helpful for my study in at least two respects.

Firstly, disturbances in the moral order are important as a conducive condition for change in religious identity (involving diffusion or resistance to diffusion of religion). For Mol (1976, 9) "identity, order, and views of reality are all intertwined." Personal and social identity require some order or stability and therefore the sacralizing process is used to safeguard and reinforce "this complex of orderly interpretations of reality, rules, and legitimations" (Mol 1976, 15). Disturbances in the moral order, therefore, are also disturbances in at least some parts of identity and it is at these times that the sacralizing process is most active (Mol 1976, 62). This part of Mol's approach is certainly consistent with my interest in the impact of intergroup relations on changes in religious identity, but, of course, he explores the deeper levels of identity and their relationship to religion, which I do not.

Another part of Mol's approach which is helpful has to do with ardor or strength of feeling. Since resistance to domination and threat is such an important part of my approach, I find Mol's emphasis on the strong feelings and efforts given to the defense of identity useful. Quoting Erickson (1963, 24), he "mentions the way individuals defend their identity 'with astonishing strength encountered in animals who are suddenly forced to defend their lives'" (Mol 1976, 2). It will be seen that such defense of identity, or as Tajfel (1981, 255-256) would say, certain valued aspects of identity, will contribute both to diffusion and resistance to diffusion.

Summary Statement

In closing this theoretical section, I will attempt to summarize in a paragraph a theoretical statement. The dependent variable or behavior to be explained is the variation in responses to the three diffusing religions, these variations broadly classified as acceptance, acceptance with conscious change, and rejection. The independent variable on the macro level is again broadly classified as conducive and nonconducive conditions found in the relationships which a receiving group has with the sending group *and* other surrounding rival groups. These relationships will be perceived in certain ways by members of a receiving group which will make them receptive or resistant to a religion being introduced.

A conducive condition for the diffusion of a religion exists when the religion being introduced is not perceived by members of the receiving group as being part of a threat to the moral order of their group, but rather as a source of strength for the group, creating self-esteem and enhancing the identities of group members in their resistance to rival groups or other dominating groups. It may be elite groups who receive the outside religion and then facilitate its diffusion to the larger society or the outside religion may be received at a lower level of society and endorsed by leaders later.

A non-conducive condition exists for diffusion if the diffusing religion is associated with a serious challenge or threat to the moral order of a receiving group and acceptance of the outside religion is perceived as weakening or devaluing valued aspects of social identity, especially ethnic, national, or social class identities. Resistance to the diffusing religion may be quite strong. Resistance may employ various revivals of or innovations in the traditional religion. Another rival outside religion may be accepted to aid in resistance, causing diffusion of the rival religion.

If the receiving group has few means for resistance to a diffusing religion being forced on them, the outside religion may be accepted, but changed in significant ways that preserve the distinctive identity of the receiving group. If the dominating religion is inclusive, changes will be introduced or "added" so that a gap will be evident between the official religion and popular religion. If the dominating religion is not inclusive, changes will be expressed through independent organizations and religious expressions.

I realize that by focusing on social identity, I am leaving out other parts of the reformulation and reorganization of groups so richly described by Wallace (1956, 1967) and Martin (1990), as well as of deeper levels of the meaning of identity as examined by Mol (1976). However, social identity appears to be a key link between the individual and groups. Also, religious identification is a means of participation in groups that formulate and reformulate moral orders. Real life, of course, cannot be fit into an abstract theoretical statement. As complex as a theory is, life is much more complex. The advantage of starting with such a statement is that the way is open to identify exceptions and make elaborations.

The Methodology

This study will undertake a broad-scale review of the historical data of the three religions, Buddhism, Christianity, and Islam. The focus will be on the initial periods when these religions (or versions of them) were introduced to groups and societies from the outside. However, each of these religions has undergone numerous changes and the causes of innovations in religions and the diffusion of these innovations are also related to the theory. That is, just as the diffusion of religions is affected by various social pressures, similar pressures may have similar results in the development and spread of later innovations.

Only three religions are being considered, although other religions and ideologies have diffused to a lesser extent, for example, Hinduism, Confucianism, and Manichaeism Because of its religious overtones and the broadness of its diffusion, Marxism could also be considered in a broader review. Certainly, the diffusion of and innovation in religions and ideologies follow similar patterns. However, consideration of the diffusion of the three selected religions should provide sufficient data (actually more than enough) for dealing with the theory advanced.

The difficulty, of course, is that even though I am dealing with only three religions (that have diffused in a relatively short time in comparison to the history of the human race), the number of cases is enormous, especially for Christianity in the last 500 years. A sampling approach could be used to look more carefully at a small set of cases. A case study approach itself, which has been the preferred method for detailed study and description, does not allow for comparisons that are needed in the move towards explanation. Actually, there needs to be some balance to the enormous number of village, community, ethnic group, and even national studies. This can be a kind of "raw empiricism" or the endless piling up of studies.

I decided that in this first review, at least a partial control on the data is exercised through attempting to be comprehensive. Therefore, I attempt to review the diffusion of these religions and their major variations from their origins to the present. Although clearly not all cases of their diffusion may be mentioned, much less examined, the review is aided by the fact that there are large areas and long periods where diffusion or resistance to diffusion took place under similar conditions and with similar results.

Interestingly, the experimental model can be simulated in the history of some areas of diffusion. An example of one of the best simulations is that of Korea and Japan. Over the last century, Christianity was brought to these two lands having similar religious traditions. Also, Christianity was brought by the same groups, carrying the same message, and using very similar methods. Yet certain conditions were quite different because of different relationships between the receiving countries and both the sending countries and nearby countries. In the case of Korea, a major threat came from a non-Christian society and Christianity became supportive of nationalism. In the case of Japan, the foreign threat was precisely from the nations from which the missionaries came. As very well known, the results of diffusion have been startlingly different. This is one of the best examples in which it is possible to isolate distinctive variables, but in general over the period of diffusion of the three religions there are many cases where similar conditions (in the religions that are diffusing and the receiving groups) make it possible to isolate those conditions (in intergroup relations) that are distinctive.

Nevertheless, since this is an historical review with a great deal of selection and interpretation by myself and others (my sources are almost all secondary), the theory cannot be demonstrated in any strict sense. My hope is to encourage more detailed historical studies and, especially, studies in which current data are used. Much of the history is fairly familiar, but rarely are comparisons made between areas.

One of the major difficulties in historical studies is obtaining indicators and measurements of the variables being examined. In the first place, as already noted, self-identification will be considered the standard as the indicator of religious affiliation rather than any external standard of "true" belief or allegiance. However, in many societies, especially ancient ones and others with few reporting facilities, religious affiliation must be inferred. Religious movements are noted for their lack of attention to counting. Furthermore, the diffusion being considered took place over many centuries when records were not kept systematically.

Campbell and Curtis (1994) considered alternative measures in national surveys of religion, bringing up to date the work of Sigelman (1977). This work, although it was limited primarily to industrialized countries, has great importance for a sociology of missions because it can show the great variations in religious beliefs that exist within and between societies (and religions) regardless of what official religious

A Theoretical Perspective and Methodology

views may be or official religious identities. In regard to the latter and with special relevance to the present study, Demerath (1994, 108-109) has noted that in many societies religious identity is ambiguous, having several levels of meaning. It is even possible to identify with one religion and practice another. These are the kinds of distinctions that need to be made in careful studies. In the present broad review, it was only possible to consider broad estimates of adherents.

In addition to the counting (estimating) of adherents, however, there are other indicators of the acceptance of a religion, such as numbers of places of worship, numbers of native clergy as compared with foreign clergy, and evidence of influence in literature, artifacts, and construction. Up until recent centuries, in many societies, the religion of the ruler was the tacit religion of the society and this may have been backed by force. In the large empires, various religions may have been tolerated, but even in the empires there were periods in which variety was not tolerated. Because of the broadness of approach, the present study will make little use of a variety of specific indicators, but I mention them for possible use in more careful examination of particular cases in contemporary studies.

Clearly, then, in an historical review, one of the major indicators of the acceptance or rejection of a religion is the attitude of the leaders of groups. This is particularly true in earlier societies when a single society tended to have a single dominant religion promoted by the leaders as a means of maintaining social unity. Elites have always been important in determining what is considered "foreign" and "native," that is, what is acceptable as an aspect of identity for members of the group. Some outside religions are first accepted by the elite who then bring about religious change through various forms of pressure on the rest of the group. At other times, change is exerted upwards as ordinary members of a group or marginal groups accept a new religion and the leaders finally make the change.

This book will not undertake a systematic use of measurements of religious change nor will the process of change itself within societies receive major attention. I leave this to later studies in the sociology of missions. I am dependent primarily on historians and missiologists as to what they report regarding adherents or simply the allegiances of groups. Barrett's (1982) statistics on religious adherents, especially in Africa and the Americas, were very useful.

The diffusion of the three religions are treated in historical order with the diffusion of Islam coming between chapters on the diffusion of Christianity. Also, the later diffusion of Christianity requires extra treatment because of the large number of cases. The chapters review the historical data and then discuss the data in relation to the theoretical approach already stated. The purpose is to consider history not as a narrative, but as a series of events.

A concluding chapter seeks to bring together the major findings of the previous chapters and point to possibilities for future research. I have included an appendix, which expresses my views regarding some theological and missiological implications of the study.

Chapter 3

Buddhism

A New Moral Order for a New Set of Rulers

Christianity and Islam began their diffusion very soon after the death of their founders, but Buddhism did not begin to diffuse from its home base in India until over two centuries after the death of its founder, estimated to be about 483 B.C.E. Buddhism was one of several innovative religious movements in tension with the dominant Brahmanism, the latter having been building up since about 900 B.C.E. (Thapar 1969, 306). Thus, Buddhism developed as a dissenting religion. It was a "deviant sect," along with several others in India. It was during the Mauryan empire that Buddhism appears to have been favored, particularly by the Emperor Aśoka, the grandson of the founder of the dynasty, Candragupta, who began his career about 321 B.C.E.

Romila Thapar (1969, 306) notes that the less fortunate of the four castes tended to favor new sects and that the third caste (vaisyas), made up primarily of merchants, landowners, and wealthier cultivators, was gaining strength prior to the ascendancy of the Mauryas. Above them were the priests and the aristocrats. Aśoka's grandfather and father were said to be members of non-orthodox sects, antagonistic to Brahmanical ideas, and Aśoka became identified as a Buddhist. This was in the beginning of the second century B.C.E. and thus some 250 years after Buddha lived. In contrast to Brahmanism, Buddhism "demanded a relaxing of the social rigidity encouraged by the caste system" (Thapar 1969, 306) and was actually a spearhead of the sects that had been questioning the older Brahman traditions and were at times regarded as atheistic.

At the time of the Mauryan ascendancy, a much wider variety of peoples than ever before were brought together under one rule. According to Thapar's (1969) analysis, the Mauryan kings needed a new ideology that would aid in the governing of a variety of peoples through a complex imperial structure. They did not want to be dependent on the older upper castes and the ceremonies and rituals of the priests. Aśoka promoted the principles of "Dhamma," which emphasized toleration, non-violence, and social welfare (Thapar 1969, 308). Asoka was so enthusiastic about the value of "Dhamma" that he sent missions of "the officers of Dhamma," a type of priesthood, to neighboring countries and to various Hellenic kingdoms in the west (309). "Dhamma" was not identical to Buddhism, but was certainly based upon it and the point was made that Buddhism provided an ethic that was supportive of a peaceful and prosperous rule over diverse peoples. At the same time, Buddhism had a strong element of anti-elitism based on universalistic principles and the possibilities of individual salvation.

Thapar's analysis is important because it shows that the advancement of Buddhism in its country of origin was associated with a shift in the moral order that accompanied the rise of a new set of rulers. The new rulers needed support against the older authorities and an ethic for the newly ascendant groups. This analysis also helps to explain why Buddhism was more successful than Hinduism, its mother religion, in spreading to other societies. In Southeast Asia particularly, Hinduism and Buddhism were jointly influential, but Buddhism ultimately had greater success with the broader populations. Also, with its ethic for rulers we see why Buddhism appealed repeatedly to leaders of newly established states as a source of strength for their new orders.

Although Buddhism continued to enjoy great prestige throughout India, forty years after the death of the great Mauryan, Asoka, the older Hindu influences returned to prominence with the empire of the Guptas (Noss 1949, 179-180). Thus, Buddhism could be considered a variation of Hinduism that ultimately developed independently rather than within Hinduism. Unlike Shi'ism or Protestantism, the adherents of Buddhism came to identify themselves as a distinct religion from their "mother" religion. However, two great versions of Buddhism have developed, (1) Hinayana, with its major form, Theravada and (2) Mahayana.

Buddhism of the Old School - Theravada

The Buddhism that diffused to the south and east became foundational for the civilizations that developed there, being adopted by groups which were preliterate. It became established as the official religion of many societies and an important aspect of the identities of people throughout the region.

Probably one of the earliest societies to accept Buddhism outside of India were the Sinhalese of Sri Lanka. These were people who had migrated from northern India (the base of the Mauryan empire) and who were in a continuous struggle with the Hindu Tamil peoples of South India and Sri Lanka. The fifth century writing, the *Mahavamsa*, although full of legends, clearly shows that Buddhism was associated with the national or ethnic identity of the Sinhalese (Ludowyk 1962, 55). Buddhism aided the Sinhalese to distinguish themselves from their traditional enemies, the Tamil people, who continued to be identified with Hinduism. Thus, the religion from an advanced, but non-threatening society, aided the Sinhalese in opposing pressure from nearby societies, at least partly by affirming and enhancing an already existing distinction. After Buddhism virtually disappeared from its country of origin, it continued to be strongly maintained in Sri Lanka, as well as in other Southeast Asian countries.

Indian culture of the great Mauryan empire also had a strong influence on the developing kingdoms across the Bay of Bengal. In present day Myanmar (Burma), there can be no doubt that the early people known as Pyus were Buddhist, as were the Mon people. Hinduism and Buddhism were to some extent rivals in Southeast Asia in many societies, but Theravada Buddhism eventually achieved the dominant influence. M.H. Aung (1967, 23) notes that although India clearly had an important cultural impact on the peoples of Myanmar, Theravada Buddhism from Sri Lanka had an even more important impact. The Mons, who were "less democratic than the Pyus" adopted both the Hindu idea of the divine king and the Hindu law code of Manu, but "the Siva cult, which became so popular in the Khmer and Javanese empires, could make no great headway among the Mons because of their long tradition of Buddhism" (Aung 1967, 24).

The Mon people, although they came to be dominated by other peoples, became the most culturally advanced in the region and their influence, which included being teachers of Buddhism, extended throughout mainland Southeast Asia. Hinduism often appeared to appeal to rulers, including the Mon rulers, but Theravada Buddhism was accepted and renewed by a new people, the Burmese, who came into the region from the north and dominated the Mon people.

Indian culture with its strong Hindu elements seemed to have had a great influence in other early kingdoms in mainland Southeast Asia and somewhat later in Indonesia. The Funan (first to sixth century) were overthrown by the Chenla, who in turn were incorporated into the even larger Khmer Empire, whose power increased in the late seventh century. Indian scholars, artists, and religious leaders were prominent in the court, especially among the Khmer. Hinduism tended to be the main royal cult, while Buddhism diffused throughout the kingdoms and also received royal patronage. Eventually, Hinduism was dropped in favor of Theravada Buddhism introduced from Burma (Robinson and Johnson, 1982, 116). When the Thais came on the scene, the pattern of pervasive Buddhism became established at least by the late twelfth and early thirteenth centuries. "Despite the court Brahmanism, Thais of all social classes considered themselves Buddhists" (Robinson and Johnson, 1982, 117). A little later Theravada Buddhism became the official religion of Laos in the fourteenth century.

Several important groups did not receive Theravada Buddhism as it diffused, primarily from Sri Lanka and the Mon people. One important set of groups were the minority mountain tribal peoples who remained isolated from the various kingdoms and continued in their animism. Another important set of groups that eventually followed a different religious route were the peoples on the edges of mainland Southeast Asia, who were ethnically Malay. One group was the people of Champa who had initially been receptive to Hinduism. They had to struggle for centuries to maintain their independence from the Khmers to the west and the Dai Viet to the north. Eventually, they largely accepted Islam.

The ethnically similar people to the south, the Malays and the Indonesians, largely followed a similar path of eventual rejection of Buddhism. Initially, Hinduism or Buddhism or a mixture of the two, was prevalent among the rulers of the new states. The Hindu concepts of a god-king (devaraja) and of court ritual were particularly useful for the establishment of states as it was on the mainland to the north. During the latter half of the fifteenth century, however, kingdoms in the Malay Peninsula and Indonesia converted to Islam with the exception of the island of Bali, where "a Hindu-Buddhism mysticism survives today" (Robinson and Johnson 1982, 118). Islam was allied to the rising trading class and also contributed to resistance to domination from the outside. Soon after coming to the throne of Malacca in 1446, the new king refused to continue paying tribute to the Buddhist Ayuthaya kingdom (Siam) and was able to defeat its forces.

A final exception to the reception of Theravada Buddhism were the Dai Viet, who accepted Mahayana Buddhism from China along with numerous other cultural influences, such as Confucianism and Taoism. They overran the Champa kingdom that earlier had helped them resist the Mongols. With the conversion of the Dai Viet, Buddhism became the dominant religion on mainland Southeast Asia, the exceptions being the animistic tribal peoples and the Malay people on the southeastern edges. Except for the people on Bali, Indian cultural influences lost out to Islam among the Malay people in what is now Malyasia, Indonesia, and the southern Philippines.

It may be noted that it is the older or Theravada version of Buddhism which became the dominant form in South and Southeast Asia. In this form the monk is the central figure and the religion is less elaborated than in Mahayana. Although "the *average* Hinayanist" prays to a supernatural personality represented in the image of Buddha, the more learned monks know that although "prayer increases merit...there is no *answer*" because Buddha is in Nirvana (Noss 149, 179).

This older version of Buddhism formed a foundation for the civilizations that developed in South and Southeast Asia. There had been no previous literature and Buddhism brought both literature and scholar-monks. At the same time, Buddhism became strongly associated with the ruling authorities and was officially promoted over a long period. In accordance with the theory of this book, it is important to note that where Buddhism became strongly associated with authority and a broad social identity, a gap developed between "what Redfield (1957) calls the 'big tradition' (the 'official' beliefs as defined by the elites) and the 'little tradition' (the version of a religion to which everyday people adhere)" (Kurtz 1995, 22-23). In other words, domination by an "official" religion is conducive to the development of an "unofficial" religion.

Mahayana or Elaborated Buddhism

Mahayana, the more elaborated form of Buddhism, developed first in India, probably because of dissatisfaction with the older traditions that were considered too conservative and literalistic (Ch'en 1963, 12). Once the Mahayanists broke from the more conservative Hinayanists, who were dominated by the monks in the homeland of India, Mahayana developed a rather different form of Buddhism. Noss (1949, 182) writes:

> Countries which responded slowly to the appeal of the Hinayana doctrines now took up the Mahayana with eagerness. And because the Mahayana was by nature expansive, it changed as it moved; the peoples among which it made its way contributed to its development.

For me, Theravada was also expansive in its way, but the "expansive nature" of Mahayana was due to the religiously competitive environment into which it entered and its ultimately less authoritarian position (at least in China and beyond) than Theravada.

In the northern diffusion of Buddhism, an invading group, the Kushans accepted Buddhism from the people they conquered and became the primary means for the diffusion of Buddhism to Central Asia from where it subsequently spread to China, then to Korea and Japan. The Kushans were people who had earlier been pushed westward where they crossed the Pamirs. They were known as Yüeh-Chih by the Chinese and regarded as allies against the wild tribes between them. The Han Empire (206 B.C.E.- 220 C.E.) through much effort extended its influence to the northwest over what is now Xinjiang, but in doing so was in recurring conflict with the tribes that had been largely responsible for pushing the Yüeh-Chih westward.

Kadfiz founded the Kushan empire in 15 C.E. and Kanishka I became a great patron of Mahayana Buddhism, initiating a tradition of constructing images of Buddha. The Kushans fought with the Parthians, who were largely adherents of Zoroastrianism. The Parthians were relatively tolerant of various religions. Some of them accepted Buddhism and even became missionaries to China. However, the Parthians had an advanced religion in Zoroastrianism and the succeeding Sassanids sponsored a nationalistic revival of Zoroastrianism. The power of the Kushans was broken in the middle of the third century by the Sassanians, the Persian successors to the Parthians. However, Kushan authority continued northeast of Persia.

In China, Buddhism encountered a people with a developed literature and with organized religions. During the Han Dynasty, Buddhist scholars, many of whom were translators of Buddhist writings, made their way from the Buddhist centers of Central Asia to China. The Han rulers developed armies that were able to defeat the northern tribes and at various times the trade routes were open for trade and the passage of scholars. Up to the end of the Han dynasty (C.E. 220), it is probably true that Buddhism was a religion of foreigners, "either fresh immigrants or persons of foreign extraction - among whom Indian or Central Asian copies of Buddhist scriptures circulated" (Zurcher 1959, 24). It was in the tumultuous centuries following the fall of the Han Dynasty that Buddhism established its roots in China.

After four hundred years of relative stability, China entered a period of great instability that lasted some 370 years until the founding of the Sui Dynasty (589-618), which was followed by the famous Tang Dynasty (618-907). It was during the period of instability between the Han Dynasty and the Sui and Tang Dynasties that Buddhism was widely accepted in China. Numerous dynasties rose and fell and large numbers of Chinese migrated to the south under pressure from the northern tribes. The final breakdown of Chinese rule in the north came at the beginning of the fourth century and for the first time in recorded Chinese history, a sinicized Hun ruler, "commander of five Hsiung-nu hordes," brought an end to Chinese sovereignty in the north that was not restored for almost three centuries (Zurcher 1959, 58).

The reception of Buddhism in China took place in two major patterns. On the one hand, Buddhism was accepted and given state sponsorship by the foreign, formally tribal, rulers in north China. Although it is well known that these foreign rulers adopted Chinese culture, it should be noted that the religion which they soon promoted was not the traditional Chinese religion of the court, Confucianism, but the religion imported from central Asia, primarily by scholarly translators of scriptures. The Buddhist scriptures were impressive to the receiving societies, especially those in the north, many of which were ruled by people who recently were tribespeople.

While Buddhism became favored by the new foreign rulers in the north and the numerous foreign settlers, another movement towards Buddhism took place among the Chinese gentry, many of whom became displaced. The gentry amounted to a disinherited social group. Some of the Chinese gentry helped the foreigners rule but many others migrated to the south. There is considerable literary evidence, cited by Zurcher (1959, 71-73), that Buddhism penetrated the Chinese gentry primarily after 300 C.E. Buddhism had been introduced by foreign scholars well before this time, and there were some Chinese adherents, but it was during this time of turmoil and displacement that the new doctrines of Buddhism found acceptance among the gentry, both in the north and the south.

There was some resistance from the traditional Chinese religion, Taoism, which had some similarity to Buddhism, and from Confucianism, which was previously most closely associated with government officialdom. There was a persecution of Buddhists in the north in 446 C.E. instigated by Chinese government officials under the foreign Emperor, but after the death of the leading officials involved, the measures against Buddhism were relaxed and then were revoked under the next emperor (Ch'en 1963, 147-153). Over a century later, there was another brief suppression (574-577) of Buddhism in the north by the sinicized emperor, who had decided that Confucianism should be favored (Ch'en 1963, 190-194). Again, the next emperor was more sympathetic to Buddhism.

In the south, where there was greater intellectual debate and less official sponsorship, reaction against Buddhism took a different form. In the south, instead of official persecutions, the opposition took the form of treatises attacking Buddhism on various grounds. Ch'en (1963, 136) attributes this to the weakness of the Chinese governments in the south and to the strong tradition of moderation in the Confucian tradition.

Following the reunification of China under the Sui (589-618) and Tang (618-907), Buddhism solidified its place of acceptance at all levels of society. The Tang imperial clan favored Taoism, but generally followed a policy of toleration of all religions, which now included Nestorian Christianity, Islam, and Manichaeism. There continued to be anti-Buddhist writings from intellectuals, especially the scholar-bureaucrats. A strong, but short-lived, suppression of Buddhism developed, reaching a climax in 845, which also included Manichaeism, Nestorianism, and Zoroastrianism. Although the successor emperor revoked the suppression in 846, the creative age of Buddhism in China was completed.

The growth of Buddhism in China formed a base for the further expansion of Buddhism to Korea and Japan. Both of these countries were behind China in cultural development in numerous aspects from writing to art to government. Ethnically and linguistically, Korea is closer to Central Asian groups than to China, but its location brought it under Chinese cultural influence.

The Han Dynasty established colonies in Korea, one of which, Lelang or Lolang (108 - 313 C.E.), survived the parent dynasty (Cumings 1994, 6). During this time of weakness in China, three kingdoms developed in Korea and in the fourth century, one of the kingdoms, Koguryo, expanded in power. Buddhism is said to have been introduced to Koguryo in 372 C.E. and two years later to Paekche by monks from China. Two other kingdoms to the south, Paekche and Silla, were weaker than Koguryo; however, Silla gained strength and by the mid-sixth century asserted control over the central area with help from China.

Although Buddhist monks were sent to these kingdoms from China at least by the fourth century, it was in Silla that Buddhism was most strongly embraced by the elite and made the state religion around 535. In the meantime, Koguryo was invaded by Sui and then Tang forces, but was able to defeat them in striking victories (Cumings 1994, 8). Koguryo finally succumbed to combined forces from Tang China and Silla. Paekche also fell to this combination of forces, but not before its many trading ships had carried Buddhism to Japan. There was now a single state for the peninsula in 668 C.E., which was at its height of power and civilization until 780 C.E. During this time Buddhism flourished and Silla monks were sent to China and India. At the same time, a Confucian academy was established and Confucianism was influential along with Buddhism (Cumings 1994, 11). By the late 900s, new kingdoms had developed, claiming to be revivals of Paekche and Koguryo, and Silla power did not extend beyond the capital district.

The three kingdoms were unified in 936 under the kingdom of Koryo during which time Confucianism was increasingly upheld as a new ideology. However, Buddhism continued in its influence as witnessed by the fact that the entire Buddhist canon was put on woodblocks of movable type in 1234, two centuries before Gutenburg. Under the Yi dynasty (1392-1910), the influence of Buddhism in the government was restricted and Confucianism further advanced.

Buddhism was introduced to Japan from Korea at a period when a centralized monarchy was being consolidated "out of a federation of tribes" (Robinson and Johnson, 1982, 198). The Soga clan rose to prominence with the accession of the emperor about 531 C.E. The Soga clan, which intermarried with the royal family became strong supporters of Buddhism. The regent, Shotoku Taishi (574-622), was a devout Buddhist. There was a strong reaction against Soga domination in the Taika Reform of 645, but Buddhism remained and spread through all classes of society in the following centuries. Robinson and Johnson (1982, 198) comment, "Confucians did not like to go abroad and teach among 'barbarians,' so in Japan the Buddhists had the field to themselves for centuries." Korean influence declined, but like Korea, Japan sent monks to China and India. Chinese cultural influence was great, but Japan did not consider itself subordinate to China. Outside of the Mongolian unsuccessful attempt to invade Japan in the thirteenth century, there was no military threat from China.

Tibet lies between India and China, but was protected from both by its high mountains. A strong kingdom developed in the seventh century under the first Tibetan emperor, Songzen Gampo (620-649.). He defeated and unified a large area of Inner Asia and held his own against the Tang emperor of the time. He built Lhasa, constructing a Buddhist cathedral. There was opposition to Buddhism from regional nobles in the name of the previous animistic religion. About 840, Buddhism was persecuted by a new king, but later in the 10th to 13th centuries, the regional rulers sponsored the return of Buddhism.

Tibet was important in the official acceptance of Buddhism by Altan Khan of Mongolia in 1578. Tibetan became the language of ritual. The Buddhists gave legitimacy to Altan Khan and he, in turn, gave patronage to them. It is worth noting that Mongolia received its Buddhism from Tibet rather than from China, the traditional enemy. The Mongols which had settled in Central Asia became largely assimilated to Turkic groups and with them converted to Islam. The road through Central Asia, by which Buddhism had come to China, became a road for Islam to enter northwestern China.

The story of the diffusion of Buddhism to the East ends almost four hundred years ago. However, towards the end of the 19th century and especially in the 20th century, there has been some diffusion to Western countries, apart from the diffusion that has occurred with migration. Benz (1976, 305,308) claims that Buddhism in the West has had the most impact on the United States, where he sees a "Zen boom" in American philosophy, psychiatry, and psychotherapy. Kapleau (1979, 263) remarks how in 1950 Dr. Suzuki drew "scores of painters, composers, poets, psychiatrists, and philosophy professors" to his classes on Zen. The actual number of Buddhists in North America who are not immigrants or descendants of immigrants from Asia is very difficult to determine. Morreale (1988) undertook to list Buddhist centers in North America and was able to prepare a list of 433 centers of various types and an additional fifty-five unconfirmed centers. Although there is no large-scale movement to Buddhism, there is a certain receptivity among intellectuals of a humanistic and artistic bent.

Variations Compared

Differences in the two major variations of Buddhism have already been noted, but additional comparisons may be made. In South and Southeast Asia where Buddhism has been officially sponsored for an extended time and has become a pervasive aspect of social identity, a gap developed between the official and highly literalistic Buddhism and popular Buddhism. Popular Buddhism became an unofficial innovation. On the other hand, in Mahayana, which was not always able to maintain official sponsorship, numerous schools developed in which lay participation became important.

In Mahayana, Buddhism became more "religious" in the sense that Buddha "was adored and worshipped as a divine being, who came to earth out of compassion for suffering humanity" (Noss 1969, 181). Instead of salvation being an individual discipline, primarily for monks and nuns, as in Theravada, in Mahayana the salvation of enlightenment was offered broadly to those who live by faith and compassion (Ch'en 1963, 12). The emphasis was placed on Buddha remaining a "bodhisattva" and thus a vital intermediary between the human and divine worlds (Kurtz 1995, 37).

Within the broad area in which Mahayana spread, often gaining official sponsorship for a period of time, but competing with other religions, various schools of thought and practice were developed. Tantric Buddhism, with a special emphasis on magic, developed in India, and seems to have represented a kind of "reversal to primitive ways of thinking and acting" (Conze 1975, 181). It was introduced to Tibet and was eventually elaborated into the Laminism of Tibet and

Mongolia. In these lands, unlike in China and eastward, Buddhism appears to have had prolonged official sponsorship.

Other schools developed in Mahayana outside of India and "profoundly modified the Indian impulse"(Conze 1975, 200). These non-Indian and initially Chinese developments include Ch'an (Zen) and Amidism. "Ch'an," coming from the Chinese version of the Sanskrit word for "meditation," was founded in China probably in the fifth century. Buddhism, which survived the persecution under the T'ang dynasty in 845 better than any other religion, found its greatest expression under the T'ang masters of Ch'an (Conze 1975, 201-202). Later, of course, Ch'an became influential in Japan as Zen.

Another form of Buddhism, which was greatly elaborated in China, was "Amidism" or "Pure Land School" (Conze 1975, 205). It emphasized the availability of grace to all and access to a Paradise in the West. The cult of Kwan-Yin, the Goddess of Mercy, became associated with Amidism and, like Ch'an, Amidism found acceptance in Japan and Korea. In Amidism, the "original Buddhism is completely transcended" and "the Mahayanists frankly recognize this departure from early Buddhist teaching" (Noss 1949, 193). However, "they have the belief that Gautama taught several kinds of doctrine, depending on the nature of the hearers: to the weak and selfish he outlined the eightfold arahat path; to those of greater understanding and strength of character he imparted the ideal of the compassionate and altruistic bodhisattva" (Noss 1949, 193).

It is not my purpose to enter a debate on the "true" content of Buddhism, but to try to understand why it was elaborated into a variety of schools in Mahayana, but not in Hinayana, in which the variation has been an "unofficial" addition. In the areas dominated by Theravada (the form of Hinayana that remained and diffused), Buddhism did not have to contend with already well established religions having their own literary traditions. Buddhism became foundational to the civilizations that were established in Southeast Asia and also rather closely connected to the governmental authorities. Changes introduced to Hinayana tended to be of the type that are "unofficial" rather than in the form of independent "schools." This means that there tends to be a greater distinction than in Mahayana between official or monkish understanding and popular religion, the "great tradition" and "little tradition" (Redfield 1967).

On the other hand, in the areas where Mahayana first developed (India) and to which it later spread (China), Buddhism had to contend with well established religious and moral traditions and was not able to sustain official sponsorship continuously. In China, especially, it could be pointed to as a "foreign import." Thus, Buddhism did not remain in association with a dominating power nor become the single dominant source for religious identity. If it is true, as Max Weber (1964, 195) noted, that Buddhism was favored as "a means of taming the masses," it was not generally feared for its political influence. The great persecution of Buddhism in China in 845 was of short duration, as with previous persecutions, but a decline continued from which Buddhism never fully recovered (Ch'en 1963, 232-233). In Korea also, after enjoying official sponsorship, Buddhism lost favor while Confucianism gained favor with the rulers. In Japan, a state religion, Shinto, developed alongside Buddhism. Thus, in the Mahayana areas, at least outside of Tibet and Mongolia, various "schools" developed and lay leadership became highly important.

Discussion

The theoretical approach of this book is to emphasize the importance of social group relationships and the effects of domination and resistance to domination in the diffusion of religions and subsequent changes in religions. Buddhism may offer the most difficulty in examining this approach because of the problem of knowing the number and characteristics of intergroup relationships, the consciousness of distinctive identities, and the sense of self-esteem of peoples during the period of the major expansion and elaborations of Buddhism. Much of this kind of historical information must be inferred, especially for ancient times.

The spread of Buddhism like "spilt ink" may be used to argue for social contact as a major factor in diffusion. Certainly, I would not argue against the necessity for there to be carriers of a religion in order for it to diffuse and in the period of major Buddhist expansion, intergroup contacts were more limited, being primarily with neighboring groups, than they became in the modern era. However, the history of the diffusion of Buddhism and the development of its major variations provides data for the argument that domination and resistance to domination in intergroup relations affect reception, rejection, and change in religion, as well as the development of religions in the first place.

In India itself, after the fall of the Mauryan dynasty, Hinduism reasserted itself with new rulers in central India, the Guptas, and subsequently Buddhism became associated with the nomadic invaders from the northwest, the Kushans. Hinduism also remained strong among the Tamils of southern India, who were (and are) in conflict with the Sinhalese.

As it spread eastward and southward, rarely was Buddhism introduced to a group in association with an intruding or dominating power which became a threat to the order of the receiving group. Rather, it was repeatedly received (including in its land of origin) by leaders of ascending powers for whom it was apparently perceived as strengthening the religious and moral base of their rule. One possible case outside of India in which Buddhism was rejected because of association with an intruding power is to the west of India, where the Kushans, after accepting Buddhism from the people they conquered, engaged in extended conflict with the people to the west. In that area (Iran), at least, Buddhism would be seen as associated with an external military threat. It may be assumed that the Sassanids perceived the bearers of Buddhism, the Kushans, as a threat to their national religion of Zoroatrianism, a basis for their national identity. At any rate, Buddhism was deflected to the north and from thence eastward.

Other possible cases of Buddhist association with power that threatened groups to which Buddhism could potentially diffuse may be seen in the relationship of the Khmers to Champa and of Thailand to Malacca. In both cases, which involved similar ethnic distinctions, Islam rather than Buddhism was eventually accepted by those being threatened by the Khmers and the Thai respectively. This is consistent with the perspective that the religion associated with intrusion is rejected and one that supports resistance to intrusion is accepted. Another case of rejection of one religion associated with an enemy and acceptance of another religion (or version of religion) from a non-threatening group may be seen in the case of the Mongols, who accepted Buddhism from Tibet rather than from their nearby enemies, the Chinese. Koguryo in northern Korea may be another case where Buddhism was initially rejected because of its association with intruding Chinese power. When Koguryo did receive Buddhism, China had ceased to be a strong threat. In the above cases, consistent with the theory, domination was associated with rejection of Buddhism.

In opposition to the theory it might be argued that in Vietman, Mahayana Buddhism was accepted from China during the long period of

Chinese domination. However, the Chinese rulers stressed Taoist and Confucian learning and after the end of Chinese rule in 939, "Buddhism in Vietnam became more and more an expression of national feeling and culture" (Robinson and Johnson, 1982, 194). It is also true that the international character of Buddhism must have been clear to the Vietnamese both from the non-Chinese missionaries and the presence of Buddhism (in another form) in the rest of Southeast Asia.

In the vast majority of cases of the diffusion of Buddhism, the receiving groups appear not to have been threatened by any power associated with Buddhism. Rather, it appears that Buddhism was often a support against outside threat. India and Sri Lanka did not threaten the orders of the groups to which Buddhism spread. The ocean and vast land distances separated them from countries to the south and east. This reduced the danger of military conquest from India and Sri Lanka, but did not prevent cultural contacts through traders and travelers. India did not conquer, but was conquered by the Kushans, who subsequently accepted Buddhism. The Mons, likewise, were dominated by those to whom they spread Buddhism.

The spread of Buddhism to Sri Lanka follows rather clearly the pattern posited in the theory. There, Buddhism was received from some distance and supported one ethnic group, the Sinhalese, (who had ethnic affinities with the northern Indians) in distinguishing themselves from and resisting their nearby Tamil neighbors. On the other hand, the Tamils remained largely Hindu, as did India after the Mauryas.

The kingdoms of China accepted Buddhism in the period after the fall of the Han Dynasty when the various kingdoms faced their greatest threats from rival kingdoms, not from the land of origin for Buddhism or from Central Asia. Significantly, the rulers of these northern kingdoms were recently tribal people from the north. In these cases, Buddhism offered a new and culturally respected basis for order in a very unstable world and also provided a contrast with the previous Chinese rulers. Consistent with the view that early adopters are characterized by high socio-economic status (Perry 1992, 490), in these, as in other cases, Buddhism was received by the elite of societies who were seeking to solidify their position in an unstable world, often against challenges from internal factions or from nearby power centers. Also, Buddhism certainly aided in clarifying the distinction between the receiving group and other groups and probably also contributed to the self-esteem of the receiving group because of the scholarly characteristics of Buddhism. This would appear to be true especially for the foreign ruled kingdoms of northern China, as well as for many of the kingdoms of Southeast Asia, Korea, and Japan.

Thus, Buddhism, when it was received, generally fits the pattern of a religion that is introduced "from below." It spread "from below" between societies, although it often spread "from above" within societies. Still, while it often gained the support of the rulers, sometimes after an extended period, it was more the intellectual elite than the political elite who were the major carriers (especially in northern Asia). Furthermore, Buddhism was able to attract a popular following in most societies, which, in turn, provided a base of support when rulers turned against it. Hinduism and Confucianism, both favored at times by elite groups, were not able to spread similarly at the popular level. Hinduism and Confucianism both appear to have had closer long-term associations with political elites than Buddhism except where Buddhism gained and maintained the support of elites in South and Southeast Asia.

In most of Southeast Asia, Central Asia, north China, Korea, and Japan, Buddhism was received by rulers or aspiring rulers of newly established states without a literary culture. In China, particularly in the south, where the Chinese were rulers, there is the case where Buddhism was received in a society with established *literary* religious and ideological traditions. It was a period, however, of extreme turmoil when these traditions appeared particularly ineffective. Furthermore, these traditions, Taoism and Confucianism, did assert themselves against Buddhism and at times were able to suppress it. The same is true in Korea, where Confucianism gained acceptance among the rulers, again, of a rising new kingdom. As noted above, Vietnam appears to be an exception to the pattern in which Buddhism was introduced "from below," since both Buddhism and Confucianism were introduced from China, which dominated Vietnam for a long period. However, Buddhism appears to be less "from above" than Confucianism.

Major variations in Buddhism between Hinayana and Mahayana versions may be seen as at least partially related to the different patterns of domination associated with Buddhism. That is, in South and Southeast Asia, Buddhism has enjoyed its most enduring official support and pervasive influence. The major variation, therefore, has taken place *within* official Buddhism in the distinction between official, monkish Buddhism and popular Buddhism. In the areas to which

Mahayana spread, especially in north Asia, Buddhism lost official sponsorship and was in competition with other religious traditions. Here various schools of thought and practice were elaborated and broad lay participation in leadership became normative.

The diffusion of Buddhism to the West in the last century is certainly not associated with any intruding military or political power. Although the reception has not been large and the receivers have not been associated with social groups that are clearly defined, such as particular ethnic groups, the receivers do belong primarily to a subgroup of intellectuals for whom the inner life is important, namely psychologists and artists. Also, this group is not very influential institutionally, except in some parts of the literary and academic worlds. To some extent, Buddhism offers an "oppositional ideology" to some traditional ideologies that are well established in the larger society, especially Christianity. In this sense, Buddhism is allied with "intellectualism," which since the Enlightenment, has been opposed to traditional Christianity. According to the theory, it may be predicted that Buddhism will continue to diffuse to intellectuals seeking an "oppositional ideology." that is also religious or deals with the "inner life.".

Conclusion

It is easy to see how Buddhism is thought simply to have diffused through mere contact between groups. Certainly, propinquity facilitates diffusion. Examination reveals, however, that the nature of intergroup relations played an important part in the diffusion of Buddhism, contributing to delayed or rapid acceptance or its rejection and deflection. The nature of intergroup relations and of domination patterns also affected the characteristics of the variations that developed within Buddhism. This recognition of the effects of intergroup relations, however, does not mean that the internal characteristics of Buddhism, namely, its emphasis on compassion and individual salvation, its egalitarianism, its scholarly literature, and its missionary activities did not make an important contribution to the diffusion and subsequent changes in Buddhism. Some of these characteristics seem to have given it an advantage over both Hinduism and Confucianism. It was seen that Buddhism was not received by certain societies and these cases are consistent with the argument of this book. One important society, which stood between Buddhism and its diffusion westward, was Iran with first the Parthians (who were tolerant of Buddhism) and then the Sassanid Persians as rulers, who had overthrown the Parthians. These societies were in conflict with the Kushans, who were carriers of Buddhism at a crucial time for possible diffusion westward. The Sassanids were also strongly identified with a revived Zoroastrianism.

Buddhism also failed to diffuse to most of the domains of the Malayo-Polynesian peoples, except for a period of influence along with Hinduism in Indonesia. Important inter-ethnic conflicts developed between some of these peoples and the Buddhist societies to the north. Interestingly, the island of Bali, far from this conflict line, preserves a version of Hindu-Buddhist religion in contrast to the dominant religion of the area. A diffusing religion appears often to strengthen or enhance existing social distinctions.

By and large, Buddhism was introduced successfully to groups or societies by people who did not apparently come from groups that threatened the receivers. The original country of origin, India, and many of the succeeding sending societies were far from most of the receiving societies. When the sending societies were not far away, they were usually not in a position of domination or threat. In some cases, the receiving societies were themselves dominating powers, as when the Kushans received Buddhism from India and the Burmese from the Mons. It can be said, then, that Buddhism, in most cases where it diffused successfully, was introduced "from below," that is, not from a position of dominance. However, after acceptance, it often diffused downward from the leaders.

In other words, Buddhism was repeatedly received by the elites of societies, who then became its patrons. It seems safe to assume that in these cases Buddhism was perceived as contributing positively to the order of these societies and probably as enhancing the ethnic or national identities of those who accepted the religion. At times, however, elites, for example in China and Korea, later turned against Buddhism and favored Confucianism as more supportive of their position. The elites of Southeast Asia were often able to combine their Hinduism with Buddhism.

Although largely consistent with the theory advanced about the influence of intergroup relations on diffusion, the review of the diffusion of Buddhism offers a limited number of contrasting cases of reception. This is due to the pervasiveness of the diffusion of Buddhism in the areas to which it diffused before the modern era. The areas of major resistance were primarily on the edges of the areas of major diffusion. Islam and especially Christianity offer greater opportunities to observe variations in diffusion.

Chapter 4

Christianity Before 1500

Diffusion and Variations in the Mediterranean Basin

Looking at the rise of Christianity in terms of intergroup relations and social identity, it may be said that the first participants in the Christian movement were people who were geographically, organizationally, and in religious-social status on the periphery of Jewish life. They moved from the periphery of a traditional religion to the center of a new religious movement. A second wave of Jewish participants in the Christian movement were Diaspora Jews who faced a choice of clinging more closely to their Jewish heritage or entering more fully into Gentile life. These Jewish participants perceived that in the Christian movement they could both affirm their Jewish heritage and at the same time engage the larger Gentile world through the Christian movement. However, from the beginning, there were Jewish people, first in the homeland and subsequently among the overseas Jews, for whom the Christian movement was interpreted as posing a grave threat to Jewish identity in the denial of the centrality of its great institutions of the law, the Temple, and the Holy City.

Within one or two generations the Jewish portion of the Christian movement became a minority as Christianity diffused among the Gentile populations of the Roman Empire. This development tended to confirm the view of many Jews that Christianity posed a threat to distinctive Jewish identity. In contrast to the view that Christianity posed a threat to their identity, Gentile groups on the periphery of life in the empire (such as women, slaves, and conquered peoples) continued to perceive their identities as being affirmed and enhanced in the Christian movement over against those denying their significance.

The story of the spread of Christianity is relatively familiar, but it is often thought of primarily in terms of the names of individuals and of events. Because of this bias towards emphasizing the missionary efforts and the conversions of individuals and probably also a bias favoring Greek and Latin cultures which are foundational to Western culture, there is a certain masking of the nonrandom diffusion of Christianity among various peoples and cultures. This is true especially for the first centuries of diffusion in the Mediterranean Basin, but also for the second great area and era of diffusion, which was among the numerous cultural and linguistic groups of Europe. The Mediterranean Basin, though full of diverse peoples, had been united politically within the Roman Empire, but the European tribes were only partially conquered by Rome. To the east, Rome faced foes that it could never conquer, most notably Parthia, and to the south lay the Sahara that Rome could not cross. These barriers (south and east) became barriers to the spread of Christianity, as we shall see.

The spread of Christianity in its first two phases was quite different from its spread in the modern era when Christianity accompanied an expanding Western world. In the first two phases, the faith spread in just the opposite pattern, that is, opposite to a pattern of diffusion from expanding centers of power to areas being invaded and often colonized. Instead, in its first phase of diffusion Christianity spread from a conquered part of the Empire to other conquered peoples and eventually was officially recognized in the center of power at Rome shortly after the beginning of the fourth century. Similarly, in the second phase of diffusion, Christianity spread from a declining or static empire to ascendant power centers to the north and from one new kingdom to another. Thus, in these first two phases of diffusion (throughout the Mediterranean Basin and then throughout Europe), the diffusion was "from below" rather than "from above," the latter being the dominant pattern in the modern era.

Considering the Mediterranean Basin first, Rodney Stark (1995), in his on-going project to uncover answers to the growth of Christianity in the Roman Empire, presents evidence for the importance of women to that growth. Looking at the modern diffusion of Christianity, H. G. Barnett (1953, 408) noted, "It is noticeable that wherever Christian morality has been accepted in place of one embodying double ethical standards [for men and women], female acceptors have outnumbered male." This is highly consistent with the theory of this book since women were a dominated sub-group and Christianity clearly enhanced female identity. Significantly, within the dominated group, in accordance with studies of diffusion, there were often "leading women" who were the "opinion leaders" or "early adopters."

In general, in the Mediterranean Basin, numerous societies had been overrun by the Roman armies, but even before the decline of Roman power, many of the cultures of the conquered peoples began to reassert themselves. It is important to note, in relation to the theory of diffusion already stated, that Christianity was often part of this cultural reassertion. Sanneh (1991, 51), who has given special attention to the ability of Christianity to adopt local languages, states, "What can be said with confidence, even if it has not been said with consistency, is that the expansion of Christianity had a direct effect on the emergence of renewal movements at the local level." The most obvious case is that of the Greek cultural reassertion in the Eastern Empire that became the Byzantine Empire. Another and even earlier reassertion was among the Syrian people, although this was not associated with the development of a dominant political power center. Moffett (1992, 57) notes, "Syrian tradition honors Edessa as the capital of history's first Christian kingdom, Osrhoene," possibly one hundred or more years before the time of Constantine. The emergence of Syriac as a literary language was due to Christianity and the same is true of the Armenian language. In Armenia, Christianity helped preserve Armenian identity and to "safeguard the Armenians against the Persians" (Harnack 1908 II, 346), a clear example of a religion from the outside helping to resist pressure from another direction.

Sanneh (1991, 67) comments that Christianity spread among the Coptic people in the third century and that in the period of ferment that followed, Coptic versions of scripture and other Christian literature appeared. The various distinct cultural groups often were associated with the spawning of distinct movements within Christianity. The Montanist Movement in Asia Minor, for example, was associated with the Phrygians. Deanesly (1981, 6) states, "The Monophysite schism in Egypt represented a national Coptic reaction against Greek rule." Latourette (1938, 1), who unlike many church historians pays attention to ethnicity, notes that the Armenian, Jacobite, Coptic, and

Nestorian communities may be seen as "the last bulwarks of ancient nationalities."

Regarding the tendency for variations of the faith to develop among different peoples, Latourette (1953, 276) writes that "the cleavages were largely along the cultural, racial, and national seams in the fabric which Rome had held together." Thus, Arianism strengthened the contrast of the German tribes with their Roman enemies and the Coptic version of the faith reinforced the Egyptian antipathy to the rule of Byzantium. In a similar way, Monophysitism formed a bond in Syrian Christianity in contrast to Greek Christianity and the national church of Armenia stood against the orthodox Greeks. The majority of Christians in Persia were Nestorians, which put them in contrast to the enemy of Persia to the west.

In North Africa, the Christianity that eventually became dominant there was quite Latin in expression and, therefore, associated with the ruling group. Christianity did not take deep root among the original inhabitants, namely the Berbers, who had been colonized by other Mediterranean peoples. The Punic people, descendants of the Phoenician colonists, found a native expression in the Donatist movement. When the Arian Christian Vandals came, the Donatists seem to have joined them "against their common Christian enemy, the Catholics" (Latourette, 1937, 195). Sanneh (1991, 69) believes that "the failure to produce a Punic version of the Bible was an ill omen for the church in North Africa, for it left indigenous populations excluded from any meaningful role in Christianity."

Some of the variations that developed took the form of popular religion, which could be either syncretistic or puritanical (an emphasis on a "pure" or "spiritual" religion in contrast to the religion of the official church leaders). Sometimes these influences could be mixed as in Gnosticism and later, Manichaeism. Very early, especially in Asia Minor, Gnosticism with its dualism between the spiritual and the material was brought into Christianity. The Gnostics became dominant in some churches and Marcion, in particular, was able to gather his followers (who were forbidden all sexual union) into churches (Latourette 1953, 127).

Probably the most successful sub-movement within early Christianity was the Montanist movement that arose in Phrygia in Asia Minor in the latter part of the second century and persisted into the fifth century (Latourette 1953, 129). As with many movements within Christianity to the present, it opposed the laxity that had developed and like the Pentecostal churches of today, it stressed the gift of the Holy Spirit and the imminent return of Christ. Tertullian of North Africa was a convert to Montanism and remained critical of the majority church until his death at the close of the first quarter of the third century.

The Donatist movement was likewise a "purifying" movement, although on a different basis. There developed serious divisions primarily in North Africa between those who wanted leaders who had not yielded under persecution and the officially recognized leaders. The Donatists in North Africa, the Novatians in Rome and elsewhere, including Constantinople, and the Meletians of Egypt, all opposed leaders who had yielded in some way to persecutions. These groups persisted into the fifth century, but eventually were suppressed as Christianity gained political power.

In a real sense, Roman culture collapsed into the Western Church and Greek culture into the Eastern Church, with the major difference being that in the latter case, the political structure remained strong and unified in the Byzantine Empire whereas in the West there was a proliferation of secular political structures on the one hand and a unifying of religious power in Rome on the other.

To the south a great natural barrier existed in the form of the Sahara Desert, as well as the jungle beyond. There was an extension of Christianity to Ethiopia from contacts along the Red Sea as early as the first half of the fourth century (Latourette 1937, 236). To the east were hostile peoples, never conquered by Rome nor by the later Byzantine Empire. However, Christianity made considerable headway in the Persian Empire, as Moffett (1992) has shown. What is especially significant in terms of the theory of this book is the comment by Samuel Moffett (1992, 137), "When Rome became Christian, its old enemy Persia turned anti-Christian." Latourette (1937, 228) also comments that "it is significant that severe persecution of Christians in the Sassanian territories began soon after the avowal of the faith by Constantine." The association of Christianity with political power in the West seems to have pushed Persia towards Zoroastrianism; certainly it was away from Christianity.

Beginning with the conversion of Constantine, there was a great increase in the power of organized Christianity to enforce unity. Christianity was still a minority movement in the Empire with the majority of Christians in the East. Ramsay MacMullen (1984, 86-101) writes that although it was generally understood that religious conviction could not be compelled, the fourth century saw increasing pressure placed on non-Christians and Christians deemed heretical, sometimes accompanied by the same kind of mob actions and violence that had been previously directed against Christians. The leaders of society, who were often Church leaders, typically felt that religious unity was important enough to be imposed or enforced. However, Latourette's (1953, 172) comment concerning Christianity in the year 500 is that "the efforts to achieve Christian unity through doctrinal statements, ecclesiastical organization, and the aid of the state were proving illusory."

While Christianity in the West gained power and tended to be a rival to state power, Christianity in the East, although more "democratic" in the sense of depending more than the West on councils and a plurality of church leaders (patriarchs), at the same time became more consistently dependent on state power than Christianity in the West. However, in the controversy over icons that broke out in the eighth century in the Byzantine Empire, it was demonstrated that popular piety surrounding the government could eventually affect the decisions of those who exercise authority over the religion. Popular Greek Christian culture gained the victory over the Christian culture to the east that was further from the capital. Concerning the controversy that developed in the Eastern Church, van Leeuwen (1964, 207) states:

> Whatever part was played in this struggle by an aversion to the growing power of the monasteries and the advances of idolatry, it was also an oriental hostility towards Hellenic culture that impelled the emperor and the army of the eastern provinces to give their support to the iconoclasts. The victory of the iconodules therefore issued in a general revival of Hellenic culture.

This victory of the views of those closest to the source of authority in Constantinople meant that the division in the Eastern Church with those beyond the Empire to the East was reinforced. It also shows how a religion associated with political power and part of pervasive social identity tends to incorporate popular religious-cultural elements. This is also demonstrated in the gradual elevation of Mary, angels, and saints in popular religious devotion in both Eastern and Western churches, but especially in the West (Latourette 1953, 209).

Diffusion and Variations to the North

In contrast to the barriers that existed to the south (primarily geographical) and to the east (primarily political), there was relatively easy access to the north from the Mediterranean Basin. The flow of conquest, which had first been northward, was increasingly reversed leading eventually to the sack of Rome in 410 by the Goths and the withdrawal of Roman garrisons from Britain in the same year. The last Roman Emperor in the West was deposed in 476. The Goths, in fact, had been the first of the northern peoples to be converted. Ulfilas (c.311- c.380), a Goth himself, translated part or all of the scriptures to Gothic. It is significant that it was a variant form of Christianity, Arianism, that spread among the various Gothic groups who were in the forefront of the invasion of the Empire. The Arian form of Christianity spread among the Visigoths, the Ostrogoths, the Gepidae, and the Vandals, all of whom fought against various elements of the old Empire and its, by then, Roman Catholic leadership (Latourette, 1953, 100). Referring to the various Arian Christian barbarian invaders, Daniel-Rops (1959, 113) states that Arianism became an element of great importance "in asserting their nationality and in distinguishing them from the Romans." This shows how a variant form of an outside religion may gain ascendancy in groups that are enemies of those from whom the religion originally came. At the same time, the Arians were not able to impose their faith on those they conquered. Frend (1984, 800) comments, "The fate of Arianism in North Africa demonstrated that the Germanic rulers, however determined their rulers, could not impose their religion on the mass of the Catholic provincials, providing the church's organization survived."

The Burgundians, a Teutonic people who moved across the Rhine and subsequently established themselves in the Rhone Valley, first accepted the Catholic Christianity of the Celtic provincials among whom they settled, although later they became Arians. In the fifth century the Franks became dominant in Gaul and their king, Clovis, adopted the Catholic form of Christianity, the faith of his wife, Clotilda, in 496. It is important for the theory that the Franks were not directly involved in the struggle against the dying Roman Empire as were the various Gothic groups. Furthermore, in the fifth century, the greatest threat to the Franks was not Rome, but the Arian Gothic kingdoms that lay between them and Rome. The Franks, in fact, had remained largely pagan. Subsequently, Clovis and the Franks defeated the Arian Goths to reunite Gaul and its largely Catholic Christian population (Daniel-Rops 1981, 190-195).

During the century before the conversion of Clovis, Christianity spread from Britain to Ireland, primarily through the leadership of Patrick, who was at least a third generation Christian from Britain. Thus, Christianity had already spread among the British Celts during the Roman occupation and evidence points to an organization in existence as early as the middle of the fourth century (Hutchinson and Garrison 1959, 87). The Christian Celts, however, were surrounded by the mostly pagan Celtic population, as well as the pagan Picts and Irish (then called Scots), the recently victorious German Franks in Gaul, and the menacing Saxons and Jutes. To add to the danger, Roman forces were withdrawn from Britain in 410, the year of Rome's fall.

In spite of this pagan environment, the tiny Celtic church spread Christianity to Ireland, the most famous missionary being Patrick, who was born toward the end of the fourth century and lived beyond the middle of the fifth century. What is remarkable is that Irish Christianity, in turn, became a major force for spreading Christianity back to Britain and much further into the Continent, including Germany, Switzerland, and even northern Italy. The "wanderers of Christ" ("the perigrini," Latourette 1938, 40) from Ireland were particularly active in the sixth century during the time when pagan Angles and Saxons were invading Britain. They carried Christianity to their fellow Celts of Scotland, Britain, Brittany (Amorica) and to other peoples, including their enemies, the Germanic invaders of Britain, and to the Franks and Saxons of Europe.

A missionary effort from Rome led to the conversion of the Saxon king, Ethelbert, who was baptized by Augustine in 597. Bertha, his wife, a Frankish princess, played the part of a second Clotilda. Christianity spread gradually in Britain throughout the succeeding century, the Celtic missionaries spreading over the lands of the new Germanic kingdoms "even more widely than the continental ones from the south" (Deanesly 1950, 47). There were various wars between the Germanic (Saxon) kings in England in which the future of Christianity seemed to be at stake. In one case, after the defeat of Edwin of Northumbria, who waged "a veritable holy war against the pagans," the Celtic Britons, though baptized Christians, joined their pagan neighbors in attacking Northumbria (Daniel-Rops, 1959, 233). However, in spite of various set-backs, the descendants of the Germanic invaders gradually became Christians and by the end of the seventh century the Celtic and Germanic branches of the church in Britain had come to an agreement to follow the See of Rome and the Church of England was stabilized (Daniel-Rops 1959, 234). It could be argued that the Celtic church was never anti-Roman, but rather was isolated from Rome geographically. The enemy was the nearby invader from Germany to whom the Celtic missionaries carried their faith.

Just as the Celtic church had actively spread Christianity eastward, the Anglo-Saxon church now joined it in sending numerous missionaries to the Continent. What is particularly significant is that the English missionaries had much greater success in converting the Frisians and Germans than did the nearby and warlike Franks. The Saxons in Germany, who had not migrated to England, were the last of the Germanic peoples (except for the Scandinavians) to be converted. Latourette (1953, 349) notes that "they long resisted conversion, for they associated it with Carolingian imperialism." The English missionaries, who did the most to convert them, were recognized as their kinsfolk and were encouraged by Charlemagne in his campaign to Christianize the Saxons. He also used armed force to put down Saxon revolts and to bring Saxons into the Church.

Beginning about 800 and continuing for some 250 years, the Scandinavians raided and invaded the coastlands to the south, as well as the river system of what later became the Russian kingdom. They eventually accepted the Christianity of the peoples they conquered, but some areas of Scandinavia were not converted until the twelfth century and some people on the East Baltic coast (Lithuanians) were not converted until the fifteenth century (Latourette 1938, 194). Now it was the Saxons' turn to be missionaries and it was largely Saxon missionaries (from England and Germany) who carried Christianity to Scandinavia in the ninth and tenth centuries. This was exactly during the period when the Scandinavians were invading northern Europe.

The Scandinavians, known as Vikings or Norsemen, who settled among or next to the people they conquered were the first among their people to accept Christianity. Mission work had been done earlier, but in 934 the Saxons gained the upper hand over the Danes and the king of the Danes was compelled to be baptized. In 1018, Canute became king of both England and Denmark and in 1020 "energetically espoused the cause of Christianity" (Latourette 1938, 122).

The conversion of Norway, like that of Denmark, was highly influenced by Anglo-Saxon Christians from England. The Norwegian kingdom was created by Harold Haarfager ("Fairhair"), who died in 933, and his descendants brought about the conversion of the land with a mixture of force and persuasion (Latourette 1938, 126-130). There were various set-backs due to pagan resistance, but by the first half of the eleventh century Christianity was the predominant faith (Latourette 1938, 130). Sweden became Christian shortly after Norway and again it was primarily through missionaries from England, rather than through missionaries from Germany or from the nearby Danes and Norwegians. As in the other Scandinavian countries, there was some continuing resistance from representatives of the traditional religion, who were often local leaders or rivals of a Christian leader, but a Christian king (Inge, son of Stenkil) gained power in the early twelfth century and led in the establishment of Christianity. There was more disorder after Inge's death, but after Sverker mounted the throne in 1130, Christianity was further strengthened. The Swedes were the last Scandinavians and, indeed, last of the Teutonic people to be converted (Latourette 1938, 141).

Moving to the east, the Slavic peoples were converted from two directions: the West (the Western Church) and the South (the Eastern Church). There was often a rivalry between the two sources with local rulers looking first to one and then to the other (Latourette 1938, 156-159). At various times there was a return to paganism and very strong resistance, for example from the Wends in the borderland between Poland and Germany (Latourette 1938, 180). Earlier, Slavic groups, such as the Wends, had moved westward, but Germanic peoples subsequently moved eastward and there was conflict between the groups.

Sanneh (1991, 72) states that "it was in Moravia, lying on the eastern flank of the East Frankish empire in the upper Danube, that the stage was set for a proud indigenization movement that sent ripples through the whole Slavonic world." Significantly, the strengthening of Slavonic identity through the missionaries, Constantine and Methodius, inspired the Franks to similar efforts. Sanneh (1991, 75) quotes Ofrid von Werssenburg, who wrote in the introduction to his harmony of the Gospels: "In our time many are trying to do so, writing in their own language, endeavouring to glorify their own nation. Why shall the Franks neglect such things and not start to chant God's glory in the language of the Franks?" (Dvornik 1970, 370).

Just as Christianity diffused northward from Rome, the Eastern version of Christianity also diffused northward. The initial mission of Ulfilas that brought Arian Christianity to the Goths has already been noted. The next influx of people from the north were the Slavs, who largely erased Christianity as they pressed into former Roman territory in the Balkans in the sixth and seventh centuries (Latourette 1938, 155). The Frankish rulers sought to spread Latin Christianity to the Slavs of Central Europe, which were near to the centers of German power and were under Carolingian influence. However, German domination was often resisted and shortly after the middle of the ninth century, a Moravian prince, Ratislav, invited the two famous brother missionaries from Byzantium, Constantine (Cyril) and Methodius, (from the distant rather than from the nearby threatening society) to come to his kingdom. The work of these men made "lasting contributions to the Christianity of most of the Slavic world" (Latourette 1938, 159). Whether Constantine made the first reduction of the Slavic language to writing or not, their translations were "to have lasting consequences for Slavic literature, not only in Central Europe and the Balkans, but also in Russia" (Latourette 1938, 161). There was much competition between the Latin and the Slavonic types of Christianity. Bohemia eventually looked to Rome, as did the Magyars who had invaded the area, but Slavic nationalism continued and Eastern Christianity continued to spread.

The Bulgars, a people of Turkish origin, moved into the Balkans and defeated Byzantine forces in the second half of the seventh century. Eventually, the Bulgars were assimilated by the Slavic majority over whom they ruled and they maintained a strong kingdom just north of Byzantine territory, inflicting many defeats upon the Byzantine forces. The conversion of the Slavs took place primarily in the ninth century. The Bulgarian ruler, Boris, accepted baptism in 864 or 865 at a time of special pressure from Constantinople, but also at a time when he had a chance to strengthen his power against local magnates and unite the country with a common religion and language (Latourette 1938, 241-242). At about the same time, Constantine and Methodius went to Moravia at the request of Ratislav. Earlier (845) fourteen Czech princes had been baptized by Western priests (Daniel Rops 1981, 489). Also, in the latter part of the ninth century, many of the Serbs were converted under their ruler, Mutimir.

An important development among the Slavs beginning in the tenth century was a religious movement, attached to the name of Jeremiah Bogomil, which drew on the dualistic ideas of Manichaeism. It had many sectarian "puritanical" characteristics in which the formalism and rituals of the established church were rejected and it also contained Slavic nationalistic overtones (Soloviev 1967, 633-644; Newman 1945, 172-174; Latourette 1938, 442). It was successfully suppressed among the Slavs, except in the mountainous area of Boznia where many leading people supported the movement. When this area was later conquered by the Turks, it was primarily the followers of this movement who converted to Islam. A similar movement took place in Italy and France, where it was known as the Albigensian heresy. The name "Cathari" or "pure ones" is also associated with these movements which points to the fact that they were opposed to established, and what they regarded as "unspiritual," Christianity. They were most easily sustained in mountainous areas where they could successfully resist outside domination.

The Magyar invasion toward the close of the ninth century split the northern and southern Slavs and effectively destroyed the Christianized kingdom of Moravia. The Magyars were finally defeated by the Germans in 955, but were able to consolidate themselves into a state and avoid being absorbed by the Slavic majority. In the latter part of the tenth century, their leaders looked to the Christianity of the West. Significantly, they chose what would distinguish them from their nearby Slavic neighbors.

At approximately the same time as the Magyars of Hungary were being Christianized, leading people in what is now Poland were also accepting Christianity. Shortly after the middle of the tenth century, the Polish king accepted Christianity from the West and became a strong sponsor of the faith. It is significant that Poles had joined with Germans to fight pagan Slavic groups that were between them. The Polish rulers and Polish Christianity had close ties to the Germans, yet at the same time, a direct connection with Rome and the development of an independent ecclesiastical structure offered the Poles some protection from the domination of the Germans.

As already noted, to the north and west of the Poles were other Slavic people who came under more direct domination from the Germans and who converted more slowly, if at all. Among those who were highly resistant were the Wends, the Wilzi, and the Obodrites, who had earlier occupied what is now northwestern Germany. The Saxons employed some of the same rough methods to carry Christianity to these tribes that had been employed against themselves by the Franks (Latourette 1938, 180). In the tenth century, Otto I gained relative domination over the Wends, but it took some two centuries after his death and many revolts before the area was assimilated to

German rule and Christianity, as much or more by immigration as by conversion (Latourette. 1939, 180-181). Similarly, it took several centuries for Christianity to be accepted by the Pomeranians to the east of the Wends. The Pomeranians were conquered by the Poles and their conversion was accomplished with German help.

Further east and north along the Baltic were the Prussians, Lithuanians, Latvians, Letts, Estonians, and Finns. Although the Danes, Swedes, and Poles all helped, the Germans were the major contributors to the conversion of these varied peoples. There were numerous rivalries among those introducing Christianity, as well as among the Baltic peoples. One Baltic group would seek help from the outside against another group. The process of conversion was long delayed so that it was not until the fifteenth century that it was "even superficially completed" in some areas (Latourette 1938, 194).

In the latter part of the tenth century, at about the same time as the Poles and Hungarians were being converted from the West, leading Russians (partly descendants of Scandinavians) centered at Kiev turned to Christianity. Scandinavians had earlier dominated the area, but they assimilated to their Slavic subjects and led in fighting against the Khazars, who ruled a large area to the south. The Khazars of that time did not convert to either Christianity or Islam, but a majority of their rulers converted to Judaism (Latourette 1938, 252). This unusual and little known phenomenon of the Khazar conversion to Judaism (Koestler 1976) is consistent with the theory that resistance to outside threat (Islam from Persia and Christianity from Constantinople) is conducive to acceptance of a non-threatening, supportive religion from the outside (Judaism). In this unusual case, the threat came from two directions. The Russian leaders of Kiev chose the Christianity of Constantinople and, after the fall of that city in 1453, Russia felt that it had succeeded the Byzantine Empire as the center of Orthodox Christianity (Latourette 1938, 258).

In an analysis of the spread of Christianity in Central Europe, Latourette (1938, 209-212) states that it was closely related to the eastward expansion of the German peoples: "For almost the first time in its history, Christianity became a tool of an expanding political and economic imperialism" (209). After 1500, of course, this was to happen on a much larger scale, as we shall see. In spite of the association of the diffusion of Christianity with German domination, there were influences towards conversion from directions that tended to offset German power. Both Rome and Constantinople were off-setting forces. Many peoples, such as the Poles, the Bohemians, the Moravians, many Slavs of the Balkans, and the Hungarians were led into the Church by their monarchs and the missionaries were Slav as well as German. The Scandinavians were active in the conversion of the northern Baltic peoples and the Lithuanians were eventually won by the Poles "in an effort to offset German aggression" (Latourette 1938, 210).

It has already been noted that in the early centuries there were movements, often with popular support, in opposition to laxity within Christianity. It is not surprising, therefore, with the growing size and internal control in Christianity, especially in the West, that there should be movements to purify the Church and at the same time resist domination. Dualistic thought, as expressed, for example, in Manichaeism, lent itself to an emphasis on "spirituality." This kind of thought contributed to the Bogomil movement in the Balkans, which also expressed Slavic opposition to Byzantine culture. As noted above, similar movements for purification or greater spirituality broke out in northern Italy and southern France in the twelfth century which were called "Cathari" (an eastern word) and "Albigensian" (from an area in southern France) (Deanesly 1981, 114-115). Thus, the relationship between official and popular Christianity was strained and sometimes broken in particular areas.

Some movements for greater spirituality in Christianity were kept in the Church through the monastic movements, which were revived in the twelfth century and in the friar movements, which led to the establishment of the Franciscans and the Dominicans. Other movements, however, could not be similarly contained, such as the Waldensians of northern Italy and Central Europe and the Lollards in Holland and Britain. John Wycliffe, a British scholar, translated the Bible and taught from it, but he and his followers were denounced as "Lollards." John Hus of Bohemia was a great preacher in the Czech language and also a Slav nationalist leader. Like Wycliffe and his followers, Hus and his followers were also condemned. These "uncontained" movements laid the groundwork for the Protestant Reformation that followed.

Another type of religious movement is represented by the revolutionary messianism of both medieval and Reformation Europe. The roots of millennialism are deep in Christianity and Judaism, being represented and supported by the apocalyptic visions and eschatological emphasis in the Bible itself.

Norman Cohn (1961) analyzed these movements which appeared in Western Europe from the eleventh century onwards. He (1961, 22) writes:

> The areas in which the age-old prophecies about the Last Days took on a new, revolutionary meaning and a new, explosive force were the areas of rapid social change - and not simply change but expansion: areas where trade and industry were developing and where the population was rapidly increasing.

According to Cohn (1961, 309, 312) this revolutionary apocalyptic was "in the margins of the English Civil War and the French Revolution," appeared in the nineteenth century in France, Germany, and Russia and has now jumped outside the West.

Diffusion and Variation to the South and East

As easily seen, the major direction for diffusion of Christianity from the Mediterranean Basin was northward. During the centuries before the rise of Islam, practically the only communication southward was by the Red Sea and after the rise of Islam communication southward was even more difficult for Christians. Christianity spread to the kingdom of Axum in the northern part of the Ethiopian highlands in the middle of the fourth century (Sanneh 1994, 5). In the sixth century Ethiopia (Abyssinia), under Christian leaders, invaded Southwestern Arabia to relieve Christians from persecution (Latourette 1953, 321). Ethiopia, in its isolation, was not threatened by Roman or Byzantine power, but by the nearby Arabs and possibly by tribes to the south and west. Later, Ethiopia was effectively cut off from close contact with the larger Christian world by the rise of Islam and particularly because of Egypt's fear of possible alliances with Christian Europe (Sanneh 1992, 16). Christian North Africa was overrun by Islam, but Ethiopia remained a Christian outpost in the south.

Moffett (1992) describes the spread of Christianity eastward from the borders of the Roman and later Byzantine Empire. The major problem from the perspective of this book is that unlike in the West where Roman power declined in the face of the European tribal onslaught, in the East, the Byzantine Empire continued in power and in continuous conflict along the traditional lines of hostility. Strong Christian communities grew in Mesopotamia and Persia. However, a major problem developed in intersocietal relations: in the fourth century, Christianity became closely associated with power that had traditionally intruded upon and sought to dominate Mesopotamia and Persia.

As already noted, Moffett (1992, 137) and Latourette (1937, 228) point out that toleration decreased in Persia as Christianity became identified with Roman power. There was often toleration by the Persians for the Christians that the West considered heretical. However, persecutions of Christians "coincided with war against Constantinople" (Moffett 1992, 160) and these persecutions were often extremely severe. Amazingly, Christianity did survive in Mesopotamia and Persia, but the numbers were small at the time Islam defeated the Byzantine armies and conquered Persia. There were, in fact, Christian Arab groups who joined the other Arabs against Persia and Christian minorities persisted, even under Islam. Basically, Islam inherited the long struggle of Middle Eastern people against domination from the West and reversed the direction of intrusion.

Christianity spread to small nations to the east of the Roman and the later Byzantine Empire. The Syrian kingdom of Osrhoene has already been mentioned as history's first Christian kingdom (Moffett 1992, 57). For others, Armenia is considered the first kingdom to become officially Christian, probably late in the third century (Latourette 1953, 79). Both of these kingdoms benefited, but also periodically suffered because of their identification with Christianity.

Missionaries, who were primarily Nestorian, went further east, to India, Central Asia, and China. A church was established in India which has continued to the present. There is the well-known tradition of the Apostle Thomas going to India. Pahlavi (Middle Persian) inscriptions in South India dating from the seventh century and the use of Syriac as an ecclesiastical language point to the fact that the Christian communities, all of them coastal or near to the coast, resulted from contacts with Christians of Persia, Mesopotamia, and Syria (Latourette 1953, 324).

Some groups of Central Asia, for example, the Keraits and the Onguts, accepted Christianity and there was considerable openness to Christianity among the conquering Mongols, some of whom were Christians or married to Christians. According to Moffett (1992, 401), the Christian chief of the Keraits became the patron of young Temujin (later known as Genghis Khan) and a Christian Kerait princess was the mother of three imperial sons, including Kublai Khan. There was

Christianity Before 1500 73

great hope in the West that the Mongols might be converted or at least that Mongol power might break the power of Islam. Neither event took place and Christianity in the East continued to suffer from lack of communication with the large Christian centers in the West. This separation had been reinforced in the seventh century with the rise of Islam and it was reinforced again by the continuation of Islamic power after the decline of the Mongolian empire.

Nestorian Christianity was introduced to China at least by the first half of the seventh century when the T'ang dynasty had recently risen to great power. The Sui dynasty, followed by the T'ang dynasty, represented a reassertion of Chinese power after a period of intrusion and domination by tribal people from the north. Although Christianity was tolerated by the first T'ang rulers so that monasteries were founded and literature produced, the Christian communities remained primarily foreign (Latourette 1953, 324-325). The persecution of 845, directed primarily against Buddhism, but also including Christians in its proscription (Latourette 1953, 325) was a severe blow to the small communities. Later, when China was under the Mongols in the thirteenth century, Christianity appeared again with Nestorian communities in several cities and with missionaries sent from Rome. However, following the triumph of the Ming (Chinese) Dynasty, the conditions became very unfavorable for the Christians since they had been associated with the previous rulers who had been foreign invaders from the north. Latourette (1953, 601) states, "So completely did Christianity disappear in China that we do not know either the date or the manner of its demise." A new start had to be made in the sixteenth century.

Thus, the diffusion of Christianity eastward from the Mediterranean Basin remained on a comparatively small scale. A promising beginning in the Near East (Mesopotamia and Persia) was negatively affected by the continuing hostilities between East and West and the attendant barrier that was reinforced by the rise of Islam. Diffusion to Central Asia, particularly to Mongolian groups, again had promising beginnings, but Mongolian power was not sustained in a manner that might have given Christianity the opportunity to be the basis for a Mongolian civilization. Even so, Nestorians are said to have shaped part of Genghis Khan's written law (Moffett 1992, 401).

In both India and China, Christianity became encapsulated as the religion of special populations. In India, the caste system aided in the separation of Christians into a special caste and in China it was the foreign character of the Christian community that doomed it to isolation and, during anti-foreign movements, to elimination.

Discussion

As with the diffusion of Buddhism, the review of the diffusion of Christianity and some of its changes in its first fifteen centuries provides some general support for the theory, but also some difficulties. To mention a difficulty first, the failure of Christianity to diffuse on a large scale to the Near East may be accounted for in terms of the theory by the association of Christianity with the threatening power to the West. However, there was little Western threat in India before the modern era and Christianity was apparently introduced "from below," not from a position of power. In China, where Christianity was similarly initially introduced "from below," at least it may be said that it had (or acquired) associations with foreigners who had been traditional invaders from the north. I have stressed the importance of the quality of intergroup relations for the diffusion of religions, but clearly the absence of close or continuing relations between groups is a negative factor itself and the small Christian communities in the east were isolated for long periods of time. Natural geographical barriers to the south and east reduced or completely blocked the communication that is important if diffusion is to take place. However, consistent with the theory there was a major barrier created not simply by geography, but by inherited hostilities that were perpetuated in continuing conflict between powers associated with Christianity and Islam. The failure of Christianity to diffuse on a large scale across the barrier of hostility to the east is very consistent with the theory which states that a nonconducive condition exists for diffusion when the outside religion is associated with a source of threat.

Turning to the areas of successful diffusion for Christianity in its first millennium and a half, it was seen that, like Buddhism, Christianity diffused primarily "from below." This is certainly consistent with the theory. Thus, in the Mediterranean Basin, Christianity was not associated with a dominant political power as it spread among the conquered peoples of the Empire. In the second phase, it was primarily from a fallen Empire in the west and a greatly weakened Empire in the east that Christianity spread northward to the numerous developing kingdoms of western, central, and eastern Europe. However, as with Buddhism, the similarity of the diffusion to "spilt ink" masks many of the variations in rate and direction of diffusion that were affected by intergroup relations.

The negative effect on diffusion of domination and force from the direction of the diffusing religion is a basic part of the theory. The theory, therefore, has some difficulty in accounting for diffusion in Europe. Force does become a factor in the diffusion of Christianity among various kingdoms, the most glaring being from the Franks towards the Saxons and the Saxons towards the Slavs and others to the east. However, the examples of force tend to hide the many cases in which missionaries, who offered no threat, ventured forth to win kingdoms for their Lord. In most of these cases, elites accepted Christianity from foreign scholars who were beneath them in political and military power, but above them in learning. Even in the cases where force accompanied or followed missionaries, as with the Franks and Saxons, there was knowledge of a further (and sometimes very influential) source of Christianity in faraway Ireland, England and, especially, in Rome and Constantinople. In many cases, the missionaries from the more distant and less threatening groups had greater success than those associated with nearby groups, for example, among the Saxons, the Frisians, the Moravians, and the Norwegians. Also, repeatedly, the most serious threat to a leader accepting Christianity was a rival leader or tribe rather than an outside kingdom.

In some cases there may be seen a tendency for groups to accept an alternative form of faith to the form represented by the enemy. For example, Gothic groups, who had been fighting Rome for many years, accepted Arian Christianity. Also, Phrygians, Punics, Syrians and Egyptians developed different versions of Christianity than that of the dominant power. Medieval heretical religious movements had nationalistic overtones and may be regarded as "oppositional ideologies." These cases are consistent with the theoretical statement that dominated groups may seek to change the accepted religion in a way that preserves their distinctive identities and supports their independence.

In the initial period of diffusion, the internal religious and moral orders of many groups were clearly destabilized in the Mediterranean Basin by Roman power and it can be argued that Rome, likewise, was destabilized culturally by its contacts with numerous other societies, having a variety of moral orders. In this confusing world, Christianity offered an identity that for many people increased self-esteem.

In the second period of diffusion, the European tribes could hardly avoid perceiving the great contrast between their societies and the literate and complex civilizations of the Mediterranean. What is important is that in the cases in which Christianity diffused, it was able to contribute to rather than reduce the distinctive identities of the receivers and, at the same time, increase self-respect and the dignity of minority groups and tribes.

The contribution of Christianity to self-esteem has been shown convincingly by Lamin Sanneh in his tracking of the process of "translating the message" (Sanneh 1991). Translation of the scriptures has been one of the primary means by which groups came to perceive Christianity as affirming their distinctive cultural identities. A parallel may be seen in the many translations of Buddhist scriptures in the East. Europe became a patchwork of peoples who had both accepted an outside religion and maintained strong distinctive identities. This is very consistent with the theory that describes a conducive condition for diffusion to be when the receiving people perceive the outside religion as contributing positively to their distinctive identities, as well as supporting them in opposition to other groups..

The internal characteristics of Christianity are being "held constant" in this analysis, but in fact there are certain consistencies with Buddhism. For example, Christianity is an even more missionary religion than Buddhism. They are both universalistic and egalitarian in appeal, offering salvation to individuals, regardless of social status. They both emphasize compassion, although compassion might have been easily missed by those groups, for example, the Saxons and later the Wends, who resisted Christianity, not to speak of Persians and Arabs. It is also true, of course, that both religions (Buddhism and Christianity) offered a literate expression that was a major attraction for aspiring scholars and the otherwise upwardly mobile. In some cases, of course, the receiving groups had developed literatures, for example, in Persia, China, India, and the Roman Empire. The internal characteristics of the religions are not being given major consideration, not because they are unimportant, but in order to isolate crucial conducive conditions external to the religions.

Conclusion

The primary diffusion of Christianity in the first millennium and a half was, like that of Buddhism, to contiguous areas within two large areas: the Mediterranean Basin and Europe. This, in itself, masks variations in the diffusion process. There was some limited diffusion to Central, Southern, and East Asia, but by and large, a major barrier to diffusion was formed in an area where hostility had long existed between the peoples of the Mediterranean Basin and the peoples to the east. This barrier was originally in Persia and was later reinforced and expanded by Islam. This blockage is consistent with the theory regarding non-conducive conditions for diffusion.

Numerous cases of diffusion also appear to be largely consistent with the theory. This is true especially if attention is paid to the variations of Christianity that appeared among minority ethnic groups. This may be seen, for example, in the Montanists, the Donatists, the Monophysites, the Nestorians, the Arians, and, indeed, in the Eastern Church itself. Christianity was received by the Armenians from a source that was less threatening than nearby Persia and the new religion supported Armenian nationalism. Celts, Franks, English Saxons, Frisians, and various Slavic groups received their versions of Christianity from sources less threatening than their immediate neighbors. By and large, in both the Mediterranean Basin and Europe, Christianity diffused "from below" between groups, namely from positions of non-threat, often from conquered groups to conquering groups and from non-powerful missionaries to elites. However, once received, Christianity often diffused "downward," from positions of high status to low status within groups. This subsequent downward diffusion was often resisted and variations from official expressions developed..

The strongest argument against the theory is found in the cases where diffusion was associated with force, as in the cases of the diffusion from Franks to Saxons and from Saxons to some Slavic groups. Even in these cases, there were also non-threatening representatives of the new religion present and support for national or ethnic identity was developed very early, for example, through translation efforts and the development of indigenous clergy.

Timing is seen to be important since diffusion was often slowed when receiving groups were in conflict with sending groups, but speeded up when threat was reduced. For example, Christianity diffused northward from the Mediterranean Basin and eastward in Europe most effectively when power in the sources was declining or not threatening.

In regard to major variations within Christianity, after Constantine the pressure towards uniformity was supported by political power. The poorest elements of society have tended to want to incorporate magic into religion, as Weber (1958, 283) noted, "Peasants have been inclined towards magic" due to their dependence upon nature with its "elemental forces." What may be considered a positive aspect of this magical or superstitious approach to life is a concern with spirituality. The pervasiveness of Christian identity combined with the authoritarian structure of the religious organization meant that gaps would develop between official and popular religion (the "great" and "little traditions" of Redfield 1967). At times, religious authorities came to recognize and even sponsor changes introduced by popular religion. At other times, dualistic, puritanical, or millenarian movements were considered dangerous and were repressed. The gap that developed between official and popular expressions is consistent with the theory regarding acceptance followed by change.

The diffusion of Christianity and the development of variations that have taken place within it in the modern era, in addition to providing better historical records, offer considerably more cases in which conditions may be contrasted. Before that can be discussed, however, there was the great diffusion and growth of the third religion to be considered: Islam.

Chapter 5

Islam

The Rise of Islam Among the Arabs

The diffusion of a religion is in continuity with its rise and this is as true for Islam as it is for Buddhism and Christianity. From earliest times, Buddhism involved communities gathered around teachers and monks. Governmental sponsorship or favor has been an irregular occurrence. Christianity likewise consisted originally of communities of believers that spawned other communities. Political involvement did not occur until Constantine, but the "two kingdom" principle continued. Islam, however, from its beginning united the religious, social, and political areas in a single struggle. Although Mohammed had a prophetic message and gathered followers, he was involved in a struggle for political, as well as religious leadership. In short, he sought to establish a complete new order.

Islam brought its new order to a people who were in disorder and under great pressures from outside influences. At the end of the sixth century, the Arab people were divided and surrounded by dominant powers. Earlier, Rome and Egypt had found ways to bypass Arab trading centers so that trading opportunities were literally passing by the Arabs and economic decline had set in.

North of the Arabian peninsula there were powerful empires, Byzantium to the west and Persia to the east, each seeking to dominate the area between them and to the south as they had opportunity. The Arab Ghassanids, and later the Lakhmids, in the north became Christianized and came under Byzantine influence. In the south, the Arabs of Yemen were invaded and ruled by the Christian Abyssinians. A southern group, the Himyarites, became Jewish and the rivalry between Christians and Jews led to more fighting and another invasion from Abyssinia. When the Arabs asked for Persian help to oust the Abyssinians, the Persians obliged, but stayed on to rule. Nutting (1964, 24-25) states, "Thus, as the sixth century drew to a close, the Arab world found itself the pawn of rival empires - of Byzantium and Persia in the north, of Persia and Abyssinia in the south."

Into this fractured and disordered group of Arab societies, Mohammed the prophet brought a new religion and a new order. The people of his town of Mecca were deeply involved in idolatry and corrupt practices. Mohammed received and began preaching a simple message of a single God who demanded loyalty and spiritual discipline. However, there was an extended struggle before the message won broad acceptance.

Under pressure from his relatives in the ruling tribe, the Qoreish, with its two branches, the Omayyad and the Hashamites, and with a special invitation from people impressed with his message, Mohammed fled Mecca in 622 for Yathrib, which was renamed Medina. Mohammed became the religious and temporal leader of Medina and with various groups plotting against him, he also became a warrior leader. Fighting continued against the Qoreish with both successes and failures, but Mohammed's reputation as a prophet grew and important converts were made from those formerly opposed to him. It was not so much his military leadership, but the power of his personality, his message, and his political skills that added to his followers. In the year 630 he entered Mecca unopposed, proclaiming mercy to all his enemies, and compassion and charity have continued to be major themes of Islam. Mohammed's followers increased, with numerous tribes paying tribute.

After the death of the Prophet in 632, the succession to political and religious power became an issue and has continued so down to the present. However, the message of Mohammed united the Arabs, a crucial part of that message calling for a social revolution. Consistent with the approach of this book, Nutting (1964, 37) comments, "Mohammed was able to uplift the Arabs and give to the underprivileged citizens who received his call a new dignity in being a Moslem

Arab." Somewhat analogous to the later rise of the Mongolian Empire, the Arab peoples were united and broke out of their original homeland, establishing their rule over a large area. But unlike the Mongolians, the Arabs carried a religion, Islam, under which they had been united, to the areas they conquered. Furthermore, their religion spread much further, beyond areas of Arab conquest, especially to the east.

It is important to recognize, as noted at first, that Islam was not regarded simply as a "religion," but as a total way of life, the basis of a civilization. Of course, this was true for Buddhism, especially in those countries where it was not challenged by other religions, and also for Christianity, especially in Medieval Europe. It is in the modern West that religion has been most clearly defined as a separate aspect of life. However, Islam leads both Buddhism and Christianity in its unification of civil and religious life. It is not surprising, therefore, that the earliest conflicts within Islam were over succession to the religious-civil authority, which was unified, and the major distinction (Sunni and Shi'a) still remaining within Islam has its roots in these conflicts.

Because of the Islamic unitary view of life in which religion and society are closely allied, a single form of Islam tends to become dominant in Islamic societies and to be very closely allied with the government. It also follows from this that changes in Islamic countries have often been accompanied by a drastic or revolutionary change in government. This has been true both in Arab countries and in countries to which Islam has diffused. For example, Sanneh (1991, 220) writes of the repeated reform movements in West Africa "fed by the perennial premillennial figure who appears at the head of every Islamic century to set right the affairs of the people." In these cases, the reform movements arise against the "compromising rulers." The "religiousness," "spiritualism," or "puritanicalism" of popular Islam and its revolutionary character is still being seen today. This, of course, is consistent with the view that a gap tends to develop between official and popular levels of piety in religions that are both inclusive and authoritative.

The Initial Diffusion of Islam Under the Omayyads

Association of the diffusion of a religion with conquest is counter to a basic thrust of the theory. However, the simple association of the diffusion of Islam with conquest has been grossly exaggerated and perhaps basically misunderstood, especially by people in the West who, in the past, faced Islamic armies. Other factors were important for diffusion. Furthermore, little or no diffusion took place in some areas of conquest and a great deal more diffusion took place later where there was no conquest.

Probably the most important fact for the initial diffusion of Islam was that the Arab armies brought liberation to a number of the peoples they conquered. Carmichael (1967, 61-78) points out:

> Thus a potent stimulus of the Arab military expansion was the fanatical orthodoxy of the Byzantine Empire, expressed by the persecution of the Aramaic-speaking population of Syria. It helps to explain one of the most striking things about the advance of the Muslim armies, which were all relatively miniature: their success against the superior force of the vastly more civilized Byzantines. The decisive part of this explanation may lie in the deeply rooted hatred of local Christians for the savagely intolerant and obtuse policy of the Byzantine state. They were utterly disaffected and uniformly welcomed the advance of the Muslim tribesmen - all the easier to do since at first the new religion of Islam did not seem to be so very new, after all, especially not to Monophysite Christians.

The Syrian people had long been under Greek domination, but had sought to express their independence and distinctive identity. Van Leeuwen (1964, 209) states that Ostrene (Osrhoene), with its capital in Edessa, had become a Christian state by the beginning of the third century and that "in Syrian literature there was expressed an intense national pride which went so far as to claim for Edessa the status of God's 'elect', in the place of the Jewish people, who had rejected Christ."

Egypt also was a center for national self-consciousness expressed in the Monophysite views and forms of worship, which had been severely repressed. Not long before the coming of the Moslem army, Coptic monks had been flogged and tortured and the Coptic Patriarch thrown into the sea in a weighted sack (Nutting 1964, 60). In addition to freeing societies from the heavy hand of Byzantium, the tolerant policies of the Omayyads towards other religions (not Arab dissidents) clearly had a strong appeal.

North Africa presents another case of an area that was settled by Greek and Latin colonists and long dominated by outsiders. There was a strong church in North Africa that was largely Latin in flavor. The indigenous Berber population was not an essential part of it and the Punic people, descendants of the Phoenician colonists, were disaffected. Once again, it can be said that the Arabs gave the indigenous population an opportunity to be free from and even to dominate those who formerly dominated them. Furthermore, the Berbers were quickly recruited to join the Arabs in conquering Spain and threatening Europe. It is true that there was tension between Arabs and Berbers, primarily over discrimination by the Arabs, which led to a rebellion by the Berbers. The Omayyad emir coming to Spain after the Omayyad fall in the east, was able to pacify the Berbers of North Africa and Spain and also institute "a system of generous pay and privileges" that enabled him to create "from these erstwhile rebels a well-trained and disciplined standing army of forty thousand men" (Nutting 1965, 109).

The other striking conquests of the Omayyads were eastward, which included the Persian Empire and beyond, deep into Central Asia. The traditional enemy of the Persians was the Byzantine Empire, not the desert tribes; nevertheless, the Arab advance was strongly resisted. In 637, a vast Persian army, which had so recently defeated the Byzantines, was beaten by the tribesmen of Arabia. Ctesiphon, the eastern capital of Persia, was plundered. Nutting (1964, 59) states:

> By 644 the all-conquering army of Islam had overrun three-quarters of the territory of modern Persia...Mass conversions followed these new conquests. The fire-worshipping Persians, not being permitted the same religious toleration as the Jews and Christians of Palestine and Syria, abandoned their Zoroastrian beliefs and flocked to join the Moslem faith.

Other scholars state that there was relative tolerance towards the Zoroastrians, if they did not resist and because they had "a Book" (Bakhash 1989, 11; Noss 1949, 469). Even though there was fairly rapid conversion, especially in the mixed urban populations, it was not until the ninth century that a majority became Muslim (Bakhash 1989, 13).

In the generation after the conquest of Persia, Arab armies pushed on into Central Asia and what is now Pakistan so that by the zenith of Omayyad power in 715, Arab rule stretched from China and India's borders to the Atlantic ocean. However, the power was brittle. Already the Alid Shi'a sect had become the mouthpiece for all the oppressed classes of Iraq and Persia, "whether they were Arabs who were persecuted for wanting a successor of Ali on the throne or non-Arabs who were underprivileged by reason of their racial origin" (Nutting 1964, 79).

The Dissolution of Arab Power Under the Abbasids

In addition to the liberating force of Arab conquest, another factor which, according to the theory, contributed to the diffusion of Islam was dissolution of Arab power. The original outbreak of Arab power was very largely an ethnic surge and the Omayyad leadership was relatively "secular" in its rule. As they conquered, the Arab armies were usually quite tolerant of established religions, especially of Judaism and Christianity. In fact, initial policy was not to convert people to Islam so that the taxes to be paid by non-Moslems would remain high. Another important feature of the Arab conquests was the rapid inclusion of conquered peoples into the government and the armies. This was so rapid, in fact, that very shortly after the Abbasids assumed power from the Omayyads some one hundred and twenty years after Mohammed's death, the Turkish military won control over the rulers. Even before that, Persian influence in the Islamic religion had become important. In other words, in spite of the rapid spread of Arab power, its unified control of the conquered areas was rather short. Islamic civilization remained after the decline of Arab power and, in fact, was often developed and perpetuated by other peoples such as Greeks, Persians, Turks, Berbers, and Indians.

The Abbasid rebellion against the Omayyads was a war between Arab tribes, but the Abbasids made use of discontented Arab groups, such as the Shi'a Alids and oppressed non-Arabs, especially Persians. In 762 Baghdad, not far from the ruins of the old Persian capital, was chosen to be developed as the new Abbasid capital. Surprisingly, in only a generation the Abbasids began to disintegrate, not from outward attack, but from internal weakness. However, even during the disintegration, there was a remarkable flowering of civilization centered in Baghdad. What is clear is that Arab domination was open to the upward mobility of Persian and Turkish peoples so that the sophisticated culture that developed represented an amalgam of earlier Middle Eastern, including Greek, influences and new invading forces from Central Asia.

Nutting (1964, 136-137) summarizes the dual development of disintegration and flowering:

> Paradoxically, the cause of this inner collapse was the very same factor that had contributed most to the Abbasid golden age - the predominance of foreign influence on Arab thought and action and the abandonment of that Arab racial supremacy which Omar had sought to maintain. The process of racial dilution had been going on since the great conquests of the Omayyad era...Thus even in Omayyad times the idea of an Arab military aristocracy became less and less a reality. Now all pretensions to Arab supremacy were cast aside. Even in the matter of the succession to the caliphate the Abbasids set no store by Arab blood. Not only were Haroun and al-Mamoun half Persian, but of the thirty-seven caliphs who followed Abul Abbas, thirty-four were born of Persian or Turkish slave mothers and only Abul Abbas himself, Haroun's father and his son al-Amin were of legitimate Arab parentage. Greek and Persian cultural influence dominated the social, cultural and political life of Bagdad, and Arab influence took a back seat. With Persian vizirs running the government and Persian governors administering the provinces, the caliph's bodyguard and the imperial army became filled with Khurasanis....
>
> Only the Arabic language held its own for the five hundred years during which the Abbasid caliphate dragged on. From being a language of poetry in the pre-Islamic days and of religion at the time of Mohammed, it became the medium for expressing the ideas of science and philosophy and the language of diplomacy from central Asia to Spain..

Thus, in a significant way for the theory of diffusion in this book, the founders of Islam were *not* the wielders of political and military power for many centuries because of the collapse of Arab power. The Arabs were the God-fearing and egalitarian tribespeople, carriers of a new spirituality and often initially the bearers of liberty from outside religious oppression. The founders of Islam and its initial carriers were spared association with a long dominant ruling power, except in Spain. Arabic remained the classic religious language, carrying in itself a spiritual force, greater than the force of Latin in the West. The Qu'ran was and still is regarded as basically nontranslatable and the sacred Arabic language is used as possible in worship. As Sanneh (1991, 186-214) points out, Islam as it spreads does not encourage indigenization. Non-indigenization tends to feed the tension, already noted, between reforming movements and secular governments.

In addition to the dissolution of Arab power and its subsequent disassociation with the diffusion of Islam, there were areas of Islamic power where Islam failed to diffuse. In the west, where the Omayyads continued to rule after their replacement by the Abbasids in the east, a brilliant Islamic civilization developed in Spain, but the indigenous population, in spite of numerous conversions to Islam, remained largely Christian. Eventually, Christian forces from the north were able to defeat the Arabs and their allies so that by the end of the eleventh century, Arab influence in Spain was clearly on the wane. The Arab rule in Spain actually outlasted Arab rule in the areas that were first conquered in the east. Thus, however brilliant and basically tolerant the Islamic rule, in the end, the Iberian peninsula returned to the rule of indigenous people and remained primarily Christian.

Another significant conquest in the west took place during the Abbasid period (following the Omayyad fall) when a decentralization of power took place. Sicily was conquered by the Aghlabids of North Africa responding to a call by Sicilian rebels for help against Greek domination. This conquest was begun in 827, completed in 902, and Islamic rule continued for almost 200 years (Nutting 1964, 136). The Norman Christian conquerors of Sicily and Malta, who retook them between 1060 and 1090, recognized the advanced Islamic civilization, patronized the culture and recruited Arabs for the government and army (Nutting 1964, 153). Of course, it is true that rulers often prefer the use of minorities, in this case foreigners, rather than people "of the land" to aid in government. At any rate, Sicily and Malta are additional examples of conquered areas not converting to Islam.

The conversion of Persia to Islam probably remains the greatest anomaly from the point of view of the theory of this book. From the intergroup relationship perspective, however, as already noted, Islam had shown itself remarkably open to upward mobility by Persians so that Persians gained considerable influence under the Abbasids. As early as the ninth century, Iranian rulers re-emerged and the Persian language entered a period of revival.

In addition, the Persian case fits the part of the theory which states that a conquered people faced with little choice will accept an outside religion but change it in significant ways to preserve their distinctive identity. This process was certainly not a simple one. Bernard Lewis (1993, 276-277), in his analysis of the rise of Shi'ism, rejects the nineteenth century view of it as primarily based on ethnic and national antagonism of the Persians towards the Arabs. According to Lewis

(277-281), more recent scholarship sees support for the various Shi'a sects (some moderate and some extreme) as arising from a combination of discontented Arabs and Persians who were dissatisfied with orthodox Sunni Islam identified with the Abbasid state. The Abbasid state had originally drawn on their support to gain power, but later repudiated them. "It was in North Africa, Egypt, and Arabia that Shi'ism won its earliest and most resounding successes" (Lewis 1993, 277), but later Sunnism was restored. This argument, however, shows that shi'a was from early times a mouthpiece for the oppressed and those opposed to orthodox rule (Nutting 1964, 79). For the theory of this book, it is not necessary that Shi'ism developed in Persia alone or is confined to Persia. What is significant is that ultimately this "oppositional ideology" became the view of the majority of Iranians under the Turkish-speaking Safavids by the sixteenth century.

Diffusion to the Turks and Central Asia

Under the Abbasids the Turks (in their various groups) began their role as defenders of Islam. Later, one of the great defenders of Islam from the Crusader invasions in the twelfth century was Saladin. Saladin was from northern Iraq, of Kurdish descent, and his father had been in service to Turks. The Turks had been invading the Middle East for centuries. The Abbasids made Turkish slave soldiers (Mamelukes) their protectors, but the policy backfired because the Turkish soldiers soon controlled the government. Earlier, in the middle of the tenth century, the Seljuk Turks shifted from the Kirgiz steppes of Turkistan to the country around Bukhara "where they became fervent Sunni Moslems" (Nutting 1964, 163-164). The Seljuk Turks later gained domination over Persia and in 1055 entered Baghdad. They soon moved into the highlands of Asia Minor that had been cleared of the Byzantines. In 1194 the Seljuk Turks were deposed by other Turks, the Shi'a Khwarizms (at the invitation of the Abbasid caliph), but the whole area was soon overrun by the Mongols, traditional enemies of the Turks.

The eventual defeat of the Mongols by the Mamelukes in 1260 near Jerusalem introduced a long period of Turkish domination of the Middle East which led eventually to the fall of Constantinople in 1453 and the establishment of the Ottomon Empire over the whole area, including the Balkans. Timurlane introduced a brief but cruel interlude to the ascendancy of the Ottoman Turks. Timurlane converted to Shi'a (the "oppositional ideology") rather than Sunni Islam and destroyed many of the monuments of Sunni orthodoxy, but his death in 1405 brought an end to the second Mongol threat to orthodox Islam.

The 500 years of Turkish rule of the Balkans enabled the faith of Islam to spread to certain specific groups. One group that was receptive over time to Islam was the Albanians, who are ethnically distinct from the Slavs in the Balkans. Conversion was slow and not until the sixteenth and seventeenth centuries did the majority of Albanians become Moslems (Latourette 1938, 613). The other receptive group was in Bosnia-Herzegovina. There, as noted in the chapter on Christianity, the group considered heretical by Roman Catholic and Orthodox churches and severely suppressed (the "Bogomils"), were receptive to Islam brought by the Turkish conquerors in the fifteenth century (Latourette, 1938, 442; Newman 1945, 173-174). However, on the whole, in the Balkans, the policy of ruling through the Orthodox Church actually served to strengthen Orthodox Christianity in the area.

Thus, in the Balkans, it was only minority groups who were receptive to the outside religion. As already seen, although Islam was initially carried to Central Asia by Arab armies, the Turkish and Mongol acceptance of Islam was more commonly as conquerors who entered and settled in Islamic lands. The Mongols to the east of Central Asia, who were traditional enemies of the Turks, remained mixed religiously, but eventually became primarily Buddhist of the Tibetan variety. The eastern-most Turkish people, the Ouighour or Uigur people, accepted Islam and were the means of spreading the faith to the Tungans or Hui people of west China, thus creating the Islamic minority of China.

Diffusion to the East

Central Asia and Persia became bases for the spread of Islam further east and south into India and Southeast Asia. India was invaded by several waves of Islamic peoples from Central Asia so that northern India was ruled by Moslems for extended periods. The last of these rulers were the Moguls, who extended their rule over all of India in the sixteenth century.

In general, Islam was not highly successful in its diffusion to India. That is, the Indian sub-continent remained primarily Hindu during the centuries of domination by Islamic rulers. The primary areas of conversion to Islam were the northwest, in what is now Pakistan, and in Bengal, in what is now Bangladesh. In the northwest, many of the people were descendants of the Islamic invaders and others were certainly more closely related to them than were the people to the south. Whether partial Islamization in northern India is attributed to preaching or to the use of inducements, the fact is that numerous lower caste people converted to Islam (Rizvi 1975, 287-288). In the Islamic community they lost their low caste position. However, generally in India, as in the case of the Balkans, the Islamic rulers carried out their administration through the legatees of the earlier traditions (Edwardes 1961, 128).

Major religious movements took place under the impact of Islam in India. Within Islam there was already the movement of Sufism, a reaction against the cold formality of orthodox Islam. In the tenth and eleventh centuries, influential Sufi thinkers appeared in Persia (Noss 1949, 749-756). The Sufis, including the Dervishes, although formally Sunni, represent a mystical strain that developed from outside influences, primarily in the Middle East and India. In India, the doctrine of "bhakti," with its tradition of literature, was certainly in major part a Sufi response to the presence of Islam (Edwardes 1961, 129-130). Once again, as with Shi'ism, the "interplay of dogmatic religion with popular piety" produced various forms of Sufism (Lewis 1993, 281).

The Sikh movement was initiated from a deliberate attempt to unite Hindu and Muslim believers and resulted in the formation of a separate religion. Kabir was a writer in the "bhakti" tradition and one of his disciples, Nanak, who was born in 1469, became the founder of Sikhism or "Gurmat," "the Guru's doctrine." (Edwardes 1961, 190-191). By the seventeenth century, the Sikhs had become an organized community with a military bent. In the case of the Sikh movement, the stimulation from and the resistance to an outside religion produced a religious innovation.

Although Islam had relatively little success in diffusing to the South Asian and Southeast Asian mainlands, it was carried across the seas to the Malay Peninsula, Indonesia, and the Philippines. Islam entered an area in which population and political-military pressures were primarily from north to south. The Cham people, who were originally a seagoing Malay people and lived in what is now southern Vietnam, were quite receptive to Islam. Although their kingdom eventually fell to the

Vietnamese in the fifteenth century, they have remained an Islamic minority group. The Malays of the Malay Peninsula had greater success in resisting Thai pressure from the north. The new center of commerce on the west coast of the peninsula, Malacca, was in an area over which both Siam and Majapahit of Java had contended (Harrison 1966, 54). Although Islam had been brought by traders to various ports, the conversion of Malacca in the early fifteenth century gave Islam its most powerful base for its growing influence throughout the islands to the south and east.

Siam made repeated attacks and demands for heavier tribute, but after 1460 Malacca "was strong enough to take the offensive and assert her authority northwards into Kedah (whose ruler acknowledged Islam c. 1474) and into Patani" (Harrison 1966, 59). The spread of Islam was "associated with adventurers and traders who founded new states or who procured or promoted a shift in allegiance among rulers of existing states or disrupted commercial empires" (Tarling 1966, 30).

Another historian, Zainu'ddin (1970, 58-60), describes the process of conversion:

> In many north coast Javanese towns the struggle for independence from Hindu-Buddhist Madjapahit may have encouraged the rulers to accept Islam, particularly in those places where the rulers were perhaps merchant adventurers who, like the original ruler of Malacca, moved from open piracy to a more respectable version of it--the compulsory levy of import duty and harbour dues...Possibly as the Moslem trading communities grew in size and prosperity, the rulers, through contact with leading and wealthy traders, felt that adherence to Islam gave them greater legitimacy than they could otherwise claim from their somewhat shady pirate origins.

A new source of danger appeared as Islam was spreading to the trading centers of Indonesia. Christian Portugal, followed by its major rival for trading rights, the Dutch, entered the area. Malacca fell to the Portuguese in 1511. However, this only caused the growth in importance of other Islamic trading centers, such as Atjeh and Makasar (Zainu'ddin 1970, 81-95). Whereas first Islam had given the traders and their port cities a new ideology with which to oppose the Hindu-Buddhist kingdoms, now Islam provided them a distinctive ideology to oppose the intruding Western Christian nations. Quoting from Benda (1958, 65) Tarling (1966, 65) comments: "Islam was 'a rallying point of identity' and symbolized 'separateness from, and opposition to, foreign, Christian overlords'. The European impact tended still further therefore to domesticate what had once been another alien influence."

Muslim merchants and state-builders continued to spread Islam to the east and north into what is now the southern Philippines (Mindanao). The arrival of the Spaniards in Luzon and the Visayas (central Phillipine islands) drew a line between the Christianized areas of the Philippines and the area of opposition in the south. Both Islam and Christianity built on traditional rivalries. Resistance from Islamic groups in the south to the government in the north has continued to this day. In Indonesia, although the large majority of the population accepted Islam, certain interior groups, notably the Bataks, and certain outlying groups in northern Sulawesi, Flores, and Timor became receptive to Christianity. These are groups for whom foreign pressures were often secondary to pressures from the majority population. Once again, in this easternmost area of diffusion for Islam, religious differences followed lines of local rivalries.

Diffusion to Africa

Africa, south of the Sahara, offered a formidable challenge to Islam. The two areas of earliest influence were in west Africa above the rain forest and along the coast of east Africa. A series of Islamic kingdoms were established above the rain forest. Berbers, migrating south because of Arab pressure, established Senegal. An Islamic revival among these nominal Moslems became the basis for a strong state that controlled the area from northern Spain to the rain forest in the eleventh century (Wiedner 1962, 32-33). Berber power was relatively short-lived and Islam spread to "Ghana and most other Negro states throughout the western Sudan, but many preferred to emigrate rather than accept any part of the new faith" (Wiedner 1962, 33).

After 1235, Mali became a strong Islamic kingdom controlling the trans-Saharan gold-and-salt exchange and Timbuktu became a center of brick buildings and Islamic education (Wiedner 1962, 34). The Songhai were the next to emerge as a strong Islamic state which launched attacks "in the name of religious revival" (36). After their decline in power, Mali and Hausa re-emerged. By this time, the pattern in West Africa was well established. Although migrations of Islamic peoples (mostly Berbers) into the area from the north did occur, the few attempts at conquest were short-lived. Islam became the religion of the strong kingdoms and petty states that succeeded one another or existed concurrently above the rain forest. At the same time, various large groups, such as the Ga, the Yoruba, the Akan (Ashanti and Fanti came from the Akan people), and numerous other tribal groups to the south were able to maintain their independence and traditional religions to the south, primarily in the shelter of the rain forest. Later, Christianity found its major acceptance among groups that were to the south of the Islamic kingdoms and in tension or conflict with them.

The other area for early Islamic influence was the narrow East African coast. Arab traders and others had long visited the coast, but a series of settlements was established from the Zambezi river to modern Somalia in the ninth century, collectively known as Zenj (Wiedner 1962, 99). The Zenj or Zeng Empire was the spawning ground for Swahili and Kiswahili from Persian, Arabic, and Bantu mixtures. Although the trading centers were important for centuries, Islam did not spread to any great extent to the Bantu of the interior from the plantations and port cities along the coast. East Africa became famous for its trade in slaves obtained from the interior. In the middle of the nineteenth century Arab traders greatly expanded their trade in slaves, raiding into central Africa. In the interior of Africa, unlike in the Middle East and North Africa, the Arabs were not a liberating force. However, even here, because of European intrusion and domination, they were able to inspire groups to oppose the Europeans, as in the Maji-maji uprising of 1904 against the Germans in Tanganyika (Reusch 1961, 322-326).

Diffusion to North America

The most recent diffusion of Islam, in which it was accepted from outside the group (not diffusion through immigration), has been in the United States where it has been accepted by many African Americans. Although there undoubtedly were Muslims among the involuntary migrants from Africa, the modern movement by African Americans towards Islam may be dated from the establishment in 1913 of a "Moorish Science Temple" in Newark, New Jersey by Timothy Drew after which the movement spread to Pittsburgh, Detroit, Chicago, and cities of the South (Lincoln 1989, 344-5). Elijah Muhammad (born Elijah Poole in Sandersville, Georgia in 1897, died in 1973) succeeded to the leadership of the movement. Lincoln (1973, 241) writes of a period of great growth from the middle 1950s to 1964 when membership reached between 30,000 and 100,000. Writing some sixteen years later, Lincoln (1989, 347) refers to there being 100,000 Black Muslims.

Throughout its life, the Islamic Movement among African Americans has faced a dilemma: how to maintain a strong anti-white sentiment and rhetoric and at the same time maintain the self-consciousness of being devout adherents of the Islamic Faith, which holds to an all-embracing human equality (Lincoln 1973, 242-243). One result has been the formation of two wings in the movement, one under Wallace Muhammad, Elijah's son, who has attempted a rapprochement with mainline Islam, and the other led by Louis Farrakhan, who has emphasized the original "fall of America" theme (Mamiya 1982; Lee 1988). The Black Muslim movement has suffered some rejection by the orthodox, particularly in the United States, but even Louis Farrakhan has drawn closer to mainstream Islamic faith and Black Muslim leaders have been cordially received as "Moslem brothers" in the Middle East and other areas (Lincoln 1973, 243-244; 1989, 354; Lee 1988).

Discussion

A review of the diffusion of Islam contradicts the common assumption, especially among Christians, that Islam was spread primarily by the sword. It is true, of course, that Islam accompanied Arab and other Islamic armies, but in numerous areas the Arabs, especially, set people free from outside domination and in other areas, Islam clearly has been perceived as a support against domination, for example, in the Balkans, India, Indonesia, Africa, and the United States.

Another important fact is that Arab power was relatively short-lived with Arabs giving way to Persian and Turkish influence and power in the early period of the Abbasids. This means that the founders of Islam, in which the Arabic language occupies a special status as the language of religion, were relieved from association with domination to a great extent.

The Turks, very much as European tribes accepted Christianity, accepted Islam from the people they conquered. However, in spite of a brilliant and tolerant civilization in Spain (one area where Arab power remained the longest) and also in Sicily and Malta, Islam was not able to establish roots in these areas. Another area, which largely rejected

Islam after a rule of some five hundred years by Islamic Turks, was the Balkans. The exceptions in this area, which are consistent with the theory regarding the receptivity of minorities for which an outside religion offers support against other outside domination, are the Albanians, a minority ethnic group in the Balkans, and the Bogomils of Bosnia-Herzegovina, an oppressed religious group.

To the south in West Africa, Islam was carried primarily by traders and immigrants and became a support to ascendant elites in establishing states. This follows a common pattern to be seen in the reception of Christianity by ascending elites in Europe and the acceptance of Buddhism by ascending elites throughout Asia. This was also a major pattern for the reception of Islam in Southeast Asia. There, Islam was a strong counter-force, not just to small rival groups, but to major outside powers, at first from Hindu-Buddhist power centers and then from Western Christian expanding powers. In Indonesia, as in mainland Southeast Asia, certain distinctive groups in the protected interior and to the east were the least receptive to Islam and later the most receptive to Christianity. In Africa, Islam has also acted as a counter-force to Western colonialism. Nevertheless, Islamic association with slave traders has not been helpful to its diffusion in large areas of Central Africa.

Probably, the strongest counter argument to the theory (the theory emphasizing the negative effect of domination and the positive effect of introduction "from below") is found in the case of the diffusion of Islam to Persia. This case (along with cases of Christianity being carried by conquerors) gives the greatest challenge to the theory. Mitigating factors should be considered. The Arabs were not the traditional enemies of Persia, but rather it was Byzantium, and the Arabs were unsophisticated tribespeople who, very early, welcomed Persian participation and even leadership in their religious thought. In other words, Islam encouraged upward mobility from within, especially after the Omayyad period. It is difficult to know how much weight to give to the fact that Persia was internally weak. That is, there had been a long Sassanid rule ending in a series of weak rulers and the Zoroastrian religion had been diluted from its original monotheistic form (Noss 1949, 459-468). The long struggle with Byzantium had placed a terrible burden on the people and encouraged dissatisfaction with the rulers. In some cases like this, there are nationalistic revivals of power and religion. However, the Arab conquest was overwhelming and there were few areas for escape, Zoroastrians eventually emigrating to India.

Whatever may be said regarding Persia being the clearest case of an outside religion diffusing through force, the theory does state that when there appears to be little alternative to acceptance of a new outside religion, a different or oppositional version of the religion is likely to develop that expresses the distinctive identity of the receiving group. As already seen, all of the areas conquered by the Arabs asserted their independence, but in addition, it was in Iran (Persia) that eventually the traditional "oppositional ideology" in Islam, Shi'a, became the dominant expression. Furthermore, it is significant that important religious innovations developed in the dominated societies of Iran and India, notably Sufism and Sikhism, the latter forming a new religion.

In general, Islam has had an ability to tolerate and absorb many variations. As in Christianity (from whom it borrowed the word for "heresy" (Lewis 1993, 275-293)), in Islam there has been harsh repression of or opposition to those considered "unbelievers." Given the nature of Islam with its unitary view of religion and society, this has often involved political struggle. As Kurtz (1995, 213) points out in his discussion of religious conflict and "the politics of heresy," "the problem of heresy is primarily a problem of *authority*, that of beliefs and structures." This involved political struggle among Christians well into the seventeenth century in Europe, but given the nature of Islam (with religious and political authority in close alliance), political struggle is still endemic in many Islamic countries.

The view of this book is that an authoritarian structure combined with pervasive single religious identity tends to produce a distinction between "official" and popular religion, the "great" and "little traditions" of Redfield (1957). The latter may be tolerated, as in Sufism, if it does not become dangerous to the authorities. However, in Islam as in Christianity (the "prophetic religions') popular religion may represent an attempt to 'purify" the official religion, which is regarded as too compromised. In modern Christianity, this may mean the forming of a new denomination, but in countries where Islam is pervasive, it is more likely to mean the development of a reform or revolutionary movement causing a political struggle.

Lewis (1993, 282) speaks of the importance of understanding what "underlies" some of the religious movements in Islam today:

The problem is of more than purely historical interest, since in our day, in Iran, in Egypt, and in other Islamic countries, new religious movements are stirring beneath the secularized surface: brotherhoods and creeds are replacing the wrecked parties and programs that have never really responded to the needs and passions of the peoples of Islam.

While Islam faces the problem of political struggle in those countries where Islamic identity is pervasive, in countries where Islam exists alongside other religions, as in Africa, India, China, Europe, and North America, the tension between the conservative popular or traditionally religious Islam (often identified as "Islamic fundamentalism") and the civil authorities is greatly reduced. This is because the civil authorities are secular or do not claim to be Islamic. In these countries Islam has established vital and disciplined religious communities existing alongside other religions. In other words, when a religion holds to a unitary view of life, but exists in a pluralistic society, it will tend to produce strong communitarian life as it brings its followers together in the midst of a non-believing society.

Conclusion

The theory of diffusion stated in the second chapter receives support from the review of the spread of Islam. The greatest problem for the theory is to account for diffusion that accompanies conquest. However, it was found that some of the initial diffusion of Islam, although associated with a conquering army, was to societies which were under heavy domination or threat from the Byzantine Empire. Persia, though not under the Byzantine Empire, was exhausted from long fighting with Constantinople and under weakened leadership. Islam allowed for the upward mobility of Persians who gained considerable influence within Islam. Persian culture revived within Islam and eventually the classic "oppositional ideology" of Islam, Shi'a, found its home among a majority of the Persians so that Iran became the major center of an alternative expression of Islam.

Islam failed to diffuse to large areas under extended Islamic rule. These include Spain, Sicily, Malta, the Balkans, and to a large extent, India. Sufism, within Islam, and the Sikh religion outside of Islam, were spawned by contact with Islam. Many Africans, especially those subject to Arab slave raids, have been resistant to Islam.

At the same time, many groups or societies have received Islam, not because it was forced on them, but because they perceived it as a means of enhancing the strength of their groups. The Turks came as conquerors of the Middle East (receiving Islam "from below") and became major defenders of Islam. Other tribes of Central Asia and of Africa found in Islam an enhancement to their identity and strength. In Southeast Asia, Malays and Indonesians found in Islam a support in their struggle to resist nearby Buddhist societies, but especially Western colonialism. Finally, both Africans and African Americans have been strengthened by Islam in their resistance to dominant whites.

Islam's powerful unitary view of life which combines its religious and political aspects has meant that religious and political conflicts have often been indistinguishable. On the one hand, Islam has allowed for a relatively high variation of religious expression, but on the other hand has taken strong measures of political control. This has also meant that purifying reform or revolutionary movements have periodically been generated to oppose "compromising" official rulers. However, outside of the areas of Islamic rule and in pluralistic societies, Islam has also been able to offer a disciplined community life. This may be seen in the United States as well as in Europe.

Chapter 6

Christianity After 1500

Part I The Societies in Asia

The year 1500 is a convenient beginning point for considering the modern diffusion of Christianity because it was at approximately this time that European countries, initially Portugal and Spain, began having increasing contacts with groups which were far from Europe and which previously were largely unknown to Europeans. For the first time the great seas became highways instead of barriers to continuing global interactions. Europe was the center for Christianity and Europeans (and their descendants in the Americas) became the main bearers of Christianity to the areas where Christianity was represented by very small minorities or not at all. With the exception of Latin America and the Philippines, for the most part the interactions began slowly and it was not until after the middle of the nineteenth century that the greatest diffusion took place. This was associated with the quickened pace of international contacts together with the establishment of many new colonies following the industrial revolution.

The enormous number of large societies and small groups to which Christianity diffused after 1500 makes it necessary to divide the treatment into two chapters: Part I, The Societies in Asia and Part II, The Societies in Oceana, Africa, and the Americas. The former were primarily the societies that were literate, having old civilizations. The latter were primarily preliterate and consisting of small societies.

Once again, it is important to note that I am not reviewing the missionary effort in diffusing Christianity (some of which was quite dramatic and sacrificial and, probably for this reason and the relative ease of obtaining the records, has captured the most attention). I am primarily interested in the nature of contacts and relationships (both between receiving groups and the groups from which Christianity came and between receiving groups and other groups) and the response of whole groups, some groups being quite small, while others were large societies with numerous sub-groups. In addition, I am interested in different patterns of change or variations within the diffusing religions based on continuing intergroup relations. The review can only give highlights while trying to cover the major patterns.

Diffusion to the Middle East

Christianity started in the Middle East and a number of Christian communities continue there from the early days, but in the push for diffusion since 1500 that has come primarily from Europe and North America, there has been only a very small new response. In fact, massive resistance has been the rule. This is hardly surprising given the long history of conflict and hostility between Europe and the Middle East.

When Christianity developed, only part of the Middle East had been colonized by Rome. Following the collapse of Roman power, hostility between West and East continued and was expressed in the conflicts between the Byzantine Empire and the peoples to the east and south. This hostility was exacerbated by the Crusades conducted from Europe. The tide of conquest was first reversed by the Arabs and later by the Turks and the hostilities remained. The Middle East became and still is the center for a moral order based on Islam with its scriptures and attendant large body of scholars. Arend Th.van Leeuwen (1964, 215) states that although Islam cannot be reduced to a protest movement, it did inherit a conflict with Hellenism "striking back a thousand years before Muhammad" and it thus represents a "countermovement directed against the dominating influences of Hellenism." This is certainly consistent with the view of this book that religious change is often associated with resistance to domination.

Diffusion to South Asia

There was already a Christian minority in India when the Portuguese arrived in 1498. Christians with historic relations to Syria were located primarily along the southeastern coast where the Portuguese first anchored. Over the next two centuries, a portion of the native church came under Rome, but another portion remained independent. In the nineteenth century, a group seeking to purify the Syrian church withdrew and formed the Mar Thoma Church (Latourette 1953, 1316).

The Portuguese approach was to establish themselves by force in a series of posts along the eastern coast of India. The Moguls had not yet established their empire, but Muslims ruled a number of kingdoms and came in conflict with the Portuguese. The southern end of the subcontinent was under the rule of Hindus (the Kingdom of Vijayanagar). The Portuguese intermarried with the local people and frequently enforced Christian instruction (Latourette 1939, 249), even instituting the Inquisition in Goa (Edwardes 1961, 145). One group in particular, the Paravas, sought protection of the Portuguese against the Moslems, were later instructed by the famous missionary, Francis Xavier, and became a strong Christian group that has continued to the present century (Latourette 1939, 253-254). Apparently, the Paravas were a low caste group, but they and the other converts (many of mixed birth) became virtually a new caste located in the port cities and coastal areas ruled by the Portuguese.

The Portuguese were followed by the Dutch and the English, each of whom formed companies to pursue trade in the East (the East India Company formed in London in 1599 and the Dutch East India Company in 1602). At the same time, the unified power of the Moguls began a gradual decline. The Hindu Marathas gained power in the seventeenth century and are credited with reviving Hindu political independence (Edwardes 1961, 174). After the sack of Delhi in 1739, the Mogul Empire rapidly disintegrated and India developed a number of centers of power, some of which looked to the British for support. After the uprising of 1857-59, the British government clarified their overriding authority in India, giving the British either direct or feudal control over what is now India, Pakistan, and Bangladesh.

Roman Catholic mission work continued after the decline of Portuguese power and it was joined by a Protestant effort, though smaller, in 1706 (Latourette 1939, 277). The Protestant effort was associated with the growth of British influence, even though Danes, Dutch, and

French had footholds in India. However, it was the Germans who provided the first Protestant missionaries. These worked primarily in the south and carried out scripture translations (Latourette 1939, 277-282). The East India Company, although not entirely opposed to the spread of Christianity, sometimes sought to hinder the work of missionaries out of fear that Indians would be offended and commerce hurt (Latourette 1944, 66-67, 69). However, the nineteenth century saw a tremendous advance in missionary efforts, that involved both a revival of Roman Catholic work that had declined in the eighteenth century and the infusion of Protestant missionaries from many lands. This has continued to the present century. Colonial rule was ended after World War II following a strong nationalistic movement. The South Asia mainland was subsequently partitioned into India, which is primarily Hindu, and the two Islamic nations of Pakistan and Bangladesh.

The reception of Christianity in South Asia has been quite mixed. Latourette (1944, 214) wrote concerning the effect of Christianity after some four hundred years of missionary effort from western countries, "The large majority of Hindus and Moslems and the main structure of Indian life were as yet but little affected." A pattern did appear, which to some extent has been repeated in many Asian lands. Latourette (1944, 212) describes it:

> The Christians, both Roman Catholic and Protestant, were overwhelmingly from the depressed classes and the tribes of primitive or near-primitive culture which had never been fully assimilated to Hindu civilization. In the South numbers of Christians were from the Sudras, social strata which were midway between the depressed groups and the higher castes. For the most part the natural leaders of the country, the higher castes, were only slightly affected.

One of the striking examples of receptivity to Christianity was the response of minority ethnic groups in the hill country of northeast India. They were first reached in the 1860's and by 1914 there were followings among "the Garos, the Rabhas (mixed with the Garos), the Nagas, the Abors, and the Miris" (Latourette 1944, 168).

A similar receptivity was found among peoples in the Khasia and Lushai Hills in the northeast and east, the latter being people of Mongolian strain (Latourette 1944, 148). Writing of the area that is now in Bangladesh, Barrett (1982, 165) states, "Mass conversions took place in Mymensingh in the late nineteenth century, and growth is still considerable among the tribes of the Chittagong Hills."

The mass movements to Christianity of illiterate, low-caste Hindus were primarily in the south, but also accounts for most of the Punjabi Christians in what is now Pakistan (Barrett 1982, 543). It is important to note that consistent with the theory of this book, the tribal and low caste converts accepted the Christianity presented to them without any conscious attempt to make changes in it. This will be seen to be a general pattern across Asia in the diffusion of Christianity to minority groups.

Susan Billington Harper (1995) has recently written of this phenomenon. Regarding the tendency of Nadar converts to adopt Western cultural symbols, she (1995,15) writes:

> Reasons for these choices have less to do with perceived judgments about the relative value of Western and Indian cultural systems than with the dynamics of South Indian caste mobilization under British imperial rule. Western cultural symbols served as important tools in competitive bids by the Nadar caste to improve its social ranking through the rejection of stigmatized indigenous cultural symbols and practices.

Harper's (1995, 16) view regarding resistance through religious change is highly consistent with the approach of this book:

> The mass movements to Christianity must be understood as part of - indeed, as a catalyzing agent in - this broader effort to reject caste traditions and to adopt new, more respectable forms of social identity...Far from being a weak concession to domineering missionaries, Westernization represented a symbolic challenge by long suppressed lower classes to an oppressive indigenous social order. In this context, indigenization along the lines expected by Western orientalizing indigenizers would have been viewed as just another form of indigenous oppression.

The diffusion of Christianity to South Asia has been very uneven, as Barrett (1982, 373) notes, "The faithful are concentrated mostly in the extreme south, where Christianity was first established, and the east, where important minority groups have been converted." Barrett (1982, 370) estimates that in mid-1980 Christians were approximately four percent of the population in India, but in India's large population that is almost 30 million people. In Bangladesh and Pakistan, the percentages of Christians in mid-1980 are .5 five percent and 1.8 percent respectively (Barrett 1982, 165, 542). These, of course, are strong Muslim countries.

Sri Lanka (formerly Ceylon) experienced domination from a series of nations with which Christianity is associated: Portugal, the Netherlands, and Great Britain. Like other Asian countries it has been free from outside control only since shortly after World War II. Portuguese and Dutch occupation resulted in many forced conversions. Soon after control passed to the British, there were many defections and the number of Christians decreased markedly (Barrett 1982. 635). The vast majority of Sinhalese (primarily Buddhist) and Tamils (primarily Hindu) have not received Christianity. At present Christians make up approximately 8 percent of the population (which is a higher percentage than in India), of which the majority are Roman Catholics (Barrett 1982, 635). One interesting feature of the response, pointed out by Latourette (1939, 287), is that in the sixteenth century certain social groups, the Careas, "a fisher caste on the coast between Colombo and Negombo" and the Paravas, as in India, "who were pearl fishers...embraced the faith en masse." Today, there are still concentrations of Christians in these areas.

Harper (1995, 14) concludes regarding the whole of South Asia:

> Most cultural systems in South Asia have been influenced by Christianity, but South Asians have, on the whole, remained stubbornly hostile to evangelization, with only 3 percent of today's population claiming to be Christian. Foreign missionaries were clearly instrumental in stirring up a greater awareness of ethnic and, later, national identities among some Indians. But the relative marginalization of Christianity in India has occurred at least in part because of the resourcefulness with which certain sections of Indian society responded to the Christian challenge by revitalizing their own traditions and identities and, in consequence, constructing a cultural wall against conversion.

Diffusion to Southeast Asia

Unlike India and Sri Lanka, the mainland of Southeast Asia avoided European control for several hundred years after 1500, with the exception of Malacca, which came under Portuguese control in 1511. The long Malay Peninsula distinguishes that region from the mainland to the north and the Peninsula is occupied by people who are ethnically distinct and who became religiously distinct from the people to the north, as seen in the previous chapter.

In Myanmar (Burma) there was relatively little knowledge of the Europeans due to limited contact, even though Portuguese mercenaries had been used in the sixteenth century (Tarling 1966, 69-70). It was not until 1824-26 during the first Burma War that Myanmar suffered its first loss of land to the British and then was completely annexed after the third Burma War and the acceptance of British authority by the Chin tribes in 1895 (Tarling 1966, 144-147). Thailand never came under foreign control, perhaps partly because it was between areas of British and French domination. Towards the latter part of the eighteenth century, the French helped to restore a king in Annam (northern Vietnam), who in turn favored Christianity, although Christianity continued to be periodically persecuted until the French took control after the middle of the nineteenth century (Latourette 1939, 299; 1944, 231).

In Myanmar (Burma) it was among the peoples who lived primarily outside the ancient kingdoms that Christianity was received by the largest groups of people. These peoples were primarily tribal in their structure and animists in religion, having not received Buddhism or Islam. In the nineteenth century, there was a high receptivity to Christianity brought by Baptist missionaries to a number of minority groups in the hill country: the Karens, Chins, Kachins, Lahus, and Was (Latourette 1944, 225). The British domination was not a threat to the minority groups, but rather meant a relief from the domination of the majority population (Latourette 1944, 231). In Myanmar, only the Shan minority group did not respond to the same extent as the other hill people. The Shan had their own state structure in the past which had sometimes been dominant. They also had a closer relationship to the majority people and like the majority, they were primarily Buddhist (Barrett 1982, 202). The receptivity to Christianity among the majority populations in Myanmar, Thailand, Laos, and Cambodia, all from old Buddhist kingdoms was negligible. As an example, a 1921 census showed a .16 percent of the majority people in Myanmar as Christian whereas 15 percent of the Karens were Christian (Latourette 1944, 226). In 1970 95 percent of all Baptists, the largest Christian group in Myanmar, were of tribal background (Barrett 1982, 202).

Thailand and the other areas of the old kingdoms did not have as large tribal enclaves in their hill country interiors as did Myanmar, nor were the tribes quite so isolated. Nevertheless, the response to Christianity has been the greatest among these "Montagnards." Barrett (1982, 665) notes:

> Although citizens, Thailand's Christians are often considered foreigners due to their ethnic origin. Most Catholics are Vietnamese and Chinese with a growing number of Montagnards. Protestantism is strongest among Chinese and has also made recent gains among Montagnards.

Before European contact, what is now Vietnam had kingdoms in the north and south and a variety of religious influences, which included Buddhism (primarily Mahayana), Confucianism, Taoism, Hindu-Buddhism and Islam (the last two primarily in the south). In terms of the number of ancient kingdoms and of religions, the eastern coastal region that came under French control was the most diverse on the Southeast Asian mainland. After having obtained footholds along the coast in 1787, between 1858 and 1882 the French took over the whole region that became known as French Indo-China. The war of 1858 to 1862 was fought because of the persecution of Roman Catholic missionaries (Latourette 1944, 246). In fact, the Christians of the area had suffered persecutions since at least 1645 and especially in the first half of the nineteenth century (Latourette 1944, 247-251; Barrett 1982, 744). Although Christians (primarily Roman Catholic) are now a small percentage of the population (estimated in mid-1975 to be 7.5 percent, Barrett 1982, 742), the response has been considerably higher among the majority peoples than in the other lands of mainland Southeast Asia. Significantly, there are also a number of new religions, the largest of which are the Cao Daist Missionary Church (some 2.8 million members) and the Hao Hao (some 1.5 million members), both found mostly in the Mekong Delta.

The other areas of French domination, Cambodia and Laos, have had a negligible response to Christianity. Cambodia is the site of the ancient Funan and Khmer kingdoms and the Lao are very closely related to the Thai. Both are strongly Theravada Buddhist. As in the case of the other countries, the minority tribal groups (of which Laos has the most) have been the most responsive to Christianity.

Turning to the south, Malacca on the Malay Peninsula represented the gateway to the many islands in what is now Indonesia. Malacca was taken in succession by the Portuguese (1511), the Dutch (1641), and the British (first in 1795 and finally in 1824) (Latourette 1944, 295). The port cities of the Peninsula, chiefly Malacca, Penang, and then Singapore, had mixed populations of Malays, Chinese, Indians, and Europeans. There was little receptivity to Christianity by the Malays (primarily Islamic), but considerable response from the two immigrant populations, the Chinese and Indians (Latourette 1944, 240). In addition, there has been receptivity to Christianity by the tribal people, especially in East Malaysia (Sarawak). In 1970, Christians formed only 5.4 percent of the total population of Malaysia, but 10 percent and 19 percent of the populations of Sabah and Sarawak respectively, both on the island of Borneo and with populations consisting primarily of Chinese and aboriginals (Barrett 1982, 474).

Stretching to the south and east in a giant arc from mainland Southeast Asia are numerous islands, which today belong to two major nations, Indonesia and the Philippines. The peoples are ethnically similar (Malays with numerous sub-groups), but they took different religious routes, with some overlap in the southern Philippines (Islamic minority) and eastern Indonesia (Christian minority). Beyond lie the Pacific islands, which will be considered in a separate section.

As seen in previous chapters, the Indonesian islands received considerable influence from India, as did mainland Southeast Asia. There were a number of small states and at least one empire (Majapahit) that accepted Hindu-Buddhist religious practices, especially in their ruling circles. This influence was very faint in the Philippines and there were no kingdoms developed there with state structures. The continuation of Hinduism is seen chiefly among the Balinese, but also in some mountainous areas of Java, and Hinduism and Buddhism have both seen something of a revival since Indonesia gained its independence in 1945 (Barrett, 1982, 383).

Unlike mainland Southeast Asia, except for Cham, the islands of Indonesia, especially in the west, were affected by the coming of Islam in the two centuries before the coming of the Portuguese. As seen in the previous chapter, Islam became important to the rising trading class and grew in strength under the domination of foreigners, particularly the Dutch.

After taking Malacca in 1511, the Portuguese were drawn towards the famous sources of spice and established their influence in the islands to the east. In the east also, with groups distinct from those in the main islands to the west, there was a response to Roman Catholic Christianity which may still be seen in the Lesser Sunda Islands, especially Timor. After the defeat of the Portuguese by the Dutch in 1605, the Dutch were the major Christian influence for the next 300 years. After the French conquered Holland in 1799, the Dutch East Indies Company was disbanded. The British entered the picture, occupying Java in 1811, but Dutch authority was reestablished in 1816. From 1825 to 1830 there was a major resistance on Java to the Dutch in which 200,000 Javanese died (Seekins 1992, 22).

Latourette (1953, 1321) summarizes the response of the people in Indonesia:

> The main gains of Christianity were among the animists. They were chiefly in the island of Celebes, notably the northern peninsula, Minahassa, where a mass movement into the state church occurred, and from the Bataks, a vigorous folk in Sumatra among whom the Rhenish Missionary Society had an extensive enterprise.

Barrett (1982, 382) estimates the Christians in mid-1980 to be approximately 11 percent of the population of Indonesia, "95 percent having come into Christianity from an animistic background." After an abortive coup d'etat in 1965, some 250,000 alleged communists were killed. This, along with a requirement that everyone belong to one of the four recognized religions, has pushed many people towards the minority religions, Christianity, Hinduism, and Buddhism, rather than towards Islam (Barrett 1982, 384).

One additional area, the Philippines, is usually included in Southeast Asia, although it is quite distinct culturally from the rest of the area. The Philippines, like the eastern islands of Indonesia, shared more characteristics with Oceana than with mainland Southeast Asia. Although they had trading relationships with the societies to the west, they consisted mainly of a multiplicity of small societies on scattered islands. The islands that now make up the Philippines did not have kingdoms or even trading centers that could compare with those of the main Indonesian islands. They did not even have the attraction of spices as did the islands of eastern Indonesia. Before the Spanish came, Moslem merchants from Borneo were coming to the islands, beginning to establish trading centers and teaching their faith. They were beginning to introduce the concept of territorial states as opposed to simply kingship groups headed by datus (chiefs) (Seekins 1993, 5). However, the arrival of the Spanish arrested the Islamic influence that was coming from the south (Latourette 1944, 307-308).

The Spanish were more powerful than either the Portuguese or the Dutch and had the means to carry out their goals of conquest and conversion, beginning in the latter half of the sixteenth century (Magellan having been killed on Cebu in 1521 and Villalobos having been unsuccessful in an expedition in 1542). Unlike Latin America, the Philippines did not offer the strong lure of gold. Trade with Spain had to be by way of Mexico and the Philippines were considered important primarily as a base for trade with China. Philip II, for whom the Philippines were named, was "a religious zealot" and the fact was:

> The Philippines, as the Spanish outpost in the Far East, although having some commerce, were chiefly a base for Christian missions, in which missionaries won the larger part of the population, and from which missionaries went to the East Indies, Indo-China, China, Formosa, and Japan. Indeed, at the outset, the Philippines were esteemed primarily as a strategic centre for Spanish political and religious conquest in the Far East (Latourette 1939, 308).

There were some who escaped conquest, particularly tribal people in the mountains of Luzon and peoples in some southern islands, primarily Mindanao, who were both Islamic and non-Islamic groups. Nevertheless, the Spanish conquest was much less harsh than in Latin America (there was little demand for native labor for mines and plantations and the King forbade slavery in 1573). Furthermore, as in the Americas, church leaders and missionaries spoke and worked for the protection of the Filipinos (Latourette 1939, 318-319).

The Philippines began to feel the winds of nationalism in the nineteenth century. Many studied in Europe and Masonry, of the Continental anti-clerical, politically liberal type, was introduced. A secret society, the Katipunans, was organized and in 1896 a rebellion broke out. Nationalistic heroes, Aguinaldo and Rizal, emerged (Latourette 1943, 264; Seekins 1993, 18-20). There were a number of religious movements against the Roman Catholic Church (especially the domination of the Spanish friars over the Filipino priests), beginning just before the middle of the nineteenth century, that drew on the nationalistic spirit and found opportunity in the weakening old order. The largest such movement brought about the founding of the Philippine

Independent Church in 1890 (organized in 1902) (Barrett 1982, 564). Barrett (564) states,

> The PIC attracted a vast following in its early years, including many priests and nearly 50 percent of the entire Catholic community. However, when the Supreme Court of 1906 ordered the return of all Catholic properties appropriated by the PIC, peoples' attachment to their parish churches resulted in large numbers returning to Catholicism.

Another estimate of the Roman Catholic membership that followed the movement led by Aglipay is one in four (Seekins 1993, 102). Either way, the movement was quite large. It might also be argued, in accordance with the theory of this book, that the presence of the United States as a new colonial power enhanced loyalty to the Roman Catholic Church as a balancing force to the new authorities and the new cultural influences. However, the courts of an independent country might not have made the same decision as the U.S. courts, which favored the established church.

There have been other indigenous church movements, the largest of which is Iglesia ni Christo, which also has a larger membership than any of the missionary founded Protestant churches (Barrett 1982, 564). Protestants entered the Philippines with the American annexation in 1898, but in mid-1980 those affiliated to Protestant churches numbered approximately 5 percent of the population compared to some 80 percent Roman Catholic and some 20 percent "Filipino indigenous." (Barrett 1982, 562). Clearly there is a large number of "doubly affiliated" people, which Barrett (1982, 562) places at 15 percent of the population. Anglicans and some other non-Roman Catholic groups have found receptivity among tribal groups.

The Philippines appear to be an anomaly in the diffusion of Christianity in Asia and, in fact, share many characteristics with Christianity in Latin America. These will be discussed later.

Diffusion to East Asia

When European nations began going to the Far East by sea in the sixteenth century, China was a powerful empire. The Portuguese gained a precarious foothold at Macao probably in 1514, but failed in attempts to establish other posts (Latourette 1956, 296-297). Before the Ming Dynasty fell, the Dutch obtained footholds in the Pescadores and Taiwan, building a fort in southern Taiwan in 1624. An opponent of the conquering Manchus, known in the west as Koxinga, threw off the Dutch in 1664. During the nearly three centuries of Manchu rule under the Ching Dynasty (1644-1912) the Empire reached its greatest territorial extent (Latourette 1956, 309). Contributing to China's strength were Emperors K'ang Hsi (1661-1722) and Ch'ien Lung (1736-1796), two very competent rulers with exceptionally long reigns. It was not until the nineteenth century that the then industrializing nations were able to have a strong impact on the Middle Kingdom (Latourette 1956, 310-311).

The Nestorian Christian communities that existed during the Tang Dynasty (618-907), and especially the Mongol Yuan Dynasty (1279-1368), had disappeared, as well as any Roman Catholic communities left from the Yuan Dynasty. The new effort would be by sea. The great missionary, Francis Xavier, had died in 1552, off the coast of China. However, another Jesuit, Matteo Ricci, following the policy of gaining the respect and friendship of the ruling classes, had "amazing success" (Latourette 1939, 338-341). The Jesuits won particular respect in the court for their scientific work and there were a number of conversions among people of high rank. There were periodic persecutions instigated by rivals and a rule was made against Chinese becoming Christians. Latourette (1939, 345) writes regarding K'ang Hsi's reign, "Since the Emperor was known to be friendly, the rule against Chinese becoming Christians became something of a dead letter and the Church had large accessions in both Peking and the provinces." In 1692, through the good offices of a friendly Manchu prince, an imperial decree was issued that allowed Christian worship and protection of church buildings (Latourette 1939, 347).

Later, the Emperor was made angry by the way his opinion, as well as that of a majority of missionaries, in the famous "rites controversy" was opposed by representatives from Rome. The Legate was commanded to leave, others were banished, and missionaries were required to obtain an imperial permit after examination of their opinions (Latourette 1939, 352-354). An attempt was made in 1720 to mollify Emperor K'ang Hsi, but it failed and, in addition, there was a general decline in missionary efforts due to the weakening of Spain and Portugal, the French Revolution and the wars of Napoleon, and the abolition of the Society of Jesus in 1773 (Latourette 1939, 354-356). Under Emperor Ch'ien Lung (1736-1796), although he apparently had no special enmity against Christianity, there were periodic persecutions of Christians and by the end of the century, Christians were still an "infinitesimal" minority (Latourette, 1939: 364).

In the nineteenth century, the Manchu Ching Dynasty, that had already been showing signs of weakness, continued to decline and at the same time, the newly industrialized countries of the West, and then Japan, took advantage of this weakening. The Opium War (1839-1842), which forced the sale of opium on China, the Anglo-French invasions of 1858-1860, the Taiping rebellion (1851-1864) with its semi-Christian ideology, and the whole period of unequal treaties, all helped to intensify anti-foreign feeling in China. The Boxer Rebellion in 1900 was a serious anti-foreign outbreak, but there were many other expressions, including the Communist Revolution itself. The Manchus were finally replaced by a Republic in 1912, which in turn was followed by a long period of periodic war and upheaval. China was united under Communism in 1950 and in the last two decades has seen a gradual opening of relationships to the West.

Paul A. Cohen (1963, 265), who described the growth of Chinese antiforeignism, particularly from 1860 to 1870, expressed a view that is highly consistent with that of this book when he said,

> As intriguing as it might be to do so, I have studiously avoided any "metaphysical" explanation of its causes, such as the stock charge that the Chinese are basically unsusceptible to religious experience as understood in the West. My impression is that the Chinese response to Christianity was conditioned not by metaphysics but by history...

Latourette (1944, 254) comments that in the nineteenth century, China was more "impervious to Christianity than was India." It was more united politically, "there were no depressed classes to welcome that faith as a way of escape from their hereditary bondage" and the animistic tribes "were not so large or so widely scattered a part of the population in China as in India" (Latourette, 1944, 254). It is significant that an important movement, the Taiping Rebellion, took place in the middle of the nineteenth century. The movement adopted many Christian ideas and might have been successful in overthrowing the Manchus if it were not for Western aid to the army of the rulers.

In 1914, Christians in China were "slightly less than one-half of one percent," which was about half the percentage that Christians formed in the population of India, but, as in India, they were primarily from "the humbler ranks of society" (Latourette 1944, 356). The period leading up to World War II saw tremendous efforts by mission bodies and missionaries so that churches were established throughout most of China. Donald MacInnis (1988, 7) estimates that there were almost three and a half million Roman Catholics and about a million Protestants by 1950. However, after 1950, missionaries were expelled and the church came under heavy pressures. Now, in the closing decades of the century, with foreign associations greatly reduced, Christianity is seeing tremendous growth. No one knows the actual number of Christians in China, since church leaders say they "are too busy to count." Estimates are of Protestants having from six to nine million members and of Roman Catholics as having close to four million members (Woo 1992, 1993). The basic fact is that churches are crowded and multiplying. Church leaders consider themselves in the "post denominational" age. The Roman Catholic Church (officially another religion from the "Christian Church," as the Protestants are called) is hampered by the unrepaired relationship to the Vatican.

No mention has been made of the response of the minorities in China that has been so notable in other countries in Asia. About seven percent of the population of China are in an official list of 55 "nationality groups" (Shinn and Worden 1988, 84). Some large groups in the west and north are Buddhist (e.g., the Tibetans) and Muslim (the Hui and other groups). Groups in the south and southwest are more tribal in structure and religious tradition, but many have been partially assimilated or in other ways have worked out an accommodation with the majority society. Nevertheless, in accordance with the pattern in the rest of Asia, it appears that some of the tribal groups in southern and western China have been quite responsive to Christianity. After the turn of the century, especially, there were numerous minority people in southwest China who sought to become Christians.

However, not all tribal people were responsive. Ralph Covell (1990) reports on work among the Independent Nosu, who were not generally receptive to Christianity. However, the time for sustained contact with this group was limited to the years after World War II to 1950. There is some evidence from the efforts that were made (and not made) by missionaries (and their organizations) in the nineteenth century that tribal people in China were not a high priority. It was possibly felt that the tribal people should not be given attention that would detract from efforts to reach the very large numbers in the majority population. It might have been feared that Christianity would be associated with people not respected by the Chinese. It was also possible that missionaries were afraid that the tribal people would be "superficial" Christians because of their tendency to come in large numbers. This is consistent with nineteenth century individualism and perhaps negative views of European tribal conversions.

An "Asian pattern," (high receptivity by minorities) which has been seen most clearly in India and Burma, but not so clearly in China, appears again in Taiwan. Taiwan was ruled briefly by the Dutch in the seventeenth century. Missionaries brought Christianity to Taiwan a second time (following the expulsion of the Dutch) in the second half of the nineteenth century. At this time the British became dominant in Taiwan and made opium a major import. As in Mainland China, anti-foreign sentiment was strong. Taiwan was taken from China by Japan in 1895 and ruled as a colony until the end of World War II after which it was returned to Chinese control. Taiwan has three major Chinese-speaking groups, the majority Taiwanese-speaking group, the Hakka-speaking group, and the post-World War II immigrants from the Mainland, primarily Mandarin-speaking. Some aboriginal groups were assimilated to the majority population, but after World War II (when I served in Taiwan), there were some ten different aboriginal groups consisting of less than two percent of the total population.

A Christian church developed among the Taiwanese majority population in the nineteenth century that grew during the period of Japanese rule and continued to grow after World War II. There were many Christians among the Mainland Chinese who came to Taiwan after 1945. In 1970, it was estimated that approximately 20 percent of the Mainland Chinese identified themselves as Christians. Nevertheless, in the total population, only about four percent identified themselves as Christians (Grichting 1971).

By an "Asian pattern" I am referring to the movement of aboriginal people to Christianity beginning under the Japanese, who attempted to suppress it, and expanding after 1945. Today, the proportion of Christians among the aboriginal people is probably greater than in the United States and in the Taiwan Presbyterian Church, the largest Protestant Church, they make up approximately 40 percent of the membership. This pattern is highly consistent with the statement concerning the reception of an outside religion that is not associated with domination and that has the effect of enhancing the identity of new adherents.

In the same era when Christianity was entering the Philippines and China from the sea, it came to Japan and had a remarkable reception. After a period of phenomenal growth in the second half of the sixteenth century, Christianity was severely suppressed by the rulers. Latourette (1944, 331) quotes the decree issued in 1614 which declared that Christians "have come to Japan ... longing to disseminate an evil law, to overthrow right doctrine, so that they many change the government of the country and obtain possession of the land. This is the germ of great disaster and must be crushed." One leader, Nobunaga, had thought that Christianity would aid him in the unification of Japan, but his successors, Hideyoshi and Iyeyasu, "in time felt Christianity to be a threat to this" (Latourette 1944, 323).

The door to Japan was forced open by the Perry mission in 1854, somewhat later than China was forced open, but once opened, Japan industrialized more rapidly than China. This enabled Japan to become a strong power, defeating China in 1895, Russia in 1904, taking over Korea in 1910 and Manchuria in 1932, invading China in 1937, and carrying on a war against the United States and other countries from 1941 to 1945. After its defeat in this war, Japan rebuilt and has become a world economic power.

In spite of strong missionary efforts and even the discovery of Christian villages left from the early days, the proportion of Christians in Japan has remained very small, estimated to be 3 percent by Barrett (1982, 419). Interestingly, some 50 percent of Japanese households have copies of the Christian scriptures and large numbers of people, especially students, express interest in Christianity (Barrett 1982, 419-420). In the nineteenth century there was a positive response to Christianity by many Samurai, who had been ejected from power by the Meiji restoration (Martin 1990, 139). There has been no Christian movement among the tiny aboriginal (Ainu) group, who make up only .02 percent of the population. The contrast between the response to Christianity in Japan and Korea, both rather homogeneous societies and adjacent to one another, is enormous.

Korea lies between China and Japan and has been dominated at different times from both directions. Although highly influenced by Chinese culture, which included both Buddhism and Confucianism, the Koreans are ethnically and linguistically more related to the Mongols than the Chinese. Korea was made a colony of Japan from 1910 to 1945, during which time the Japanese language and religion were imposed. Christianity came to Korea by way of the Manchu court, but after a number of conversions, Christianity was officially attacked in 1785 (Latourette 1939, 362). Christianity was periodically persecuted and numerous executions took place, but Korean Christians showed great courage and determination.

In the latter part of the nineteenth century, Protestant missionaries came to Korea. Korea was forced to capitulate to Japanese forces in 1876 and soon after this large numbers of Koreans were receptive to Christianity. There was fighting between China and Japan near Pyengyang in 1894, after which the people became more open-minded "for the bewildered populace found that they could trust the missionaries" (Latourette 1944, 422). There was very rapid growth in the churches in the five years between the Russo-Japanese War and the formal annexation of Korea by Japan (Latourette 1944, 423). Martin (1990: 139) notes that because northerners were discriminated against by the Yi (Korean) dynasty, they turned to Christianity the most enthusiastically. Church growth slowed after annexation, but significantly, the Japanese became harsh towards Christians and some Korean church leaders were arrested. Most importantly, Christianity became identified with Korean nationalism.

With a view that is similar to that of this book, Martin (1990, 138) describes important factors in the receptivity of Koreans:

> The missionaries were the friends of the Koreans, especially given that the Japanese were the enemies. What followed from this was the adoption of Christianity by many Korean intellectuals as a political vehicle of nascent Korean nationalism. Almost everywhere else in Asia Christianity had some association with what was alien. But in Korea, given that Koreans were doubly alienated, from their ancient background and from the Japanese, Christianity went native and became genuinely popular.

After World War II, Korea went through the terrible disruption of the Korean War and the subsequent division of the nation. Since World War II, Korean Christians have increased enormously. Barrett's (1982, 441) estimate is that in mid-1975 Christians were 25 percent of the population of South Korea and that by the year 2000, they will be about 42 percent. Christians are also very numerous among the Koreans who live in China and Japan and among those who have migrated to the United States. There have been many schisms in the Korean Protestant, especially Presbyterian, churches and many indigenous churches have developed. Some mix indigenous religious traditions with Christianity and some are clearly messianic, such as the Unification Church and the Olive Tree Church. Barrett (1982, 441) estimates the indigenous church Christians as making up a little less than half of all Christians. Pentecostal churches have been growing most rapidly in the last decade since 1982 showing "a decadal growth of 742 percent compared to a Presbyterian growth rate of 135 per cent and a Methodist growth rate of 130 per cent" (Martin 1990, 146). Because of the rapid growth it is difficult to estimate the percentage of Christians in the population, but Barrett's estimate is that professing Christians made up some 30 percent of the population in mid-1980.

Discussion

It was my own experience on Taiwan with the aboriginal people that first drew my attention to what I have called an "Asian pattern" and stimulated my investigation of the diffusion of Christianity, as well as of other religions, throughout history. Very briefly, it has been seen that the diffusion of Christianity to the old societies of Asia has shown the general pattern of non-receptivity by most members of the majority societies, but receptivity by members of minority groups and some low status groups. Apparent breakthroughs in which elites in Japan and China were receptive were cut off by rival groups or others in authority. A major exception to this pattern may be seen in Korea. However, Korea has a significant parallel to the minority peoples of other societies in that it was under pressure from two sides, China and Japan, and in this century was annexed by Japan (a country not identified with Christianity), who imposed its culture, including its language and religion.

Also, in a manner highly consistent with the theory of this book, China received an ideology (Marxism) from the outside that enabled it to eject foreign intruders. (Some might argue that the earlier and milder ideology of democracy did not support sufficiently the rapid independence China desired.) For me, the most relevant statement to the theory of this book uttered by Chairman Mao was when he said at the victory celebration in 1950, "China has stood up!" Now that the association of Christianity with foreign domination has been greatly relieved, if not entirely canceled, there is a high level of receptivity to Christianity in China. It may also be noted that Marxism supported Vietnam and Cuba against outside domination.

The receptive minority groups were usually people of tribal background or low social status or both, who were close to dominant large societies. India, Burma, Malaysia, Indonesia, and Taiwan are particularly notable for the small groups who were receptive. It must not be assumed, however, that minority tribal groups were always immediately receptive. Ralph Covell (1990, 89), for example, reports on a group which was resistant to Christianity, the Independent Nosu of West China. Over the years they developed a general resistance to outside influences. As late as 1945 they had "simmering hostility" towards the majority Chinese people which often "broke into open warfare." Interestingly, the Nosu have a complex writing system which supports their traditional religion. Whether having more time would have brought about a greater change is not known, but apparently *successful* independence by a minority group reduces the receptivity of that group to an outside religion or requires a longer period of contact for receptivity to develop.

This is supported by some of the other cases in which receptivity came only after a time of initial opposition from the small group, Christianity being seen as simply another outside influence to be resisted. Korea, for example, was highly resistant until the end of the nineteenth century and the growing domination of Japan. Some minority groups may reach what they consider a satisfactory accommodation to the majority group which they do not want to jeopardize by accepting an outside religion. The Ainu of Japan may fall into this category as well as some of the minority ethnic groups of China, Thailand, Laos, Vietnam, Cambodia, and Indonesia.

The exceptional case of the Philippines has already been noted and it will be seen that the pattern here is very similar to a major pattern presented in the next chapter, especially as seen in Latin America. That is, the receiving people(s) do not form a large society with a traditional moral order preserved in literature and with the means to organize resistance. The Philippines had more characteristics of Oceana than it did of Asia and in terms of a reception pattern may be grouped with Latin America on the acceptance of Christianity under pressure from a dominating power.

Indonesia was not able to resist as well as Japan, but it did have another world religion, Islam, which fortified it against the Christianity of the colonial power. However, Indonesia is much more heterogeneous than Japan, with numerous minority groups, some of which have been receptive to an outside religion.

For those who theorize that not having a literature and having an animistic religion are the major prerequisites for receptivity, Korea is an important case study. Unlike other receptive groups, Korea was not a small society nor one that was preliterate, as were many of the receptive tribal groups. Korea had (has) its own system of writing and well established religious traditions in Buddhism and Confucianism, as well as Shamanism. What is most important for the theory of this book is that Korea, as stated above, was dominated by outside powers, most recently Japan, and the carriers of the new religion were not from the dominating power, as they were in almost every other Asian country. Christianity became a means of affirming Korean identity. The very opposite was the case for Japan, as well as for the other old societies of Asia. Christianity was regarded among the older societies and in Korea before Japanese domination as a dangerous foreign ideology threatening the traditional moral order.

It is true that the old societies of Asia had cultures which included a literature. It could be argued that literature facilitates the transmission of culture from one generation to the next and therefore contributes to the stability and longevity of the established moral order. However, in the case of Korea a literate society under pressure has been receptive to an outside religion. Also, China, with its great literature, has in various degrees been receptive to Marxism and now there is a relatively high receptivity to Christianity. It is true that Taiwan like Korea was a colony of Japan for an extended time, without generating the same level of receptivity to Christianity in the majority population. However, Taiwan did not have as strong a nationalistic tradition as Korea with which Christianity could become associated. However, a tendency for Christianity to contribute to a sense of independent Taiwanese identity may be observed in Taiwan.

The macro level part of the theory is supported regarding the negative effects of domination on diffusion and the positive effects on diffusion of a new outside religion that helps preserve the distinctive identity as well as enhance the dignity of a group. On the micro level it is difficult to know the extent to which individual motives, such as self-esteem and uncertainty reduction, contributed to the willingness to accept an outside religion such as Christianity. It is clear, however, that Christian minority ethnic groups in Asia have been able to assert their distinctive identities through Christianity. The reduction of their languages to writing and scripture translation certainly has contributed to the maintenance and positive affirmation of these distinctive identities.

One aspect of the theory which will appear to be important when other parts of the world are considered is that the minority groups receptive to Christianity in Asia accepted the new religion very much as it was transmitted to them with little conscious attempt to change it. Some not only were receptive to the transmitted forms, but were defensive of them. A good example of this is discussed by Harper (1995), in which the Nadars of South India appropriated Anglican Christianity. It should also be mentioned that some new religions developed among majority groups in reaction to Western domination. One of the most famous was the religion of the Taipings, which included many Christian elements. There were also revival movements in Hinduism in India and in Hinduism, Buddhism, and Islam in Indonesia. Ahmadidya developed as an Islamic sect in what is now Pakistan, but it is considered heretical by other Muslims. New religions have developed in Vietnam and in Japan.

In Korea there appears to be the double phenomenon of acceptance of the transmitted religion in whole form and also indigenous movements within Christianity. That is, messianic religions have developed with the inclusion of Christian elements, the most famous of which is the church established by Sun Myung Moon. It should also be said that in other areas of Asia, indigenous churches have developed having organizations that are deliberately free of missionary influence. In general, however, the phenomena of deliberate attempts to develop independent expressions of the Christian faith (in organization and doctrine) have been much less common in Asia than in Africa, as we shall see. Also, since most of the churches are small, in Asia there has not been a tendency for resistance to develop on the popular level against official religion, creating the gap that is often seen where a religious identification becomes pervasive in society. However, before a conclusion is stated, other large areas of diffusion should be reviewed.

Chapter 7

Christianity Since 1500

Part II The Societies in Oceana, Africa, and the Americas

Diffusion to Oceana (including Australia)

The widely scattered islands of the Pacific were only gradually discovered by the Europeans in the three centuries following 1500. Although the Portuguese, Spanish and Dutch made contacts with several islands, in addition to being difficult to locate, the islands did not offer the attraction of rich trade to draw Europeans to them. It was not until the latter part of the eighteenth century, especially following the explorations of Cook, that the Pacific islands received serious attention from Europeans.

The missionary movement of the nineteenth century was just beginning to get underway at the same time as the explorers and traders were increasing. Thus, from these earliest days of contacts with Westerners, most islanders experienced the doubled pronged intrusion of traders (including whalers) and missionaries. These two intruding groups were often in conflict and it was soon recognized that the missionaries would not take advantage of the islanders, but instead offered them practical as well as spiritual training (Oliver, 1961, 109). The missionaries often took the part of the islanders against other outsiders, including foreign government forces and others. It is also true that the missionaries were often without direct protection and some were killed, especially in the first part of the nineteenth century. Thus, the missionaries were usually not accompanied by overwhelming force, which is consistent with their message being introduced "from below." Nevertheless, it is true that almost necessarily they were associated with the intruding Western world that challenged the traditional ways of life.

Although the work proved to be very difficult (some were killed, some "went native," and some resigned) for the London Missionary Society missionaries who landed in 1796, the king of Tahiti and Eimeo, Pomare, befriended the missionaries. His son, Pomare II, became a Christian, leading the way so that "the old gods and their cults were overthrown and Tahiti and Eimeo became nominally Christian" by 1825 (Latourette 1943, 203). Other islands in the Society group followed the example of Tahiti.

It is important for the theory of this book to note that soon other religious movements developed. In 1828 the leader of a cult, the Mamia, "proclaimed himself to be Jesus Christ and promised his followers a sensuous paradise" (Latourette 1943, 205). In the present century there have been numerous messianic movements, often in the form of "cargo" cults which prophesied the end of white rule (Oliver 1961, 178). However, Charles Forman (1994, 104) comments regarding these popular responses to dominant religion:

> However, for little understood reasons, movements of this type in the Pacific show much less staying power than do their counterparts in Africa. They have displayed meteoric careers, but most have gone into decline, and henceforth anthropological attention is likely to concentrate more on the standard churches, which themselves are also examples of social transition and which sometimes carry cargoistic undertones.

French priests established themselves on the Gambier Islands, southeast of the Society Islands, and brought those islands to Christianity. After Tahiti came under the French, beginning in 1842, about a fourth of the population became Roman Catholic, the others remaining Protestant with some Mormons and Seventh Day Adventists (Latourette 1943, 206).

In the Tonga islands there was a mass movement from Methodist influence in 1834 "marked by weeping, the public confession of sins, and the joy of conversion" (Latourette 1943, 211). This was joined by one of the chiefs, who later became king over several islands and in 1839 proclaimed laws embodying Christian principles (211-212). Samoa was affected by the Tonga Methodists, but because of agreements in London between the London Missionary Society and the Methodists, Samoa mainly followed the London Mission, but not without intertribal conflict. Roman Catholic Christianity entered the scene in 1845 and eventually became the strongest group. Even though the islands were annexed by Germany and the United States, the Samoans remained extremely loyal to their original churches.

Methodist missionaries and Tonga Christians spread Christianity to the large group of Fiji Islands. These had a number of chiefs and a history of warfare made worse by the introduction of arms. Christianity gained slowly, but there would be rapid growth from time to time when movements broke out in which there was deep emotion and contrition for sin. The conversion of the leading chief, Thakombau, in 1854 and a victory in battle in 1855 of Christian forces were major steps in converting large numbers of people (Latourette 1943, 221-222). A large group of Indian laborers were brought to the islands, but not many accepted Christianity, in spite of the strong efforts of missionaries.

The New Hebrides are particularly rugged islands and a number of missionaries and Christians from other islands were killed before the island populations became largely Christian. As in the other islands, the scriptures were translated, large numbers of people taught to read, and the quality of life improved (Latourette 1943, 226-232). The Solomon Islands and the islands of the Bismark Archipelago became largely Christian in the latter part of the nineteenth century and the early twentieth. Because of its size, conversions on New Guinea were mainly along the coast. It would be later in the present century before the interior would be reached in any force.

Valentine (1970) has made interesting comparisons between Polynesia and Micronesia (together with Fiji and New Caledonia), which he calls Area 1, and Melanesia, identified as Area 2. In Area 1, European domination was comparatively mild and generally indirect, whereas in Area 2 there was forceful and direct control by Europeans. In Area 2, apart from the movements in the early phases of contact, the response has been largely nonmillenarian and they have made adaptive modifications in their own institutions as they established indigenous and independent political institutions. On the other hand, Valentine (1970: 383) notes:

> The characteristic reaction in Area 2 has been supernaturalistic, expressed through modified indigenous religious instrumentalities, definitely apocalyptic, syncretistically acculturative, distinctly and often violently anti-European, strongly opposed to ethnic stratification, politically innovative for native politics, but no more than proto-nationalist.

These two kinds of responses (in Areas 1 and 2) are consistent with the theory that strong domination stimulates resistance and tends to produce rejection of the outside religion or acceptance with significant change.

Turning to the south, whalers were using New Zealand for refueling bases in the late eighteenth century and soon there developed a trade in timber and flax. The missionaries who came in 1814 sought to obtain land from the Maoris and at the same time agitated "against secular colonization and annexation on the part of all powers, including England" (Oliver 1961, 110). These efforts failed and in 1840 British sovereignty was extended to New Zealand. However, the missionaries continued to seek to safeguard Maoris, for example, helping to negotiate the Treaty of Waitangi that gave Maoris the rights of British subjects and "guaranteed the full, exclusive, and undisturbed possession of their lands" (Latourette 1943, 181-182). Still encroachments by whites continued and wars broke out in the 1840s and in 1860, with Maori opposition finally being subdued in 1871. In spite of these conflicts, most Maoris accepted Christianity. A chief was baptized in 1825 and growth proceeded slowly, but steadily. In 1854, it was declared that all but one percent of the Maoris professed Christianity.

Some distinctive religious movements developed among the Maoris, such as the King movement that attempted to unite them under one king and used Biblical ideas. The Hau Hau or Pai Marire movement was started by a Maori who claimed to receive guidance from the archangel Gabriel. In the end, the largest movement founded the Ratana Church by a Maori of that name in 1918 (Barrett 1982, 519-520), which became the third largest denomination among the Maoris (now eight percent of the population).

Turning to the north, the missionaries who came to Hawaii in 1820 found a culture and social order that had been shaken by their encounter with the outside world (Latourette 1943, 247). The missionaries addressed themselves to the chiefs, especially members of the royal house, and in this were helped by Christian chiefs from Tahiti. Many leaders soon professed the new faith and the church grew, helped by a "Great Awakening" in the years 1839-1841 (Latourette 1943, 249-250). It was declared in 1863 that the nation had been Christianized (251). Americans continued to gain in number and power in Hawaii and in 1893 to 1894 "they [Americans] deposed the monarch and proclaimed a republic, which they then promptly invited the United States to absorb" (Oliver 1961, 139). The Polynesian population of Hawaii, estimated to be about 300,000 at the time of Captain Cook's first visit in 1778, "had decreased to about 70,000 by 1853" (Oliver 1961, 268). Hawaiians became a minority in their land because workers were imported: Chinese (46,000 from 1852 to 1898), Portuguese (17,500 from 1878 to 1913), Japanese (180,000 from 1894 to 1939), and Filipinos (120,000 after 1906) (Oliver 1961, 268-269).

In this broad review, Australia will be included with the Pacific Islands. Because of its size and potentialities, it became an even larger area of outside settlement than New Zealand and Hawaii. In the nineteenth century the aboriginal population was overwhelmed by sheer numbers of settlers. The aboriginal people may have numbered as many as 300,000 in 1788 in hundreds of tribes and bands, speaking as many languages (Latourette 1943, 162; Oliver 1961, 26-27; Barrett 1982, 152). In 1900 they were 80,000 and a majority still retained their traditional religion, but by 1970 they numbered 138,000 out of a total population of over 12,000,000 and less than five percent still followed the traditional religion (Barrett 1982, 151-152).

There were numerous mission efforts on behalf of the aboriginals and there was religious work in all the government settlements for the aboriginals (Latourette 1945, 161). However, the space in Australia made it possible for many aboriginals to have little contact with the new population and to maintain their traditional religion.

In regard to the Pacific islands in general, Forman (1994, 106) makes an important statement:

> In other parts of the world where European empires once ruled, Christianity has often been seen as linked to imperialism and antagonistic to nationhood. Studies in those other regions have concentrated

on the relation between Christianity and imperialism. In the Pacific the problem tends to be the opposite one. Christianity has had closer links to the indigenous population than to the imperial powers, which were frequently in tension with the churches (e.g. in Tahiti, Samoa, Fiji, and Kiribati). The recent period in which the indigenous population emerged into national independence has revealed how closely the churches are tied to nationalism and the problems that result from these.

He goes on to list the involvement of clergy and churches in independence movements and governments in Vanuatu, New Caledonia, and Fiji. Thus, except for Australia, Christianity from its earliest period of introduction up to some of the most recent independence movements, has been associated in many islands with the development of distinctive national identities. Christianity has had some success, at least, in disassociating itself from outside dominating powers in Oceana.

Diffusion to Africa, South of the Sahara

When the European nations began their expansion about 1500, their primary goal was contact with Southern and Eastern Asia. The relative lack of port cities and of internal trading routes protected the interior of most of Africa from intrusion. The major trade that did develop was the trade in slaves, primarily from West Africa. Most of Africa, south of the Sahara, could be compared more or less to Europe as it was outside of the Roman Empire. The Islamic kingdoms, already mentioned in chapter 4, existed on the southeastern edge of the Sahara at the southern end of trade routes across the desert and down the coast. On the other side of the continent was Ethiopia, which had become a Christian stronghold on its high plateau. Most of the rest of Africa to the south consisted of various kingdoms, nascent kingdoms, and numerous tribes. They were in a preliterate period and migration and conflict were not unusual. However, "preliterate" does not mean that there could not be complex government and socio-economic institutions, such as in Zimbabwe (Bennett 1976, 23) and as in Europe before the coming of Christianity. Although in the area being reviewed there are some thirty nations today, there may be close to 1,000 people groups (Thomas 1987, 166).

I agree with Paul Jenkins (1986, 67-71) that the key unit in church history is the traditional sources of identity, as difficult as these are to define. I will refer to the modern political units to identify the areas of diffusion, but it is the "traditional cultural or political grouping" (Jenkins 1986, 67) that is important for understanding the responses of Africans to the introduction of Christianity.

In the latter part of the fifteenth century, the Portuguese had begun to make contacts along the west coast of Africa. They were beginning to trade for slaves, but at their post, established at Elmina on the Gold Coast in 1482, the major item was gold (Wiedner 1962, 47). After finding the mouth of the Congo River at about the same time, the Portuguese helped the king of an ascendant tribe, the ruler of the Manicongo, and were successful in persuading him to be baptized (Wiedner 1962, 48). He later returned to his old religion, but his son, Alfonso, was active in preaching Christianity. A large proportion of his subjects were baptized and the son of Alfonso became the first African Bishop until modern times (Latourette 1939, 242-243). The Portuguese helped this kingdom against its enemies and also obtained "hundreds of slaves for export" (243). By the end of the seventeenth century the kingdom died out, but to the south in Angola, the Portuguese established a strong coastal fortress at Luanda and this became a leading supplier of slaves. The Portuguese also established footholds on the east coast of Africa and had some success in converting people there, although they also met Moslem opposition in the ports to the north (Latourette 1939, 244).

The Dutch established a settlement on the southern tip of Africa in 1652 that was taken by the British in 1795. Slaves were baptized in the eighteenth century by a Moravian missionary, and though opposed by local clergy, he sought to reach the local Africans. The British trained an African missionary, but there were few results (Latourette 1939, 245-246).

The major European contact with Africans before 1800 was to obtain slaves for the Americas. The Dutch first overtook the Spanish-Portuguese lead and they were followed by the English and French. The Europeans established a series of trading depots in West Africa on either side of the first Portuguese station at Elmina during the seventeenth century and into the eighteenth century (Wiedner 1962, 59). Trading arrangements were made with African kingdoms and federations of tribes, for example the Ashanti. Established kingdoms, such as the Benin, the Yoruba, and the Dahomey were drawn into the lucrative trade in slaves. Estimates on the number of slaves purchased run from 3,000,000 to 20,000,000, but by 1860, "when the slave trade had ended, there were between seven and eight million people of African origin in North and South America" (Wiedner 1962, 67). During much of the period when this terrible trading was taking place, most of the interior of Africa was unaffected by Europeans. Contacts between Africans and Europeans in most of Africa developed slowly in the nineteenth century and came to a climax in the division of Africa among the European powers in the latter part of the century.

Perhaps the earliest contacts in the interior were made by European settlers from the Cape as they carried out hunting expeditions, but major conflict did not develop until the latter part of the eighteenth century. African groups had been migrating toward the south in the seventeenth and eighteenth centuries. Two advancing frontiers, the Dutch and the Xosa, met on the Fish River in 1775 resulting in the "Kaffir Wars" that "plagued South Africa for a century" (Wiedner 1962, 124-126). The British possession of South Africa, confirmed in 1815, meant that another group of white people were present to offset the Dutch. Missionaries also sought to protect and encourage the resident Africans. In 1809 the "Magna Charta of the Hottentots," issued by the government, prohibited debt contracts and guaranteed the freeing of laborers (Wiedner 1962, 129).

African groups, particularly from the Zulus, migrated in different directions, some back to the north. This put pressure on other African groups. The Dutch settlers "trekked" north in 1835 to 1837, defeated a Zulu group (the Matabele), and then divided, with one group moving to Natal where they defeated the main Zulu group (under Dingaan). Again, the British entered the picture and formally annexed Natal in 1843. Another trek was organized and eventually, out of the "Trekker Republics," the Orange Free State Republic and the South African Republic were organized in 1854 and 1860 respectively (Wiedner 1962, 143-149).

An important religious movement took place among the Xosa living east of the Cape Colony in 1857. Wiedner (1962, 151) describes it:

> Prophets called for the abandonment of traditional religion, the destruction of all crops and property, and the slaughter of all cattle (even those basic to the economy and the tribal social structure); then, they promised, a miracle would occur. A dramatic "whirlwind" would sweep both Britons and Boers into the sea, Xosa heroes of the past

would rise from the dead, and all South Africa would turn fertile - filled with lush grain and herds of prime cattle! The frenzy swept the crowded reserves. Property, crops and animals were destroyed. The Xosa sat down to wait for the miracle. When the "day" came, nothing happened....Thirty percent of the population was saved, (by relief supplies), but the toll of the "Xosa starvation" was staggering.

Missionary views, along with those of the British in general, remained strongly divided from those of the Dutch, the latter supported by their extremely conservative Dutch Protestantism. The Dutch remained strongly opposed to anything "that threatened Boer distinctiveness - that is, any threats to their God, to their church, to their folk identity" (Wiedner 1962, 156).

In the middle of the nineteenth century, Europeans penetrated to the central parts of Africa and in the last third of the century the European countries began to exert their influence directly on the Africans there, as well as in western Africa where the slave trade had been active. It also happened that at this time, slave trading penetrated to Central Africa, this time being managed primarily by Arabs. Between 1860 and 1910 a colonial partition of Africa took place, with support from both commercial and humanitarian or liberal interests, although the two often came in conflict. The colonial powers themselves came in conflict and in South Africa it was the colonial powers and the European (Dutch) settlers that fought.

Mission work gradually increased in Africa at the same time as the colonial partition was taking place and has continued to the present with various interruptions due to World Wars I and II and the post-World War II nationalistic movements. The major change in power arrangements in this century marked the formal end of colonialism in the decade and a half after World War II. Following the end of colonialism, numerous African nations were formed, most of which incorporated a variety of what may be termed "ethno-linguistic" groups.

The reactions to foreign domination have been numerous. Already mentioned was the movement among the Xosa in 1851 that predicted the destruction of both Britons and Boers. In 1905 the Maji-Maji revolt against the Germans in Tanzania included witches who distributed "a potion that was supposed to deflect German bullets, and prophets promised a paradise to follow the destruction of German forces" (Wiedner 1962, 213). This is not unlike what was said in the

Boxer Rebellion in China at about the same time and also in the Ghost Dance Cult in the United States.

Although these reactions to foreign domination affected literally tens of thousands of people and are important for that reason, they are also important as symptoms of resistance that, when crushed, may take other forms. Two major forms of resistance appeared and have survived to the present. One is within and the other is outside of Christianity. These will be considered after first recognizing the broad reception of Christianity.

Basically, it must be said that there has been remarkable receptivity to Christianity in all of the countries south of the Sahara. However, the growth of Christianity has been especially notable following the end of colonialism in this century. According to Barrett's (1982) statistics, except for those countries in West Africa with large segments of their populations being descendants from the Islamic kingdoms, as of 1975 the majority of the populations of the countries now existing south of the Sahara are professing Christians, with the exception of two countries. The two countries south of the West African line with the fewest Christians are Mozambique and Tanzania. Even in these countries, professing Christians are estimated to be 38.9 percent and 44.0 percent respectively in mid-1980 and increasing more rapidly (about 5 percent annually) than in most other African countries (Barrett 1982, 500, 660).

In Mozambique Islam is strong among the largest group, the Makua (18 percent), the Makonde (43 percent), and especially the Yao (80 percent), who "inhabit the region east of Lake Malawi ..., the only interior tribe below the equator to experience such a mass conversion to Islam" (Barrett 1982, 501). In addition, Barrett (1982, 501) notes that in Mozambique "all peoples north of the Save river are at least 70 percent traditionalist," adding that they were affected by religious movements in 1915 and 1934 that were suppressed by the Portuguese authorities. Likewise, in Tanzania, Islam is strong along the coast and among particular tribes along the traditional trade routes. Traditional religion is followed by 32 percent of the population, which includes 80 percent of the large Sukuma group (Barrett, 1982, 660).

However, as already noted, even in these two countries, Mozambique and Tanzania, the Christians are numerous and increasing and in the other countries, from the rain forest to the south, professing Christians make up from sixty to ninety percent of the population. One of the most dramatic instances of Christian diffusion took place in the area of the Buganda kingdom (Uganda), where the king asked for missionaries in 1875. Actually, the king was afraid of both European Christians and Arab Muslims and soon "Uganda was caught in the maelstrom of titanic forces and was thrown into internal confusion" (Latourette 1943, 415). The next king at one point instituted a fierce persecution of Christians. In 1890 British power (The Imperial British East Africa Company) was asserted in Uganda, the Muslims and the Roman Catholic Christian faction were defeated and a British protectorate was established in 1894. Following the establishment of order, there was a very large movement to Christianity. Significantly for the theory of this book, there were soon additional religious movements, for example, the "Society of the One Almighty God" grew to be one-third the size of the Anglican Church (Barrett 1982, 687). Altogether, however, Christians make up some 80 percent of the Ugandan population (Barrett 1982, 686).

Another strong movement to Christianity took place in Kenya where the large Kikuya tribe was decimated by diseases brought in by British and Indian railroad workers and turned into "a large urban and tenant class" (Wiedner 1962, 209). Barrett (1982, 434) writes of the work of missionaries who came to Kenya in the latter part of the nineteenth century: "African response to Christianity was instantaneous and immense from the earliest days of this first influx of missions, the number of converts doubling or even trebling every year for the first ten years after 1900" and "by 1916 a mass movement into all the churches...had begun." African independent churches also began to develop, beginning with a schism in the Anglican Church in 1914, and developing over 220 distinct independent churches by 1979 (Barrett 1982, 434).

As already noted, the countries that stretch along the southern coast of West Africa and continue across the continent typically included populations which were divided between those that had largely accepted Islam coming from the north and those that inhabited the rain forests in the south and followed traditional religions. Christianity has had wide acceptance among the rain forest tribes so that now the populations of these countries have large Christian minorities or even majorities. In the cases of Ghana and Nigeria, the Christians make up about 60 percent and 50 percent respectively of the populations (Barrett 1982, 323,527).

The two forms of resistance to outside intrusion mentioned above should be considered along with the striking receptivity to Christianity. The first form of resistance (within Christianity) has already been noted in the development of many independent African churches. In South Africa, for example, in the last decades of the nineteenth century, a number of independent African churches developed. This trend has continued until approximately one-fifth of the indigenous African population belongs to over 300 of these independent churches and these churches are the most successful in winning converts from tribal religions (Barrett 1982, 621).

In regard to the response to Christianity in Zaire where over 90 percent of the population profess Christianity (Barrett 1982, 758), of particular interest is the "Church of Jesus Christ on Earth through the Prophet Simon Kimbangu," which is the largest indigenous church in all of Africa. "Kimbangu began an extensive preaching and healing ministry in 1921 which attracted immense crowds" (Barrett 1982, 759). He was arrested, tried, and exiled to another part of the country where he died 30 years later in 1951 (759). Although suffering persecution, the church grew and gained the recognition of the Belgian authorities. In 1969 it was received into full membership in the World Council of Churches, the first African indigenous church to be so received (759).

Another remarkable movement was led by the Ivory Coast prophet, William Wade Harris. He began preaching on his own initiative in 1913, clad in a white robe, carrying a cross. "He demanded the destruction of fetishes and all other symbols of paganism, and taught a belief in one God, the observance of Sunday, and the prohibition of adultery" (Latourette 1943, 449). He told his followers, who numbered in the thousands, to wait for missionaries to come. Several years after the movement began, English Wesleyan missionaries learned of it and through their efforts "about 45,000 from it were gathered into their churches" (Latourette 1945, 222)

The examples of Kimbangu and Harris show that the independent movements were (and are) not necessarily strongly anti-European or syncretistic. In the great variety of movements, of course, there are a wide range of patterns in the combination of Christian and previous religious traditions. Adding to the difficulty in distinguishing the independent churches and those established by the missionaries is the fact that the latter are now largely self-governing and are therefore "independent" churches. Barrett identifies the results of the independent movements as "African indigenous" churches. In a number of cases, these churches have been aided by Black denominational churches from the United States in an often overlooked missionary effort. For my purposes, what is important is to recognize that part of the response to Christianity was for Africans to develop their own churches, which were independent of outside domination.

The other response to the introduction of outside religions is the strong maintenance of the traditional religion. In all of the countries south of the Sahara, there are particular groups which have tended to hold on to their traditional religions. Barrett (1982, 527), for example, lists 21 groups that are more than 90 percent traditionalist in Nigeria, where together Christians and Muslims make up 94 percent of the population. Barrett (1982, 323) notes of Ghana, "Traditional religions are followed by 27 percent of the population (1975), though this proportion of the population is rapidly shrinking (from 45 percent in 1960) due to conversions to Christianity." Tanzania and Mozambique are areas of particularly strong traditionalist religions (32 percent and 52 percent respectively of the populations in mid-1975)(Barrett 1982, 660, 500). In South Africa the Venda are 70 percent traditionalists (Barrett 1982, 621), and in Uganda the Jie (80 percent), Karamonjong (60 percent), and Pokot (83 percent) are largely traditionalists (Barrett 1982, 686). However, it must not be thought that these religions are static. Barrett (1982, 758) comments about Zaire:

> Movements for the renewal of traditionalist religions, with a strong emphasis on witchcraft eradication, have played a significant role, especially among the Bakongo. Some have used Christian elements, but their tendency has been traditionalist. A movement known as Kiyoka (Burning) swept through northern Angola and Lower Zaire in the late 19th century, and more recent sects of similar type are Myungism, Tonsi and Dieudonne. Eastern Zaire was also affected by the Mchape (Medicine) movement which began in Nyasaland in 1930 and subsequently spread to neighbouring countries.

Terrence Ranger (1993, 84) argues for the dynamism of traditional African religions, concluding:

> In short, I do not believe the argument for the inevitable redundancy and archaism of African religions in modern times. Wherever one looks, whether at movements or institutions, the reality seems different. Old dynamics remain vital; new principles of generalization have been developed or have become available. And in recent times the generalizing potentialities of literacy, so long the monopoly of Christi-

anity or Islam, have become available to the spokespersons of African religion.

Madagascar should be considered along with Africa, although its dominant people and language are of Indonesian origin, rather than African. After a welcome to missionaries by King Radama (1810-1828), there was a period of severe persecution under Queen Ranavalona I (1828-1861). In spite of this, the Christians continued to increase and, after Queen Ranavalona II became a Christian in 1869, "for the next 30 years a phenomenal mass movement into the churches began, and professing Christians increased from 5,000 in 1861 to over a million by 1900 (39 percent of the total population)" (Barrett 1982, 466). Growth became more gradual and after seventy years the population is divided fairly evenly between Christians and followers of traditional religions (466). There are a total of about 21 independent churches, but their members form only about two percent of the population (467).

Although it has been necessary to skip over or barely mention many of the responses to the diffusion of Christianity in sub-Saharan Africa, a general pattern has become clear. There has been a broad acceptance of Christianity, especially in this century and increasing in the last decades after the end of colonialism, but at the same time there has been a generation of a large number of independent indigenous African churches. Also, many groups have resisted the outside religion, holding to evolving traditional religions or to Islam. The association of Christianity with European dominations of various kinds appears to be stronger in Africa than in Oceana. However, a parallel argument is made by Sanneh (1991) regarding a certain disassociation developing between Christianity and its European source, although the disassociation was often inadvertent on the part of the missionaries. A major factor for Sanneh is the emphasis given to the vernacular and to the many translations of scripture. Sanneh (1991, 166) states:

> Thoughtful missionaries understood that God had preceded them in Africa, as Dr. Livingstone was at pains to point out, that translation involved esteem for the vernacular culture, if not surrender to it, that the authentic forms of the culture, consecrated by the elders, constituted the most promising signs for the Christian cause, and that, finally, linguistic investigations and the systematic inventory of indigenous resources were likely to touch off wider and longer-lasting repercussions in the culture. Even from the sternest view of the role of

missionaries in Africa, we have to recognize the immense contributions to the revitalization of Africa that this represents.

For Sanneh (1991, 185), "this matter of the overlap between the Christian revival and the revitalization of indigenous culture remains one of the most undervalued themes in the study of Christian expansion, although in Africa and elsewhere it stares us in the face at almost every turn in the road." Other patterns of domination and response may be seen in the Americas.

Diffusion to the Americas

The Spanish led the way in the European entrance into the Americas and eventually, most of the territory south of Central and South America came under Spanish domination, except for Brazil, which came under the Portuguese. The Dutch, French, and British followed and eventually dominated certain territories in the Caribbean and North America. The Europeans not only entered the Americas in large numbers, but they also introduced a large population from Africa as slaves.

The European entrance into the Americas was overwhelming because of superior technology and also large numbers of settlers, especially in North America. Because of the isolation of so many native groups and the rivalries between them, the threat represented by the Europeans was not always initially recognized, particularly in North America. In some cases, mostly in Central and South America, groups have been able to escape from the Europeans into the jungles or mountains.

The peoples of the Americas before the European invasion could be compared to those of Africa south of the Sahara, with the possible exception of the empires that came to dominate large areas in Central and South America respectively. In general, however, there were primarily numerous tribes. The various groups were not in a static condition, but in on-going relationships of conflict and federation and undertaking periodic migrations. These conditions continued after the European invasion and, in fact, were intensified.

Because of the presence of gold in the empires of Central America and the western coast of South America, they became targets for Spanish conquest. This was accomplished with the aid of enemies of the kingdoms, as in the case of the Aztecs, or outright civil war, as with the Incas. Spain and Portugal completed most of their conquests in the sixteenth century, but there remained large sub-areas within the areas they claimed that they did not control. Meanwhile, in North America European settlement began in earnest in the seventeenth century and very gradually extended inland. In North America, people of European descent were still establishing settlements in the west in the latter part of the nineteenth century. Geronimo did not surrender until 1886 and the Sioux were not pacified in South Dakota until five years later.

The two groups to which the diffusion of Christianity in the Americas should be considered (apart from diffusion by immigration) are the native or aboriginal people of the Americas and the Africans brought to the Americas by force. Roman Catholicism was the form of Christianity brought by the Spanish and Portuguese and later the French, whereas Protestantism was the major form brought by the Dutch and British. The Caribbean became an area of mixed influence. Diffusion both by immigration and the sending of missionaries, particularly over the last century, has made both North and South America places of dynamic religious change that is difficult to trace.

From the beginning the motive to convert was high among the Spanish and Portuguese. However, very early a conflict developed among the conquerors between (1) those who were willing to perpetrate violence and much abuse on the native Americans and the imported slaves in order to gain wealth and (2) those who believed that the main purpose of coming to the new world, which was conversion, should be accomplished through kindness. It happened that in Spain the most influential theologian of the first half of the sixteenth century, the Dominican Francisco de Vitoria, "asserted that the Indians could be converted, that Christians had the duty to spread the Gospel, and that no one should be forced to accept Christianity" (Latourette 1939, 90). The Spanish kings exercised close control over missionary efforts and took the humanitarian approach. The Popes of the period also strongly supported the Spanish rulers in their efforts to take a humanitarian approach. However, the European authorities were far from the scene and the sympathetic missionaries were outnumbered and "outgunned."

There were champions for the Native Americans, as well as the imported Africans, among the missionaries, the most famous being Bartolome de Las Casas. After his own awakening to the mistreatment of native Americans, he went repeatedly to Spain to argue before the throne and to obtain legal support for their protection up to the very time of his death in 1566 at the age of ninety-two (Latourette 1939, 93-97). The laws on the books and the efforts of the rulers and the missionaries had their effects, but there was also bitter opposition from the settlers and the local Spanish rulers. One missionary, Cabeza de Vaca, who had been appointed governor of Paraguay, was sent home in chains because of his efforts to restrain gross cruelties (Latourette 1939, 97).

In regard to the Africans who had been imported, Latourette (1939, 98) notes that under Spanish law many obtained their freedom and that in Puerto Rico at the close of the eighteenth century, the free people of African descent outnumbered the slaves. This was in contrast to the French part of Haiti and in English Jamaica where the slaves outnumbered the free ten to one.

In general, then, the Spanish approach was to assimilate the people they came to rule into Spanish culture, of which Christianity was a central part. Cities, towns, and villages were built around churches. On the frontiers, where Christianity was brought to the Native Americans, this meant the forming of villages around the church. Some of these attempts clearly failed, as in the case of the villages formed under the supervision of the Jesuits beginning in Paraguay and extending to other areas of South America (Latourette 1939, 154-156). However, the overall result of the Spanish effort was that the vast majority of people under Spanish rule became Christian (Latourette 1939, 159). Although the Portuguese effort in Brazil is considered to be somewhat less successful than the Spanish effort, the Native Americans under government control and the imported Africans were largely brought into the church (Latourette 1939, 167).

The nineteenth century brought a shift in the power arrangements in South America with the end of Spanish and Portuguese domination. The church was divided with many clergy participating in the revolutions against the colonial powers. Secular thought from Europe and also Protestant missionaries entered South America. Still, Roman Catholic Christianity has remained the dominant form of expression. However, certain variations in religious expression became increasingly apparent. Some of these represent combinations of Christian and non-Christian elements. Barrett (1982, 187) comments concerning "Umbanda," which he considers an "Afro-Brazilian" religion in Brazil:

This religious development, appearing within the last 50 years, is remarkable for its growth in adherents who now number over 33 million in Brazil. Similarly to high spiritism, Umbanda sees no contradiction between its own practices and the beliefs of Catholicism. Most of its followers in fact regard themselves as Catholics. Today its members are mostly urban, middle-class, with no racial distinctions...Umbanda has resisted a concerted campaign of opposition from the Catholic Church for the past 50 years and today displays great vitality, with centres multiplying throughout the country.

This type of expression is also found in the Caribbean, for example, in Jamaica the Ras Tafari movement numbered some 50,000 supporters in 1975 (Barrett 1982, 417) and in Haiti, Vodoun, which first appeared in the seventeenth century, is practiced by large numbers of people (349).

Another, but somewhat similar, type of religious mixture is found among Native Americans. In regard to this type of religion in Mexico, Barrett (1982, 487) states,

> The vast majority of monolingual Indians still practice strong christo-paganism, namely a syncretistic folk-Catholicism combining 17th-century Spanish Catholicism with traditional Amerindian religion, and in particular with Aztec and Mayan religious concepts and world-views.

This type of religious mixture appears in most of the countries of South America.

In addition to these mixtures of traditional religions with Christianity, the influx of Protestant missionaries has introduced new forms of Christianity. Some Protestant missionaries came to Latin America in the nineteenth century. For example, Moravian missionaries converted people of mixed African, white, and Native American blood as well as non-mixed Native Americans in Nicaragua in the nineteenth century (Latourette 1943, 104). However, as Mortimer Arias (1978, 22) pointed out, Protestantism began to grow more rapidly after 1930 and particularly after World War II. He estimated that the Protestant population has grown from 500,000 in 1916 (at the time of the Panama Congress of Protestant Missions) to 2,400,000 in 1936 and to 20,000,000 in 1973, representing between 7 and 8 percent of the population (Arias, 1978, 22). According to figures taken from Barrett (1982), Protestants, including indigenous groups, in mid-1980 constituted just under 30,000,000 people, which is a little over eight percent of the population of Latin America. However, there is not an even distribution of strength. Approximately two-thirds of the Protestants are in Brazil, which has a little over one-third of the population of Latin America. The other country where Protestants are overrepresented is Chile, which has a little over seven percent of the Protestants but with only 3.3 percent of the population of Latin America. In Brazil and Chile, Pentecostals account for large numbers of Protestants. In Chile Pentecostals make up some 85 percent of the Protestants (Barrett 1982, 227) and in Brazil Pentecostals are said to constitute some two-thirds of the Protestants (Freston 1994, 538). In Central America, Guatemala, Nicaragua, and southern Mexico have strong pockets of Protestantism, especially among Native Americans. In almost all the countries of Central and South America, the Pentecostal church is the most rapidly growing church and Pentecostalism has also been growing rapidly within the Roman Catholic church at the same time. As we noticed in the Philippines, double affiliation (between Roman Catholicism and other religious groups) is very common.

Although the groups are very small compared to the total populations in Central and South America, there are Native American groups that have been able to avoid successfully the invasion of outsiders and continue to practice traditional religions (outside of those who are practicing their religion within Christianity). These are the isolated groups who are surviving in the forests, but are under increasing pressure from the majority populations.

In North America, the Native American groups did not have the population concentrations that existed in the empires of Mexico and the west coast of South America. There was Spanish incursion in the southeast and the southwest in the sixteenth century, but it was the French settlement in the north and the larger British settlement along the eastern seaboard beginning in the seventeenth century that were to have the greatest impact on the Native Americans of North America. The seventeenth century Dutch settlement was incorporated by the British. In the latter part of the eighteenth century, the French nascent empire also collapsed, but a strong French community remained in Canada.

The European contacts with Native Americans in North America were not initially associated with overwhelming power as in Central and South America. The Europeans established settlements supported by farming, trading, and some fishing. Individual traders and hunters, especially the former, contacted the various Native American groups. However, conflict soon developed and continued intermittently for over two hundred years.

In some cases, Native American groups were allied with the outsiders against traditional enemies (and sometimes against other outsiders, for example, the French or the English), and in other cases federations were formed to oppose the intruders. The Europeans and their descendants were by no means always victorious in battles, but in the wars and through sheer population pressure were able both to push the Native Americans westward and allot them special territories (reservations). Some Native Americans were able to escape or in other ways maintain their separate identities, even in the eastern part of North America. In addition to the loss of life and territory through warfare, the Native Americans, as in the Caribbean and South America, suffered extremely from the diseases brought by the Europeans.

The Hurons, a member of the Iroquois family, but "in bitter and chronic enmity with the Iroquois proper" (Latourette 1939, 175), received Christianity from the French in large numbers, but in 1649 were decisively defeated by the Iroquois. French missionaries also left their mark on a number of other groups, including the Iroquois and some groups in the Mississippi Valley. Gallicanism had been strong among the French Roman Catholics, but British rule had the effect of driving the Canadian Catholics closer to Rome (Latourette 1939, 183).

Spanish missions were carried out to Native Americans in the Southeast and Southwest in much the same pattern as in other Spanish territories. The Christian villages established in the East have largely disappeared, but many established in the Southwest have continued to the present.

In the area of settlement by the British various Native American groups were receptive to Christianity brought to them by missionaries, such as Roger Williams and John Eliot, who established villages of "praying Indians". However, the Puritans as a whole were hostile and in King Philip's War (1675-76) destroyed numerous groups in New England. This pattern appeared repeatedly over the following centuries. That is, some whites would attempt to bring Christianity to Native Americans and offer kind treatment while at the same time numerous others sought to take advantage of or eradicate the Native Americans. When conflict occurred, the white authorities would intervene, bringing defeat and removal to the Native Americans.

One of the most famous examples involved the Cherokees of the Carolinas, Tennessee, and Northwest Georgia, who developed their own government and community with houses, schools and churches and also a system of writing. In spite of the intervention of missionaries during the conflict with the State of Georgia, most of the Cherokees were removed in the famous "Trail of Tears" (actually, a series of trails) to Oklahoma.

A significant reaction of Native Americans in North America to the intrusion of Europeans and to Christianity was a series of religiously based movements that began on the east coast and continued across the country. Sometimes the movements would support armed resistance and other times they would be peaceful, although often dealt with by force as the Ghost Dance Movement at Wounded Knee. Anthony F.C. Wallace (1956) used the term "revitalization movements" in his study of the Handsome Lake religion among the Iroquois to indicate how these movements attempted to revive and perpetuate the life of the group with a new moral order. This religion, as well as a number of other independent religious groups or churches, continues to exist (Starkloff 1985).

Today, Native Americans make up a very small proportion of the population in the United States, 0.1 percent (Canada has 1.4 percent registered Native Indians), but continue to be identified in more than 150 tribal groups, the largest of which are the Navajo (96,700), the Cherokee (66,200), the Sioux (47,800), the Chippewa (42,000), and the Pueblo (31,000) (Barrett 1982, 211, 711). Many Native Americans belong to churches that were brought to North America, but in 1970 there were some 19 separate indigenous churches and the largest one "has an estimated 60 percent of all Navajos in the U.S.A." (Barrett 1982, 716).

The largest group in the Americas to which Christianity was introduced from the outside are the people who were brought from Africa as slaves. African Americans constitute approximately 12 percent of the population in the United States. Enslavement, enforced transportation, mixture with strangers, and continued domination by others over centuries were all extremely destructive to the old order of life. However, the very size of the slave population, the similar origins and struggles for survival, and the continued segregation from the majority population formed the basis for the development of a distinctive African American culture. In many ways this culture has been undergirded by African American Christianity. Even after the abolition of slavery in 1861 in the United States, segregation continued, and after the official elimination of segregation in the 1950s and 1960s, discrimination and unofficial segregation continue to the present.

Christianity was introduced to the slaves by their owners and by missionaries. The growth of Christianity was slow until independent African American churches were established beginning about the time of the American Revolution, usually because they were made to feel unwelcome in white churches. It has been estimated that twenty years before the Civil War one-fifth of the Southern slaves were church members (Brown 1957, 54). This corresponded fairly well to the proportion in the majority population. Today there are African Americans in most of the major white dominated denominations, "with the largest numbers in the Roman Catholic Church (855,000) and the United Methodist Church (500,000)," but "the majority of all USA Blacks are members of over 140 separate Black denominations..." (Barrett 1982, 716). The two largest church traditions among African Americans are Baptist and Methodist. A third tradition that is developing is the Pentecostal. Three of the ten largest denominations in the United States are African American churches.

Discussion

The numerous cases in which Christianity has been resisted, received, and received with significant change since 1500 are overwhelming. Not surprisingly, there are some broad patterns. In its diffusion eastward (later, westward) to the areas dominated by large societies with literature and organized religions (Asia), Christianity met massive resistance by most majority populations so that Christians today generally are small minorities in the populations. However, in accordance with the theory of this book, numerous ethnic minorities and some low caste groups have been receptive to Christianity and have been strengthened in maintaining their distinctive identities through it. Unlike the old empires and kingdoms which were threatened by the intrusion of the West, the minority and suppressed groups were under pressure from the majority societies and their identities were enhanced by Christianity. Korea appears to be a case where a "minority nation," (the "hermit kingdom") under domination from its neighbor, was supported in its nationalism by Christianity. Furthermore, it may be noted that the groups which have been receptive to

Christianity have, by and large, accepted what was brought to them without a conscious effort to change or "indigenize" their new beliefs.

On the other hand, the response to Christianity in the areas where there were numerous small societies, namely in Oceana, sub-Saharan Africa, and the Americas, has been more complex and difficult to analyze. Nowhere did these societies have the long literary traditions and histories of complex state structures that existed in the Middle East and Asia and that influenced surrounding societies. No world religions had developed. In this respect, they were similar to Europe before the introduction of Christianity.

Whenever these contrasts are made, I like to mention the social scientific perspective which still does not seem to be widely taken for granted. That is, that the ancient civilizations are very late productions in human history and represent only a small fraction of that history. There is clearly no correlation between the ancient civilizations and human intelligence, the civilizations developing simply on the basis of need, opportunity, and cumulative experience. As a matter of fact, in spite of all the impressive creations of the ancient civilizations, the standard of living and quality of life for large numbers of people who lived in them was well below that of many people whom they considered "primitive" or "barbarian." My own view is that even now in the scholarly world, particularly in those fields that emphasize "the classics," the contribution of tribal societies to modern life is very underrated, particularly in the field of government (parliamentary rule) and law (the common law). This kind of comment is important because of the attempts by societies to dominate other societies and the ability of the more technologically advanced societies to extend their domination. Furthermore, as a result of the extension of domination in the colonial era, terms such as "advanced" and "backward," and terms that are worse, have been used to make comparisons and continue to have their effect on self-conceptions of both dominant and the dominated groups (Horowitz 1985, 147-149).

In general, in the three broad areas of small societies reviewed, there has been a mixture of the two responses, reception and reception with change, and a sprinkling of high resistance among those who have been able to isolate themselves in some way. There has been Western domination over the whole area, although it was not always strong or obvious at first and has been reduced in recent years. Missionary association with this domination has been common, but at times seems to have been successfully disassociated from it.

Oceana appears to have had a particularly high level of acceptance of the Christianity that was introduced to them. The Philippines Islands, mentioned in the previous chapter, should probably be included with Oceana in respect to the nature of their societies, but with Latin America in respect to the nature of the religion introduced and the overwhelming power that accompanied it. It might be argued that the island societies were more vulnerable than mainland societies and therefore less able to resist the intruding powers. However, it was seen that on many Pacific islands, domination from the outside was initially not pronounced and partly because domination was not pronounced or sustained, it was possible very early for the missionaries and the churches to support local rulers and their peoples against other outsiders. The Christian message lent itself to this kind of disassociation, but scripture translation was particularly helpful in this regard. Christianity became supportive of nation-building and in the major churches there has been less attempt consciously to "indigenize" the faith than in Africa and the Americas. Nevertheless, resistance has been shown in various religious movements, particularly the "cargo cults," and in the organization of independent churches.

This pattern of acceptance and resistance also may be seen in Africa and the Americas, but in these two areas two distinct patterns of "acceptance with change" are delineated. The reception of Christianity in Africa and the Americas has been more involved with indigenous independent movements on the one hand or syncretistic folk religions on the other than in Oceana. As in Oceana, and earlier in Europe, in Africa and the Americas Christianity entered a field of many small competing societies. There were many cases, therefore, where Christianity was received by people who were strengthened by it against the threat of other groups. This seems to be the case of tribal groups and kingdoms in Central Africa and West Africa who were threatened by the slave trade in the latter part of the nineteenth century. The Hurons of Canada and other groups in North America formed Christian villages that were supported against other threatening groups. Likewise, in Latin America, Christian villages offered alternatives to living in more exposed positions. However, many of these settlements suffered tragic mistreatment from the general population of European immigrants who did not share the viewpoint of the missionaries towards the Native Americans.

In addition and apart from any immediate protection against threat from other groups, Christianity was undoubtedly perceived as offering a means of general enhancement of the group. In a comment concerning Africa which could also be applied to Oceana and the Americas, as well as to the European tribes, Zablon Nthamburi (1989, 113) stated concerning Christianity, "In most places it was readily accepted either as a way of enhancing the status of a community or as a means of obtaining literary skills that were important to communication to the outside world." This is consistent with the theory of this book which emphasizes the fact that perception of the possibility of enhancement of identity with one's own group is important for establishing a conducive condition for reception of an outside religion that would provide that enhancement. However, there is a prior emphasis in the theory on the problem that a dominating or threatening relationship presents in having such a perception. According to the theory, the receiving group, without other options, may receive the religion, but change it significantly so that it will be expressive of the distinctive identity of the receiving group.

This is, in fact, what became pervasive in Africa. Nthamburi describes what has been seen in the review:

> The African indigenous church movement can be traced in part to the African reaction to the process of colonialization and subjugation of African peoples by European powers. Christianity preceded colonialization even though the two were often seen by Africans to have the same objectives. As Christianity swept the continent, reactions to Western Christianity sprang up in the form of indigenous churches.

The theory of this book terms this "acceptance with significant change." Jean Comaroff (1985) speaks of the African independent churches as "subversive bricolages" to dominant systems, "bricole" referring to an indirect action. Of course, there were some direct, but futile, wars fought against European domination in Africa, as well as in Oceana, but especially in the Americas.

In Latin America the main resistance to an imposed religion has not been so much as in Africa with the formation of independent indigenous churches, but by the development of folk religions that perpetuate Native American beliefs and practices *within* the church. In this century, Protestantism, especially Pentecostalism, has become an alternative expression to that of the dominant form of Christianity. Recently Protestants have been able to use two "conduits" for evangelical expansion, according to Martin (1990, 283-284): the minority ethnic groups and people moving from the countryside to the mega-cities. This certainly is consistent with the pattern of acceptance (seen so often in Asia) in which an outside religion is accepted that offsets a nearby previously dominating power. However, at present, the overall change is still relatively small.

In a remarkable analysis of the stability of the Roman Catholic Church, Edward Norman (1981, 69-70) describes how the weakness of the Church enabled or required it to allow two religions within itself:

> Ecclesiastical authority had neither the means nor the will to disturb an arrangement of things which was externally uniform and which, it supposed, was suited to the limited intellectual and moral capacity of the Indian subculture. Latin-American Catholicism has remained, in consequence, almost entirely untouched by formal heresy or schism.

Thus, there developed within the dominant church the well-known gap between the official version and various popular versions.

However complex and paradoxical the situation of Christianity in the Americas and Africa, it appears that the theory of this book that a dominated people will find a way to resist a religion that is imposed upon them is borne out. In the case of Latin America, the resistance appears primarily in changing the religion from within, but more recently in accepting versions of Christianity that are different from the dominant version. In North America, although again the resistance is within Christianity, because of the Protestant ethos, there is a greater phenomenon of independent churches rather than folk religious practices within the established church.

Harold Turner (1973) points to the neglected subject of the large number of movements among Native Americans that developed in response to Christianity. Included in these are a number of independent churches, the largest of which is the Native American Church. The larger phenomenon of the African American churches is well known and as Lincoln and Mamiya (1990, 15) state, "One of the major roles of the black churches in the future will be as historic resources of black culture and as examples of resistance and independence."

Thus, what is very evident in Africa and the Americas is resistance to full acceptance. Some resistance is through maintaining isolation, but much of it falls into the middle category of the theory: where there is little alternative to accepting the outside religion, it will be accepted but changed in significant ways to preserve the distinctive identities of the receiving groups. Although it is a worldwide phenomenon within Christianity, the desire to develop an indigenous theology appears to be strongest in Africa and the Americas. The minority groups of Asia appear more likely than those in other parts of the world to accept Christianity without deliberate attempts at "indigenization." However, in Africa and North America indigenization has often taken the form of independent churches whereas in Latin America it has taken the form of the introduction of folk religious practices into official Christianity.

These two patterns of "acceptance with change" are associated with different forms of domination. In Latin America Christianity has exercised an inclusive domination with a pre-Reformation view of the relationship of church to state. In Africa and North America, the dominant religious ethos has been Protestantism, which eventually (especially in North America) separated itself clearly from civil authority and encouraged religious pluralism.

Conclusion

The diffusion of Christianity since 1500 has been very extensive and has been met with a variety of responses. The theory is useful in understanding many of the responses, especially of acceptance by minorities and groups that are dominated by non-Christian neighbors, a pattern that has been quite characteristic in Asia. Rejection of Christianity by groups that are dominated by nations identified with Christianity is also consistent with the theory. Societies in Asia that were large and had traditions of literature and organized religions had the greatest resources for resistance and in general the majority of their populations have resisted Christianity.

Just as in the case of the diffusion of Islam to Iran, the successful diffusion of Christianity to the areas dominated by the nations associated with Christianity remains the most difficult to fit into the theory (primarily Oceana, Africa, and the Americas). However, the middle category of response, namely acceptance with change, although it appears to be quite complex, does seem generally to fit those cases where dominated receiving groups are not able to successfully resist or escape. In these cases, various kinds of resistance are carried on from within the new religion, some of it a kind of altered Christianity (as in

Latin America) and some of it both an altered and independent Christianity (as in Africa). Resistance often seems to be covert or delayed in its appearance. Resistance has been mitigated most successfully among the small societies when Christianity has been disassociated from the dominating powers and has provided means for affirming the distinctive identities of groups. The translation of the Bible has been especially useful in affirming the dignity of the culture of many groups whose languages previously had not been written. In addition, in Oceana, Africa, and the Americas, as with minorities in Asia, missionaries have at times, sometimes inadvertently, been able to approach people "from below" (not from a position of power) and Christianity has been perceived as contributing to the enhancement of the group.

Chapter 8

Conclusions and Some Directions for Study

The Nature of the Findings

It is important to reiterate in the tradition of Frederick Teggart that the purpose of this book is not to narrate history, but to examine a series of events. The events are the cases of diffusion of the three religions which have diffused most widely, together with some of the major changes that have been made in these religions. The book presents a perspective with which to review these cases of diffusion and the development of major variations within the religions. The central element (major independent variable) in the perspective is intergroup relationships.

I have attempted to be comprehensive, not necessarily thorough, in the review of the diffusion of the three religions. The only reason that a non-thorough, but comprehensive look at history is possible, is that there are patterns which exist in large areas and certain periods so that selections can be made that are representative of these areas and periods. The broad areas of similarities serve to highlight variations and lines of demarcation. The social sciences, of course, are preeminently interested in patterns. In a basic sense, I am attempting to set forth certain patterns that I believe may be seen in history. One approach is to describe patterns, but in simply describing patterns, the important question of cause ("why" as opposed to "what") has been neglected. The social sciences are typically more interested in relationships of cause and effect than in simply describing what takes place, as important as the latter may be in preparation for learning about the former. Theories are statements of how some effect (the dependent variable) results from or may be accounted for by some cause or causes (the independent variables).

A well known difficulty in social scientific research is in introducing enough controls to know that you have isolated the variables you want to deal with. In spite of the fact that it is impossible to have adequate controls of historical data, I have chosen to follow a major model of research in the social sciences. In this model a theory is proposed and then tested by comparing results after particular causes are introduced. However, in using historical data this experimental approach can only be a model which helps to clarify an argument rather than actually "test an hypothesis."

The major similarity to the research model is that in this book a theoretical perspective is stated at the first. I wanted to do this so that the discussion would be as pointed and clear as possible. In addition, this approach is useful because it opens the way for argument and disagreement. My findings, of course, are not "a test" of the theory, but are basically what history has to be: description, and in this case, exploratory description. The data, like all historical data, are selected. Nevertheless, the description is intended to support a particular view of one of the major causes for the successful and unsuccessful diffusion of religions. Knowing the intention is a basis for criticizing the results and that is how the historical reviews (probably any history) should be read. In this way, the reader will be thinking of exceptions, but also of additional data that further support the view of the book.

It is not so much that I am looking for disagreement, although disagreement is typical of all social scientific searches for answers, but I am particularly interested in another part of the search for answers: elaboration. Notice, however, that I have not attempted to set forth all of the causes of successful and unsuccessful diffusion of religions. I initially stated under "background variables" that there are certain characteristics of religions and certain characteristics of receiving societies that contribute to successful and unsuccessful diffusion. These are areas that may be elaborated. Thus, variations may be analyzed and clarified in the religious diffusion-decision process, in religious

Conclusions and Some Directions for Study

innovation characteristics, and in the characteristics of those who adopt outside religions. However, I am particularly interested in elaboration in the area of the theory with its two levels: intergroup relationships (macro level) and social identity (micro level).

To reiterate, then, although historical data are used, this is not an historical narrative in the ordinary sense. It is also not an attempt to uncover and list "reasons" for the diffusion of the three religions considered. There will always be many reasons for diffusion which will vary in each specific case. I recognize that historians, like social scientists (sometimes they are hard to tell apart), are also interested in "reasons," but the interest of social scientists is in reasons for classes or categories of phenomena rather than a particular phenomenon or an individual event.

The purpose is to isolate "crucial" factors. However, just to extend the argument, I realize that even "crucial" may be understood in another way (non social scientific), which I would call "historical." For example, Christianity would not have spread to Ireland except for the "crucial" fact that Patrick and others crossed the sea. Speaking historically, Patrick was "crucial," but speaking social scientifically, it is a missionary and one who was perceived as Patrick was perceived that was crucial.

In that regard, contrary to some thought, individuals and their efforts have a place in sociological analysis as a "class of phenomena." A good example of this is the place given to the charismatic leader in the study of religious movements. In regard to leaders, I have observed that the first missionary to a people (such as Patrick, as well as missionaries in recent centuries) has a very high symbolic value in subsequent religious, and sometimes national, life.

The historical data that I used were comprehensive in the sense that they were intended to include the total period of diffusion for the religions, as well as the periods in which certain major variations developed. This type of study obviously needs the balance of thorough case studies, which I hope this study will stimulate. However, one of the reasons that I wanted to be as comprehensive as possible by reviewing diffusion from the earliest periods to the present century is that probably the views people have of these religions tend to be based on particular periods.

For example, Buddhism is often associated with its ancient history and it is often forgotten, as Finney (1991) pointed out, that Buddhism is a world religion that is continuing to diffuse. The diffusion of Islam is often associated with conquest, particularly in the minds of Westerners, but a review of the total history, as well as periods of conquest by Islamic armies, shows that the diffusion of Islam did not depend simply on the fact of conquest. Likewise, the diffusion of Christianity is associated for many people only with the modern era when the Western World was expanding and extending domination over large areas. The earlier periods of diffusion, when Christianity was not associated with domination, are often forgotten. Thus, a basic reason for including patterns of diffusion from all periods of diffusion for the three religions is to bring balance, a form of "control of the data," to the consideration.

My Unhidden Agenda

The purpose of this book has been to consider in a preliminary way why Buddhism, Christianity, and Islam have diffused so widely. However, someone might say that I had an "agenda" in this book and they would be right. In fact, the explanatory research model makes it easy to discover an agenda because the theory is stated initially. However, to state my agenda more succinctly, I have a basic goal to demonstrate that the spread of religion is not well served by force, domination, or threat and that domination in religion produces overt or covert resistance. I wanted to show that religion is best presented "from below," not from a position of power, especially when it is a threatening power. I am stating this in case this goal has not been discerned from the theoretical statement. Also, I am preparing the ground for modification and elaboration of my views.

I had a second part to my agenda. In many studies, but especially in commonly expressed views, I felt that too much emphasis has been placed on the influence of culture on receptivity to an outside religion and not enough emphasis has been placed on the effect of how people are treated in intergroup relations. I have sensed a tendency with some to view certain groups as "not culturally compatible" with some religions. My approach questions this view, which may be called "intellectualist" or "mentalist" (Hefner 1993, 22-25).

Perry (1992, 488) noted that theory in the cultural diffusion tradition, represented primarily by anthropologists, emphasized that "borrowing hinges on the extent to which the element can be integrated into the belief system of the new culture" and "elements that are incompatible with the new culture's prevailing normative structure or religious belief system are likely to be rejected." My view is that it is much more important to determine *why* people may regard or perceive an outside religion as capable or not capable of being integrated and *why* an outside religion may be considered compatible or not compatible with a culture's prevailing normative structure or religious belief system. Not only do members of receiving cultures evaluate outside religions from their normative perspective, but social scientists may make presumptive judgments about what is "compatible" to cultures.

In short, I felt that so much emphasis has been placed on understanding "cultural differences" that the importance of attitudes and perceptions of people regarding their own dignity and self-respect and that of others has been neglected. Thus, I wanted to draw attention to the quality of intergroup relationships as a major, if not the major, influence on response to an outside religion and also I wanted to draw attention to the attitudes of self-esteem that people have as a result of these relationships.

Closely related to the above parts of my agenda, was a third goal: to focus not on the efforts of religions to diffuse, but on the response of people to those efforts. The work of missions, at least in the modern era, is rather well documented, but the attitudes and responses of people in receiving countries has received relatively little attention. Given the drama of missions and the availability of materials, it is easy to see why this is the case. Data on how and why people view other groups as they do is more difficult to obtain, but crucial if response to outside religions is to be understood.

The theoretical statement is based primarily on my own observations, particularly in Asia and North America where I have lived and worked. As noted above, I did some narrowing which others will need to expand. That is, I did little to develop any detailed statement regarding pre-diffusion conditions either on the side of the religions that diffused or the side of the societies to which the religions diffused. I was interested primarily in the effect of the relationships between groups on the process of diffusion. It appeared to me that domination by groups and resistance to that domination often played a crucial role in diffusion regardless of which of the three religions was involved and whatever the receiving groups or societies were like. I was also convinced that members of groups that I had known, who were either receptive or resistant to outside religions, desired self-esteem and took some satisfaction in their ethnic or national identities and to this should be added other aspects of social identities, such as gender identity, occupation identity, and social class identity. With this background, I made the centerpiece of my theoretical perspective a two-leveled statement that dealt with the quality of intergroup relationships and with perceptions and motivations of people in receiving groups.

The statement attempted to account for three basic responses of groups to religions introduced from the outside: acceptance, acceptance with conscious and significant change of the introduced religion, and rejection. The theory was stated in terms of conducive conditions for these responses as being (1) on the macro level, the quality of relationships between a receiving group and both the sending group and other groups and (2) on the micro level, the perception of members of a receiving group of the contribution an outside religion would make to the existence and strength of their group.

I felt that Wuthnow's (1987, 156, 170) concept of moral order was relevant on both levels because of the ways in which intergroup relationships often disturb or threaten established moral orders, and new religions (from the outside or reshaped old religions) are perceived as aiding in the establishment of a new order, often as "oppositional ideologies." In addition, I felt that the social identity theorists (Tajfel et al) provided insights on how an outside group may be perceived as threatening a valued aspect of social identity, particularly ethnic or national identity, and how then a perception develops that a change in religion would enhance ethnic or national identity. Recently, the importance of female gender identity has been emphasized, especially in the study of Rodney Stark (1995). Females, of course, have also been a dominated group whose identity has been enhanced by a new religion.

Very early in my studies I felt that Wallace's (1956, 1967) work on "revitalization movements" was helpful in understanding responses to mission efforts and it is clear that he relates the macro and micro levels. David Martin's (1990) "breakup of monopolies," similar to Peter Berger's (1969) "sacred canopies," and the subsequent reformulation of a "free space" also relate the two levels. These linkages of macro and micro levels are also consistent with the earlier work of MacIver (1942), as pointed out by Boskoff (1972), regarding "dynamic assessment" of changes in "familiar" settings.

Recently, I found strong support for my approach in Robert Hefner's (1993, 25) view of "the moral economy of self-identification." He brings together moral order and personal identity and recognizes how groups might adopt a religion other than that of their proximate rivals in order to maintain their identities. (I felt that it would be important to include the series of cases presented in his book). Also, although Hans Mol (1976) uses the concept of identity in a deeper and broader sense than I do, I felt that his expanded use of the concept of identity was consistent with the linking of a disturbing of the moral order with a seeking for a new identity. For Mol (1976), the seeking of a new identity is tantamount to seeking a new moral order. Thus, Mol closely links macro and micro levels.

Arguments From the Data

The historical reviews have been discussed in each chapter. Rather than repeat the conclusions from these discussions, I will summarize how the findings relate to the particular goals that I have had. In addition, because of the significance of the case studies in Hefner's (1993) book, I will comment on the relevance of these studies.

The review of the diffusion of Buddhism certainly confirms the generally held view that the spread of Buddhism has not been related to any conquests. Buddhism is well known for its emphasis on compassion and peace. It spread over broad contiguous areas of Asia, which lends support to the view that intergroup contact (a factor which I did not emphasize) is a major factor in the diffusion of religions. For my purposes, intergroup contact, or the existence of carriers, is a necessary, but not a sufficient, factor for successful diffusion. Since the last century, Buddhism has been diffusing to the West, which is not contiguous to Asia, but certainly this recent diffusion has been facilitated by increased international contacts.

However, Buddhism did fail to diffuse across two boundaries along which there was hostility and conflict: the Indian-Persian boundary and the boundary between northern Southeast Asia and the areas to the south and east occupied by Malay groups. This is certainly consistent with the theory that religions are not likely to diffuse from one group to another when the group from which the religion comes is threatening or dominating the receiving group.

In addition to this negative argument, there is evidence in the history of Buddhism that association with an all-inclusive domination tends to produce a great distinction between official and popular levels of the religion. Theravada appears to have produced a greater gap between official and popular understandings of religion than Mahayana (usually less pervasive and dominant than Theravada). In contrast, Mahayana is characterized by a number of schools of thought and by the rise of lay leadership.

In some respects, the diffusion of Christianity in the Mediterranean Basin and in Europe is similar to the diffusion of Buddhism. Again, a religion is seen diffusing to contiguous areas and being received by the elite of numerous groups for whom it represented a cultural advancement. The diffusion of Buddhism and of Christianity to many ascendant nations supports the theoretical views of social scientists who have found that early adopters are often of high status. Even when the groups themselves are marginal or of low status, as in the case of women, early adopters often appear to be in leadership positions.

Christianity failed to diffuse directly southward in Africa because of the lack of contact. However, consistent with the theory, Christianity failed to diffuse successfully to a contiguous area (nearer than Europe) because of the threat and attempted domination of the Middle East by Rome, Byzantium, and eventually Europe. The conversion of Constantine, so applauded in the West, had the opposite effect in the lands on the eastern border. As far as diffusion farther east is concerned, there was limited contact, but also, as in the case of China, there was the added negative effect for Christianity of association with dominating foreigners (the Mongols).

Some of the effects within Christianity of association with political power may be seen in the tendency for variations, often regarded as heretical, to develop among dominated ethnic groups or among enemies of Rome, namely the Goths. The fourth century is very important to observe because it begins with the conversion of Constantine and is followed by the fall of Rome. Before the fall of Rome, conversions of many tribes were to Arianism, contrasting with the faith of both Rome and Constantinople. After the fall of Rome and thus the decline of threat and domination, Arianism declined and the tribes to the north converted to Catholicism.

However, with the growth of the association of Christianity with political power there may be seen the tendency for a distinction to develop between official and popular expressions of religion. The popular movements tended to incorporate elements of traditional folk religion (with magical elements) or to be movements to restore "spirituality" or purity to Christianity or to be a combination of both tendencies.

Conclusions and Some Directions for Study

Islam and Christianity since 1500 offer the most difficulty to the theory because at first glance the diffusion of both religions seems often to have been associated with conquest and general domination. Contiguousness, namely proximity or propinquity, begins to lose its importance, especially after 1500, because of the increasing ease of communication. Nevertheless, carriers of the religions continue to be important, although it is not clear as to the importance of the number of carriers.

On the basis of some cases of the diffusion of Islam and Christianity someone might argue facetiously that certain steps will assure the diffusion of a religion or ideology. First, make sure that the religion or ideology has universal or "world religion" characteristics. To bring about diffusion, choose a country that is ruled by a small authoritarian elite (it will help if it is also cruel and corrupt) and has overextended its resources in fighting other groups. As an alternative, choose an area with no organized government, but only scattered tribal people (unfortunately, there are few of these left). After conquering the land as rapidly as possible, impress upon the conquered people that they may become fully qualified members of the religion you are bringing to them. It will help if, as soon as possible, local people are welcomed into leadership positions in the religion. It will also help if some economic improvements are brought to the people.

This approach or something like it seems to have worked pretty well for Islam in Iran and much of North Africa and for Christianity in Latin America and parts of Africa and Oceana. It does not take much imagination to see parallels to the successful diffusion of Marxism. However, for those who see conquest and domination as typical of Islam and Christianity, a careful review of the facts reveals something quite different. Conquest appears to be of secondary importance in the diffusion of Islam and Christianity and often to have had a negative effect. Furthermore, continuing association of a religion with domination produces resistance to that religion or to its current leadership.

In regard to Islam, it was seen that it represented a force that offset domination from other sources. This seems especially true of Syria, Egypt, and much of North Africa. Also, consistent with the theory of the negative effect of domination, Islam did not diffuse successfully to large areas that it ruled for extended periods, such as Spain, Sicily, the Balkans, and much of India. At the same time, minority groups in the Balkans and oppressed groups in India were receptive to Islam.

Iran, although threatened by Byzantium was not ruled by foreigners and so it was not a case of Islam freeing a people from foreign domination. My major argument against the factor of conquest as the basis for diffusion of Islam to Iran is the remarkable openness of Islam to Iranian influence and leadership. Eventually, in accordance with the theory, Iran became the major base for a form of "oppositional ideology" that had long festered within Islam. The Turks, also, soon became the dominant power and so Islam lost its association with Arab domination, although Islam continued to emphasize the crucial Arab association with its founding and with basic spirituality. The diffusion of Islam to Southeast Asia, of course, was not associated with conquest, but Islam was clearly an offsetting force to first Buddhist and later (and primarily) Western Christian domination. Also, in current North America, Islam offers an offsetting force to Christianity for many African Americans.

Islam, however, continues to pay a certain price for its close association with governmental power in those lands where it is a pervasive religion. That is, it tends to generate reform or revolutionary movements against the official authorities, which are perceived by zealous people as compromising and unspiritual. Islam's inclusive or unitary view of life, however, has meant that in religiously pluralistic societies, it is able to produce strong religious communities that offer clear moral standards and disciplined life.

The successful diffusion of Christianity with conquest appears most dramatically in Latin America and the Philippines. In addition, there was successful diffusion in association with some conquest, but mostly with general domination in Oceana and Africa. However, in the reviews it was seen that several additional factors seem more important than conquest and domination.

In all of these areas and in addition, in North America, there developed overt resistance to conquest and domination which included rejection of Christianity that has continued to this day. At the same time, in all of these areas a disassociation was made between the intruding forces and Christianity by some of the representatives of Christianity. The most successful disassociation seems to have been in the Pacific Islands, but it also may be seen in Africa and the Americas.

Many times rivalries between groups within these areas appeared to be as important or more important than the threat from the invading representatives of Christianity. One of the greatest contributors to the sense that Christianity would enhance the identities of groups was the

Conclusions and Some Directions for Study 159

translation of the scriptures into native languages. Nevertheless, continuing domination has produced certain patterns of resistance from within Christianity.

One pattern may be seen in Latin America and the Philippines, where an inclusive authority exists in Christianity. There appeared various forms of popular folk religion, some of which have been strenuously opposed by the official religious leaders and others of which have been overlooked or tolerated. Another pattern may be seen in Africa and North America where the resistance within Christianity has typically generated many new church organizations which were independent of outside control. New church organizations, especially in the form of Pentecostalism, are now becoming prevalent in Latin America also (Martin 1990). It also seems to be true that in Africa and Latin America there is a greater concern with developing "indigenous theologies" than generally in Asia, certainly than in the churches among the minority peoples of Asia.

The resistance to Christianity in the Middle East and Asia is well known and this resistance may be used as an argument to reintroduce "the cultural factor." This argument would be that the "world religions" of the Middle East and Asia preempt the need for a world religion such as Christianity. An extreme form of this argument is that members of these non-Western societies do not have a cultural affinity for Christianity, namely Christianity is incompatible with their cultures.

My approach is to see factors such as the large size, the complex organization, and the developed literatures of societies as resources for resistance to diffusion. A "world religion," having an extensive literature and an historic organization certainly is able to offer a more effective resource for resistance by a society to an outside religion than a religion with no literature and organization. It seems to me that a careful study of those who have received Christianity, particularly in Korea, but also from the majority societies in India and China, does much to undercut at least the extreme forms of the argument accounting for resistance to Christianity that are based on the presumed lack of "cultural compatibility."

Another form of "the cultural argument" is to assert that it is "easier" for people of animistic background, who do not have a "world religion" to receive Christianity than for those following one of the historic religions of Asia. Supporting this view is the fact that those most receptive to Christianity in Asia have been ethnic minorities, most of whom were animistic. My evidence against this extension of "the cultural argument" is found by comparing the tribal groups of Africa and the Americas with those of Asia. Although also followers of traditional tribal religions that would not be classified as "world religions," many of the groups in Africa and the Americas have been highly resistant to Christianity, unlike tribal groups in Asia. In fact, it was this evidence which pushed me in the direction of considering the influence on religious diffusion of domination in intergroup relations and of self-esteem.

The debate will continue, as it should. It will necessarily alternate between broad historical studies such as mine and case studies, with the latter taking precedence because of the detail they provide. However, it seems to me that the time has come to reduce the "raw empiricism" of case studies and to do more comparative case and historical studies. In addition, there is an important need for more in-depth studies of the perceptions of members of various societies of themselves and other groups. Nevertheless, case studies will continue to be important, particularly when they are grouped, and I turn briefly to an important set of such studies.

Additional Support from Recent Case Studies

An important set of studies was put together by Robert W. Hefner (1993), who also wrote the very helpful Introduction (3-44) on world religions and conversion, as well as one of the studies, which was on conversion in Muslim Java (99-125). Some of the studies had been presented at a conference on "Conversion to World Religions: Historical and Ethnographic Interpretations," held in 1988. Hefner and most of the writers use, what I also seek to use, namely a social scientific approach that is opposed to what is referred to as a "mentalist" or "intellectualist" one. (Hefner 24). Hefner (25-28) makes clear, consistent with the view of this book, that social identity, with its close relationship to self-esteem, is a central micro level factor and social, economic, and political conditions provide important macro influences on change.

The individual studies describe cases of change and resistance to change (primarily the latter), that are basically consistent with the theory I present. They describe receptivity to an outside religion when that religion appears to offset other pressures and contributes to the strength of local identity, for example, in part of Java (Hefner 99-125) and Amazonia (Pollock 165-197) and in Papua (Barker 199-230). However, most of the cases describe groups that are resistant to conversion, for example in Africa (Ranger 165-197), Java (Hefner 99-125), Mexico (Merrill 129-163), Amazonia (Pollock 165-197), Australia (Yengoyan 233-257), and Thailand (Keyes 259-283). In all cases of resistance, the religion (Christianity) being introduced is associated with intrusion and domination. In Mexico and sometimes in Amazonia and Africa, resistance was more likely to take an indirect path (acceptance followed by change) than in the other locations and in Africa resistance also produced numerous adaptations in the traditional religions. The case studies describe various positions between acceptance and rejection discussed in my theory.

My major difference with some of the studies (a difference that seems to be shared by most of the other studies) is in the weight they give to pre-existent cultures, particularly religious ideas, of receiving groups in predicting or evaluating responses. These studies tend to follow the "mentalist" approach, which the other studies do not. My view is that social conditions are the major factor affecting reception, but that pre-existent cultures are important in affecting the kinds of adaptations made of religious expression, whether in the new religion or the traditional religion. Before considering future directions for study, two special aspects of the theoretical approach will be discussed briefly.

Religion and Domination

The theory of this book makes domination and subordination in intergroup relationships a central factor in investigating the diffusion of religions. Although the history of diffusion was reviewed, little attention was given to how patterns of domination have changed within and between groups, especially in recent centuries. Social scientists have been very interested in patterns of power and authority in societies that determine how domination is exercised.

According to Max Weber (1967, 78) a political association is defined by its means, not by its ends, and its means are "the use of physical force." However, governments seek to have their power legitimated by those they govern thereby gaining authority to exercise power and easing considerably their efforts in that exercise.

Religions also are political bodies when they exercise power as James Gustafson (1961, 31) frankly recognized concerning the Christian Church: "The political structure of the Church then is the patterns of relationships and action through which policy is determined and social power exercised." Moreover, religious bodies, just as states, but even more so, seek to have their power legitimated by their members since religions have fewer resources than governments to exercise power that is not legitimated. Authority is "legitimate power" and as Gustafson (1961, 33) points out, power can be exercised both formally and informally, the latter being constituted by "personal relations and the exercise of personal influence."

Weber's (1967, 294-299) famous distinction of three main types of authority (traditional, charismatic, and legal) is useful when applied to understanding domination in religions. For example, in Christianity, the application of the principle of legal authority (the sacraments are valid, not on the basis of character, but on the basis of the office of the celebrant) was used against the Donatists. However, all movements that have succeeded in establishing either independent organizations or "contained organizations" (orders and parachurch groups) have had leaders that were recognized as having charismatic authority.

From the point of view of the diffusion of religions, charismatic authority and legal authority seem to be especially important, whereas domination by traditional authority would seem to inhibit missionary effort. That is, traditionalism may cause a religion to become overly attached to its environment and established culture. In contrast, strong and independent personalities (with charismatic authority) are needed to strike out in new directions, crossing frontiers and challenging established ways. Furthermore, systematic organization with the establishment of special offices (with legal authority) for missionary activity means that missionary work can be sustained even when there is initial failure and turnover of personnel.

Religious leaders have had a distinct advantage over other kinds of leaders in being able to claim support or authorization from the highest authority possible, a supernatural authority that is both transcendent and present. From a social scientific perspective the "ultimate source" of authority by definition is the group or community granting that authority. However, the religions that have diffused have all claimed a transcendent authority and then applied their claimed authority to develop secondary sources of authority in historical objects and institutions. Using Weber, Hefner (1993, 19-20) describes the basis for the effectiveness of the world religions:

> The real force of the world religions lies in their linkage of these strict transcendental imperatives to institutions for the propagation and control of religious knowledge and identity over time and space.
>
> In other words, the most distinctive feature of the world religions or of, again, their most institutionally successful variants is something both doctrinal and social-organizational. These religions regularize clerical roles, standardize ritual, formalize doctrine, and otherwise work to create an authoritative culture and cohesive religious structure. At times this cultural impetus may be subverted or challenged, giving rise to heterodox or localized variants of the faith that challenge its transregional integrity. Such a process seems to have regularly occurred, for example, in Sufi and folk variants of Islam, in Gnostic and folk Christianity, and as Keyes's (1993) essay aptly illustrates, in popular Theravada Buddhism...
>
> ...The world religions appear to be complex responses to the challenge of *identity and moral community*. [italics mine]....The world religions' message of Truth and a redemptive identity incumbent upon all people and their introduction of a social organization for the propagation of that message have proved to be revolutionary forces in their own right, well suited to the challenge of life in a new kind of social macrocosm.

As has been seen in the historical reviews, all three of the religions that have diffused, as well as other religions, have both supported and been supported by civil authorities. This kind of relationship was considered beneficial from both sides since civil governments wanted authority supplied by religions and religions wanted the power supplied by civil governments. However, the tensions and conflicts that have always existed between civil governments and religions became especially clear in an extended struggle between religious and state authorities in the history of the West.

Van Leeuwen (1964, 271-248) offers an analysis of "the revolutionary West" in terms of the breakup of the "ontocratic" pattern of civilization. "Ontocratic" expresses the way in which there is perceived to be a direct and comprehensive linkage between the transcendent and the rulers so that the authority of the rulers becomes more or less a direct expression or extension of transcendent authority. Furthermore, in these societies, typically called "traditional," almost all relationships take on an ontocratic quality so that individuals and groups are seen as extensions of each other. Likewise, as Robert Bellah (1969, 75) noted, in these traditional societies the distinction between believer and subject was not distinct.

What is important to recognize for understanding the relation of religion to domination is that authority in the modern West has been relativized and broken up into numerous specialized areas. For religion this has meant the development of numerous "differentiated religious collectivities as the chief characteristic of its religious organization" (Bellah 1969, 75). Where it has been possible to maintain an inclusive authority in society, then replacement of authority tends to require a radical action.

It has been seen that in Islam, for example, movements for change tend either to be repressed or to involve a complete change in government. The same has been true in societies where Roman Catholicism and Eastern Orthodoxy have been pervasive. In these and other traditional societies, organizational experience has been limited because authority has been concentrated and inclusive in its domination at the same time. Where authority has been diffused throughout societies, organizations, including religious organizations, have multiplied and people have developed experience in self-government.

Thus, there has been a historical process consisting of the break-up or relativizing of authority so that it is related to specific and specialized fields and responsibilities. This process has had and is having an enormous impact on the societies of the world, including their religions, many of which existed under monopolistic authority. In many societies there have been few organizations that include dissent, debate, and peaceful resolution of opposing forces. In addition, people have not had much autonomy and, therefore, little experience in making choices. Often, there has been an idealization of authority that does not expect or plan for mistakes on the part of those who exercise it and the consequent need for correction and reform. Then, when the need for change becomes obvious, the solution is radical and drastic. There is no "loyal opposition" that accepts the basis for authority, but disagrees with its application. Needless to say, the relativization of authority in the world is resulting in much change, and in some cases, conflict and turmoil.

Nevertheless, people, particularly the leaders of societies, seek a unifying symbolism. Traditionally, religions (or ideologies) have contributed much of this symbolism, but the authority of religions to impose a symbolism has become highly limited, especially in the West.

According to Robert Nisbet (1965, 68-69), Emile Durkheim saw the dilemma that although the state "has survived the tempest of modern history," it cannot provide sufficient moral authority for societies and the individuals within them. Durkheim's solution to provide occupational associations proved to be of "ephemeral importance" (Nisbet 1965, 69), but his vision of the need for authority, discipline, and morality in society has been an enduring contribution to the analysis of modern societies.

The three religions that have diffused, as well as other religions and ideologies, continue to offer authority, discipline, and morality in greater or less measure. The pluralistic settings of modern societies themselves may be perceived as a threat, especially by adherents of traditional monopolistic religions. Religious (and ideological) monopolies may continue to be strong where they can become identified with the struggles of minorities, oppressed groups, or developing nations. The religions that have diffused and thrived in monopolistic settings are now showing that they can thrive by offering an offsetting force to the intrusion of the perceived "immorality" or moral uncertainties of modern societies. Formerly monopolistic religions may thrive in pluralistic settings by providing moral authority and contributing to clarity of identity and to self-esteem.

As authority has become relativized and specialized, religion has been assigned authority in (or had its authority limited to) the realm of culture. Whether "culture wars" (Hunter 1991) is too strong a term for what is taking place in North America, the term expresses the reality of the current conflict in values in which religions are participants. The perception of threat to values is real, whether the threat is perceived as being to traditional values from "modernists" or to progressive values from traditionalists. It is an aid to mobilizing forces to be able to convey to others that a threat is being resisted.

The religious association with domination today has been made more complex than it was in the past when religions often had official government sponsorship. The means of exercising power or domination have always been varied and overlapping, but it is clear that the power with which religions are associated has shifted away from the powers typically exercised by civil governments which includes military-police force and laws backed by the threat of such force. Power exercised by groups and societies, including civil governments, also may be found in such sources as wealth, advanced technology, efficient organization, and large populations. These other sources of power are still important for religions, especially when state support is withdrawn. However, a basic source of power for religions is the existence of numerous and loyal adherents. Even wealth is not sufficient without adherents.

The power of religions in religiously pluralistic societies has typically been separated from those of the state, although all religions retain the power granted them by their followers, as limited as these may be. These may consist mainly of the power to regulate religious professionals, plan religious activities, and, if necessary, drop adherents from membership. In spite of "the separation of powers" that has become typical in modern societies, there is a question as to how much religions are separated from the societies in which they exist in the perception of people, especially in the perception of "foreigners." When the adherents of a religion make up a large proportion of the population of a group or society, then it is probable that the actions of that group or society will be attributed in whole or in part to the influence of the religion. Religions may often carry baggage they would like to discard.

Religion and Identity Formation

The theoretical statement made use of the concept of social identity and especially views regarding change of selected aspects of social identity. For much of the historical periods reviewed and in much of the world, religious identity and ethnic or national identity have been closely associated. However, in industrialized and industrializing societies, this strong association has been weakened and in some parts of societies there has been considerable disassociation. Individual choice and religious pluralism have become normative or at least held up as a goal in much of the world.

In a useful discussion, Hammond (1988, 5-6) draws a distinction between two kinds of religious identity: one that is largely involuntary because it "emerges out of overlapping primary group ties" and one that is voluntary and based on involvement in secondary groups. The first type of religious identity tends towards "collective-expressive" involvement and the second type tends towards "individual-expressive" involvement in religions.

It has been seen that when religious identity has been closely associated with ethnic identity, change could be rapid and would typically involve the whole group. Presumably, when religious identity is not associated with primary group relationships, then change in that identity tends to result from individual choice. This would typically be the case in North America and Europe, but also in many urban areas throughout the world. Nevertheless, the original theoretical perspective may still be applied in understanding these individual choices.

For example, in understanding the decline in mainline American denominations, it may be theorized that one cause of this decline has been that for some, the denominations were perceived as being too closely associated with established institutions and with others, the mainline denominations were too closely associated with "anti-patriotic" or "anti-traditional values" causes. Speaking negatively, in both cases choosing to be in a mainline denomination did not (does not) enhance some valued aspect of social identity. For the first group, individuals do not feel assisted in being members of modern progressive society by being in a mainline denomination. Their identity as educated and enlightened "moderns" is not enhanced. These people are comfortable with a secular identity, with perhaps an occasional "religious touch" in their lives at birth, marriage, and death. They might even drop off their children at Sunday School and attend church occasionally.

The second group which is failing to join mainline denominations prefers a clear religious identity, but one that is gained from a group that affirms "traditional" and "patriotic" values. These people choose evangelical groups that enhance other aspects of their identities which are valuable to them, in particular their identities as patriotic Americans contending for values on which they believe the country was founded.

For both groups, the secularists and the evangelicals, that have left or are not joining the mainline churches, there are numerous secondary (non primary) groups which they may choose to join that will aid in enhancing the identities they seek to form. Both groups perceive a threat from outside forces. For the "progressive secularists" the threat is primarily from dominating economic power that threatens the environment, the peace of the world, and is willing to write off the disadvantaged people in society. For the conservatives, the threat is from modern culture (often represented by "the media") that undercuts traditional values. To a great extent, the mainline denominations are in the middle of this "cultural war" (Hunter 1991) with the result that both groups (according to the approach of this book) do not perceive the mainline denominations as contributing to a positive identity formation.

As Hammond (1988) points out, people vary considerably in the extent to which their identities are derived either from primary groups (such as ethnic groups) or secondary groups and, of course, most people draw their identities from both primary and secondary groups. This discussion is meant to suggest that the social identity perspective is useful in understanding identity formation whether it is primary or secondary groups from which people draw their identities. Thus, this perspective may be applied to the diffusion of religions in earlier times, as it was in much of this book, when primary group relations dominated, and also in modern times when secondary group relations are pervasive.

Some Directions for Study

The diffusion of religions has received relatively little attention in the sociology of religion. Among social scientists, the anthropologists have led the way in the study of missions and the missiologists (some of whom are anthropologists) contributed large amounts of material. Even when the study of globalization has included consideration of religion, attention has not been given to how the diffusion of religions has affected globalization.

A major thrust of this book has been to try to understand the response of people to whom new religions have been introduced from the outside. In general, mission efforts have received considerably more attention than the object and results of those efforts. This book emphasizes that a useful beginning point for study of those on the receiving end of diffusing religions is to take account of group relationships, both within societies and between societies.

Allan Tippet (1992, 197-198), who has looked carefully at the process of conversion in groups, writes:

> My experience has been that when a group is sufficiently large to have sub-groups, especially if there are competitive values in the culture, it is always possible for one segment to respond with acceptance and the remainder with rejection. The point to press here is that such acts of fission are invariably cleavages on a basis of social structure - nuclear families within extended families, extended families within villages,

status and craft segments, or perhaps culturally established factions or supporters of rival chieftaincies.

If this can be said of relatively small groups, it can also be said of larger societies and, therefore, there is a task to analyze the existing groups within all societies, their relationships, including their rivalries and perceptions about each other and the total societies to which they belong. In addition, there are the relationships with other groups and societies that may be some distance away, but because of modern communications and the presence of representatives, including missionaries, perceptions have been formed of these distant groups. An important question which may have rather complex answers is, "To what extent are other groups near and far perceived as representing a source of benefit or of threat?"

Individualism and egalitarianism are increasing throughout the world, but this should not be allowed to hide the importance of intergroup relationships and the identities based upon memberships in groups. People carry their experiences and attitudes formed in groups into new groups that they join. A basic assumption here is that all ideas are socially influenced and, of course, ideas themselves are part of that social influence.

Probably the most difficult area to investigate, because of the difficulty (sensitivity) and expense of such study, are the perceptions and attitudes of people in receiving countries. In many societies people have never been asked their views and opinions and it may be dangerous for them to express themselves openly. Domination and lack of individual freedom in many groups are not seen negatively unless such threats originate from outside the group. To put it another way, many people accept restrictions on themselves imposed by their own group because of a perceived outside threat (and this perception is encouraged by the leaders). In any case, perceived danger or threat is an important stimulus to behavior and this is an aspect of intergroup relations that needs to be uncovered.

In many parts of the world, Western culture, with which Christianity is associated, is a perceived threat. However, it is not only perceived danger or threat that needs to be uncovered. The potential contribution of new groups to existing groups is another important perception to uncover. Many of these kinds of attitudes must probably be obtained unobtrusively or even inferred. Historical materials may also be used or may be the only source, if the study is of receptivity to religions in the past. However, I hope that also current data may be obtained under controlled conditions to give increased confidence about the effect of domination (from various sources) on receptivity to an outside religion.

One of the difficulties in the study of attitudes that surfaces and with which I have had to wrestle is the circularity of variables. That is, attitudes may be simply expressing the behavior you are trying to explain. Attitudes are the result as well as the cause of behavior. This is a major reason for making macro and micro levels of study complementary. To return to where this discussion started, intergroup relationships need to be investigated not simply on the level of perception, but also in terms of actual power and influence that are exerted by groups upon one another. This is where social scientists must depend on historians, not to speak of political scientists and economists. My own conclusion was that the study of power relationships really has priority over the study of attitudes. It is more than simply background study. These relationships formed important independent variables affecting attitudes towards aspects of social identity and self-esteem.

In regard to the study of power relationships, the relativizing and specialization of power and authority in the modern world, discussed above, complicate such study. The varied sources of power exercised by groups (military force, wealth, technology, communication, population size, etc.) and the means used (formal and informal) need to be distinguished so that reactions to the various types of power may be compared.

In addition to the responses of acceptance and rejection of people to diffusing religions, it was seen that the modifications made by receiving groups in the religions received have been quite numerous and varied. Some of the modifications seem to be more or less unconsciously made, the people assuming that they were accepting the outside religion more or less in whole form. However, many modifications have been deliberately made. Although the modifications are interesting for their cultural content, it is more useful, I believe, to clarify why groups seek to modify the religions that were introduced to them and why they chose particular areas to modify. In other words, it is useful to clarify why certain continuities with the past are chosen and why certain new elements from the outside are chosen.

In this regard, it was seen that different groups modified different "strands" of religions: ritual, organization, and theology. It would be helpful to know why different strands and combinations of (from) strands are selected to modify. Some aspects of religion are more "materialistic" than others. For example, ritual and organization are more observable than theology. The cases where ritual and organizational forms are adopted, but theology rejected are fairly well known. Is it possible that in some cases theology may be adopted and ritual and organization rejected? This may be the case of the "no-church" movement in Japan.

Any study of diffusion should begin with a review of Rogers' (1962, 1971 with F. Shoemaker, 1983, 1995) discussions of difficulties and problems in past research and his set of "middle range" theories. Some biases affecting the study of the diffusion of material items may be different from the biases affecting the study of the diffusion of nonmaterial items, such as religion. Whereas Rogers (1995, 100-114) speaks of a "pro-innovation bias" and a "source bias," which tend to favor the diffusing item and blame the individual for rejection, in studies of religious diffusion there may be a tendency for researchers to blame the source and the diffusing item (religion) and to favor the receiving society and culture, which may reject the outside religion. Probably the greatest difficulty mentioned by Rogers (1995, 121-123) has to do with the study of change over time and particularly the use of recall, which is notorious for its unreliability and built-in bias.

In general, descriptive studies and case studies are needed, but I believe that explanatory studies should not be postponed. Instead, explanatory studies should be combined with descriptive studies so that there can be more progress in understanding than can be gained simply by accumulating descriptive studies. My own hope is that more detailed studies than mine will try to answer the question which I investigated in a very broad fashion, namely, "Why have responses to outside religions varied so much?" Tentative answers to this question are more useful than endless description.

In the developing world order, global and local processes are increasingly linked. Rhys H. Williams (1991, 297-311) discusses and recommends pursuing the twofold task of analyzing global and local processes. He is in accord with Anthony Giddens (1991, 32) who wrote:

> Transformations in self-identity and globalization, I want to propose, are the two poles of the dialectic of the local and the global in conditions of high modernity. Changes in intimate aspects of personal life, in other words, are directly tied to the establishment of social connec-

tions of very wide scope...for the first time in human history, "self" and "society" are interrelated in a global milieu.

I believe that the study of the diffusion of religions makes it possible to link the global and the local in a way that clarifies what is taking place at both levels.

Appendix

A Theological Perspective With Missiological Implications

The Demarcation

As I stated in the Introduction, I am a "demarcationist," meaning that I believe there is an advantage both to the social sciences and to theology to keep them apart. In fact, I would seek to distinguish the social sciences from the humanities in general. I realize that the phrase should be "keep them apart in principle," because there is a tendency for our knowledge to converge within us and this convergence shows up at various points. Nevertheless, we can have some success in keeping them apart and it is useful to attempt to do so.

Theology is especially dangerous for the social sciences because by "theology" I am not talking simply about what is in textbooks, but what is everyone's beliefs. For many it is not simply opinion; it is commitment. Of course, one of the advantages that religious people have over those who claim to be non-religious is that the beliefs (at least the "official" beliefs) of religions are generally well known. People who claim *not* to be religious are more likely than religious people to have hidden beliefs and commitments. This is one of my main concerns about those who claim they can teach religion "objectively" in "religious studies," if they are *not* demarcationists. I would prefer courses to be taught from either a clearly religious or a clearly non-religious point of view. At least, a teacher or writer should make clear when she or he is moving from one perspective to another and this can be done best when one is conscious of religious belief..

In addition to being useful for our knowledge in both areas, I believe there are good theological reasons for protecting the social sciences and theology from each other. I find a major reason in the doctrine of sin. That is, I believe there is something in all of us that makes us want to twist facts to suit our opinions and prejudices. If we do not seek to keep social science (all the social sciences as a field) as an autonomous field with its own principles of investigation, then there is great danger that the data and the conclusions drawn will be unduly influenced by opinion. There is enough danger as it is, even after taking all the prescribed precautions.

At the same time, I have a high regard for the discipline of theology and although it needs protection too, it is not in as much need of protection as science. Of course, because of the untestable nature of the assertions of theology, it is more subject to the intrusion of amateurs, some of whom, unfortunately, are social scientists. However, the religious world and most theologians are used to a broad expression of opinions in theology (it is a "free-for-all") and that is why we have religious communities that exercise some control over theological views. Theology is also close to the emotions. A theology that is not held with emotion would not be worth much. As for its intellectual strength, theology must have broader shoulders than the social sciences because it must be concerned about including social scientific knowledge, as well as broader knowledge from the humanities, in its total perspective. The social sciences, on the other hand, are specifically interested in excluding theology and all normative views from their perspective (except as data to explain how theology and all views and knowledge are conditioned, a special concern of the sociology of knowledge). In the end, I believe that each field has its special rewards and its contributions and these are pretty well known in each field.

Missiology, of course, is a theological discipline that leans heavily on the discipline of history. Increasingly, missiology has been drawing on the social sciences, but I believe that the line between the social sciences and missiology is sharper than between history and missiology simply because history and theology are both more based on methodologies from the humanities than from science.

The social sciences also have a tradition (the sub-field of historical sociology) of using historical information and this area of interest has been growing in influence and, of course, was very important to one of the founders of the discipline, Max Weber. History is an area for exploration and argument for social scientists, but the social sciences have to depend in large measure on studies that can be replicated by gathering data under controlled conditions in the present. At least, in the social sciences there must be a continuous interaction between the latter type of study and studies from history.

As I have said at first, I believe that the use of history by social scientists will tend to be different from that of historians themselves, with the social scientists often appearing to be superficial and actually being so from an historical perspective, not to speak of a theological perspective. This is because social scientists tend to deal with classes or categories of data and also to seek to isolate a limited number of causes. You may regard my comment about superficiality as an excuse for my treatment in this book. So be it, but let us proceed with the theological and missiological postscript that is the subject of this appendix.

The Three Religions and Human Yearnings

I do not claim that the theological implications of the findings of this book are always clear and straightforward. The implications for the social sciences are difficult enough and undoubtedly will be both challenged and elaborated. I present these implications primarily as directions for thought. As you may have noted from the Introduction, I am a Christian and belong to one of its sub-sub-communities (Presbyterian Church U.S.A.). This means that my theology is based officially on the Bible, as it is for most Christians, but this does not mean that agreement is assured, even within my own faith tradition.

When I started the search to understand why there was so much variation in the diffusion of religions, I was thinking only of Christianity. Later, it became obvious that Christianity was not alone in diffusing widely. I had to deal with the theological significance of the diffusion of two other religions, Buddhism and Islam, in addition to that of my own faith. It became necessary for me, therefore, to deal with why these three religions, as opposed to other religions, have diffused so widely and continue to do so. I believe that the primary theological answer to this question is to be found in the doctrine of humanity (called "anthropology" in theology).

I believe that God has created humanity so that there are certain yearnings. All religions fulfill these yearnings to some degree, for example, the basic yearning to worship. However, these three religions that diffused so widely have specifically sought to be successful in fulfilling certain universal human yearnings. A skilled theologian or philosopher or student of comparative religion will be able to expand and deepen my description, but it seems to me that these religions had certain "yearning-fulfilling" characteristics that made it possible for them to diffuse in the periods and areas in which they have diffused. To be specific, they offered to individuals a combination of release or freedom on the one hand and security or order on the other hand. This meant that individuals could have a sense of salvation from the conditions of this earth and at the same time a sense of guidance in life. I believe that God has placed in humanity this yearning for transcendence over the conditions of this world and also a yearning for a moral order in life.

In addition, these three religions have had a wide appeal because of the attention they give to the individual and their egalitarian thrust. They offer a personal dignity to each individual. At the same time, they are intellectually challenging and have provided opportunities for the development of intellectual traditions, with some having the opportunity to become teachers and moral guides. The combination of the offer of salvation to all with an intellectual and moral tradition meant that the person of lowest status could advance to what is available to the person of highest status. Ultimately, social status, as well as ethnic membership, becomes irrelevant, making it possible for these religions to transcend social boundaries. This has satisfied a certain yearning for freedom from the constraints of the social and even the physical world and has given these religions an ability to diffuse across social and geographical boundaries.

There are many distinctions between these three religions and there are certain emphases that developed within them (including within my own faith tradition) that I do not accept as God's intention for human thought and behavior. However, my understanding of the wide diffusion of these religions from a theological perspective is based on what I believe God has created as yearnings or longings in human life that appear on both the individual and social levels.

In addition, members of these three religions have deliberately undertaken to respond to these human yearnings by spreading their religions. The members of these religions may be accused of seeking to dominate others through their religions, but as far as the members of these religions are concerned, the spread of their religions is an expression of concern for all humanity and for members of Christianity and Islam at least, this is a concern of God and therefore a mandate for believers. In the Bible, of course, this mandate is expressed very clearly.

Seeing God at Work

"No one has ever seen God" (John 1:18; I John 4:12), but we have seen God at work. Or have we? My belief is that God is at work in the world and that God works through human beings. This does not mean that God's work is always obvious, but this belief is based on the acceptance of an historical revelation that is centered on Jesus Christ. I believe that God came in Jesus Christ to redeem humanity and that Jesus sent out and empowered his followers to "make disciples of all nations" (Matthew 28:19). Thus, God has chosen to use human beings guided by God's Spirit. This means that we can observe God at work in others, as well as be used by God ourselves. Since all human thought and action are socially conditioned (we can no more escape our social and cultural conditioning than we can escape our bodies), it is important to recognize that God works through both individuals and through social conditions. The social sciences are especially useful at this point because they analyze human behavior as it is socially conditioned. However, there is one major problem that affects both our observation of and our being used by God. Once again, this is the problem of sin or our resistance to God.

My understanding is that there is human sin mixed with our thought, our observations, and our action. This mixing appeared early in the history of the diffusion of Christianity and has continued to the present. The very word, "Christianity," points to the human enterprise represented in my faith and if it is human, then it is sinful. I would not say that I am a believer in Christianity, although I am glad to say that I am a Christian, a believer in Jesus Christ. But I and other believers cannot escape culture and history any more than we can jump out of our skins, as I said above. Nevertheless, I believe God has and will use human beings to spread the Good News of Jesus Christ in spite of our sin and numerous failings. This is part of what the Bible calls "working all things together for good" (Roman 8:28). In regard to the whole historical process, even "human wrath" is made to serve God (note Psalm 76:10 and all the prophets regarding the judgment of God on believers, even through the enemies of God's people). One major consequence of the conversion of the Gentiles is that we brought into the Church our Gentile thoughts and ways. In many ways, the Church has never recovered from the massive influx of Gentiles and the Gospel has been distorted and continues to be distorted as a consequence.

Basically, I believe there is no choice but to go forward from where we are with the glory and the shame that is in the Church's history. The Church has suffered and will continue to suffer severe judgment for its sins. After all, "the time has come for judgment to begin at the household of God" (I Peter 4:17). An important part of my faith tells me that although we, as a people, suffer consequences for our sins in this life and, even worse, inflict them on others, there are also opportunities to start again and to do better. This is an important part of the Gospel and what we know as "the power of the Resurrection." In this, we see God at work and God's work will surprise us as it has in the past. There are many places where we need to change and improve our work so that the Gospel will be discerned more clearly.

It is this view of God at work that makes me believe we need to know what others, from ordinary people to social scientists, think of us and everything else. We may hear angels unawares!

Domination and Resistance

Probably the clearest implication of this book is that the Gospel of Jesus Christ is not well represented by dominating power or when it is associated with such power. It is a basic distortion of the Gospel of the Cross. Association with domination was not a problem for the period of diffusion of Christianity in the Mediterranean world with a few exceptions. One of these exceptions was in the association of Christianity with the Latin colonizers of North Africa as opposed to the indigenous population and its later association with the Byzantine Empire. Probably a consequence of this is to be seen in the conversion of the indigenous Berber population to Islam some centuries later. However, as is well known, the problem of becoming the religion of the majority and of those in power became a special problem for Christianity. The problem became very concrete with the conversion of Constantine and has been much discussed by Church historians. Significantly, while the conversion of Constantine may have favored the growth of the Church in the West, it worked against the growth of the Church in the Middle East. It became difficult for the Church to represent Jesus Christ, the Servant Messiah, and especially the power of the cross. A major area in which theology may incorporate the findings of this book is in what is implied about the distinction of the power of the Cross and other powers.

Roman power declined, but Christian association with political power continued strongly in Byzantium for many centuries. On the other hand, the decline of Roman power meant that again in the diffusion of Christianity to the tribes to the north, the association of Christianity with domination *at the time of reception* would not be a major problem. However, with the conversion of the elites and large numbers of people in Europe, the problem that came with Constantine reappeared in the development of many "little Constantines" and of the larger "Christendom."

I have respect for the great contributions of the theologians who wrestled with the question of how Christians should use power. They produced the "just war" tradition and the humane Spanish laws that aided the diffusion of Christianity to the Americas and the Philippines. I happen to believe that a state cannot exist without powers of coercion. I believe it is even necessary in a family. However, a state, just as leaders in a family, needs to have moral authority that goes beyond simply the power to exert coercion. What should be the position of Christianity in relation to power in societies where Christians form a majority continues to be a problem for the presentation of the Gospel.

Very gradually and in a complex way, improved ways of governing developed in Europe and I believe that a major contributor to this improvement was the "resistance tradition" with roots in the Bible. This development was not only in democratic government, but in a set of what are called "democratic institutions." My own belief is that tribal traditions, found both in the European tribes and in the pre-classical Mediterranean world (and may be seen in tribes around the world), were major contributors to the development of parliamentary government and the common law tradition that supported it, as well as all the other "democratic institutions" that oppose the imperial tendencies to impose rule from the position of power. The idea of law based on an inner moral law (the common law) and rule through debate in councils is much more of a tribal than an imperial approach to rule. At the same time, I believe it was the Biblical prophetic tradition (also aided by the earlier tribal tradition) which provided a major catalyst for this development. Resistance to state power was a continuous activity of the Church, especially after the collapse of Roman power, and this provided a context for resistance to all autocratic authority. At the same time, the Church became closely allied with various state powers.

The association of Christianity with state power and with revolutionary resistance reached a climax in the seventeenth century with the religious wars over territory and the Puritan Revolution. I believe it is important to realize how long this was after the coming of the Prince of Peace. The effects of this long association of Christianity with domination and coercion are still with us. I believe that the anti-Christian spirit and secular ideologies that developed in Europe are a consequence of this long association of religion with coercive power. Another major consequence of this association is the long tradition of hostility between the West and the Middle East, as well as within the West, by Christians towards Jews.

The modern diffusion of Christianity began even before democratic principles of government became established in Europe and North America. The industrial revolution, of course, provided a means for the European states, followed by the United States and then Japan, to extend their domination around the world. It also happens that the new wealth of the industrializing countries funded extensive mission activity. It took two chapters of this book to give only the highlights of the results of this activity that took place after 1500, but especially since the nineteenth century.

Now after two World Wars and the loss of colonies, the peoples of the world have asserted themselves in establishing political independence. Marxism, of course, was able to capitalize on this desire by the former dominated nations for freedom from domination by the former colonial powers. This is epitomized in the statement by Mao Tse-Tung in 1950 before throngs of people assembled in Tien An Men Square, "China has stood up." These breaks with outside domination are relatively recent events and the effects of the previous dominations are still present.

Two recent great blots on Christian history, the slave trade and the Holocaust, are very fresh in memory. Some may disclaim these as "Christian history," but how can we escape responsibility when they appeared in lands with Christian majorities and after a long period of Christian influence in society? Even the Crusades of over 700 years ago are not forgotten by people in the Middle East. Today, the picture is complicated by new forms of domination, for example, economic and cultural domination. These affect the whole moral orders of societies and the perceptions people have of what is brought to them from the outside. My historical review was for the period when military and political domination were more obvious. The implications of other forms of domination need much further analysis.

Cultural domination may turn out to be the most difficult to analyze and for missionaries to avoid. The Anabaptists, the peace churches, and the Pentecostals all had experience as resistors of dominant cultures. (The growth of Pentecostals in Latin America has been noted.) Some groups with sectarian (resistance to dominant culture) experience sometimes become dominant cultural influences themselves and yet remain largely unconscious of their cultural ties because of their sectarian origins. This phenomenon is particularly prevalent in the United States where formerly sectarian churches have become dominant in some areas and closely linked to local cultures while, at the same time, church and state remain formally separated.

Great attention has been given to the subject of culture, the classic study being H. Richard Niebuhr's *Christ and Culture* (1951). One reason that I undertook this study is that I thought missionaries, steeped in studies of culture, had neglected attention to intergroup relations. Nevertheless, I must admit that cultural conflict is involved in intergroup relations. Cultural differences, however, are not the cause of conflict so much as domination of one group over another and the sense of forced change. The key to healthy change is the sense of selfhood and freedom of choice.

Margaret Mead's (1975) study of cultural transformation of the Manus between 1928 and 1953 (*New Lives for Old*) is primarily concerned with the question of rapid change by a people. A major point for her is that it does not seem difficult for people to make rapid changes if it is done "under their own steam" (1975, xi). People do not mind change and, in fact, often welcome change, as long as the selections are their own. When it is their own choice, then they have a sense of continuity in identity. I want to deal with a theological approach to identity next.

As a member of a religious tradition that has supported resistance to domination, including military resistance, I am sympathetic with some views, such as liberation theology, that seek to identify and actively oppose some modern oppressions. How could I be otherwise when the rights I enjoy have been won by the sacrifice of many before me? At the same time, I am aware that some sociologists have not been impressed with the effectiveness of liberation theology in winning the allegiance of large numbers of people (Hewitt 1989; Martin 1990, 238). As much as I want people in other societies to enjoy the same rights that I have, I realize that the choice of goals and means for resistance should be made by people who are to be most directly affected. Furthermore, it is clear that people in many societies perceive domination from outside their society as a greater threat or as more hateful than domination from within their society. At any rate, outside domination is often more easily opposed than internal domination and to some extent, internal domination draws strength from being opposed to outside domination.

From a theological perspective, it is a human responsibility to submit to God's domination, but it is a domination characterized by Jesus Christ. To accept God's rule in Christ is to know freedom. This belief is expressed by, "You will know the truth and the truth will make you free" (John 8:32). This freedom is given, but we also have to work it out "with fear and trembling" (Philippians 2:12). The struggle is because it is our continuing sin that we resist God's rule in our lives and the world. True, the story of redemption is that "while we were yet enemies, Christ died for us." (Romans 5: 8), but although Christ has taken away the enmity, resistance to God is still the problem of our lives, both our personal lives and our social lives. Each one has personal weaknesses which limit her or his effectiveness in the mission of God in the world, but the mission of the Church as a whole is probably affected most by our unconscious social sins.

Some of our most deadly resistance is not in our immediate consciousness. A prime example of that resistance is the way Christians have participated in racial discrimination even though they might not personally have harmed some one else. I am sure this applies to such places as Germany, the United States, and South Africa, all of which have had a strong Christian presence. I certainly have experienced this personally in enjoying a warm Christian community that tacitly approved terrible injustices.

When the domination of God is accepted by humans, then an injection of iron into the spiritual blood takes place. The Jesuits and Calvinists are both good examples, as are the members of the peace churches. Acceptance of the domination of God means that all lesser dominations are questioned and if necessary resisted. This kind of phenomenon may be seen in history, for example, in the Islamic liberations in the Middle East and North Africa and in the Puritan Revolution. At the same time, another phenomenon may be noticed from Cromwell to Castro: when humans get rid of one kind of domination, they often replace it with another which may be just as bad or worse.

The lessons of freedom seem to be best learned slowly. One of the most difficult lessons is to oppose and love at the same time. We see this in Samuel and Nathan and all of the prophets. In the political world it produced only after many centuries what is called the concept and practice of "loyal opposition." There are many societies that do not have this tradition or it is not well established. For them, to disagree in public with someone (or their policy) is to be considered a deadly enemy, a security risk, and possibly a traitor. Public debate is therefore rare and when it does take place, there is no strong tradition of decorum (as in *Robert's Rules of Order*). It has been said that in some societies the Church is the only place where people may disagree with one another in public. However, the Church is not likely to be highly different from the surrounding society. Martin (1990, 282) noted that Pentecostalism in Latin America, although offering a "free space" to people, also offers an autocratic leadership that is familiar to the majority in the society. The church can contribute the lessons of freedom in its own life, but sometimes they are learned slowly and even painfully.

I come from a church (Presbyterian) which is almost obsessive about government in the church and society. Today, in the United States, government is more likely to be considered a nuisance than to be actually evil, as it was often considered in the days of the Presbyterian Church formation. More efficient church and para-church organizations have jumped ahead of us in many areas of mission. This sounds like an excuse and may be. Actually, we share a decline in membership and mission involvement (in personnel more than finances) with other Mainline churches. Nevertheless, we still have our share of people with "iron in their blood" (I knew and know some of them) and, more to the point, I believe there is still a place in the world where my church along with other churches can contribute to societies the lessons of freedom by the life of the church itself.

In closing this section on domination and resistance, I would say that if God's purpose in Jesus Christ is to reconcile us both with God and with one another, as I believe, then Christianity is most effectively diffused when its diffusion is consistent with Christ's own way of ministry that led to the Cross and Resurrection. The peaceful, humble, serving way of Jesus Christ is not well represented by a dominating and threatening force. The power of the Cross (as described, for example in I Corinthians 1) will not be discerned by those who confuse it with other kinds of power. Sadly, for many non-Christians, the Cross of Jesus Christ does not stand for peace and reconciliation and new creation, but rather for dominating force and the denial of identity.

New Identities

In the Christian faith the most important identification of a person is that of "child of God." This is an identification which may be claimed, not as a right but on the basis of an act of redemption (John 1:12,13). In this act of redemption, the One worthy of the identity "child of God" became the "child of humanity" ("Son of Man" was his favorite name for himself) and suffered all the consequences thereof. God, through that identification with humanity, even to suffering what we deserve, has made it possible for us to be restored to the human identity which God originally intended for us, known in the Bible as "the image of God" (Genesis 1:26,27; Colossians 1:15-20).

The "child of God" and restored "child of humanity" identifications do not rule out or cancel other identifications, but do subordinate them. This is analogous to the fact that the domination of God does not rule out other dominations, but subordinates them to God's domination. However, the new identity of "child of God" does not simply subordinate other identities, it brings new meaning and worth to them. This is certainly not always obvious in the history of the church (for example, the feminine identity) and has to be worked out "with fear and trembling."

One of the main points of this book is that the Good News, which is an offer to be not a "stranger and sojourner" any longer, but to be a "citizen with the saints and a member of the household of God" (Ephesians 2:19), is gladly heard by those who have unclear identities or who have lowered self-esteem. A great danger to the spread of the Gospel is if it is Christians or those associated with them who have made them lose their self-esteem.

I saw a great response by aboriginal people in Taiwan to the possibility of identifying themselves as "children of God." They had a confused identity, being members of tribes first, then in succession becoming part of China, Japan, and China again. In becoming Christians, all identities became relativized, but their tribal identities were enhanced within the basic identity of "children of God." An important contribution to this process was made by the translation of the Bible into their languages, languages which had not previously been reduced to writing. Another contribution was made by their self-government in which their church judicatories used their languages. Sanneh (*Translating the Message* 1991) has described the impact of the translation of the Bible on the strengthening of national identities during the diffusion of Christianity.

People become aware of their identities as special groups through their contacts with other groups. It is well known that groups simply think of themselves as "people" or "humans" in their pre-contact days and this term then often becomes the name by which they are known by other groups. In societies with many sub-groups, the majority group is less conscious of itself as a distinctive group. Churches of the majority group also do not think of themselves as "ethnic churches," even though they are as "ethnic" as churches of minority groups.

I was never asked my national origin when I lived in the southeastern United States (where one is considered either Black or White) until I moved to the Northeast where there are people from many different European nations. Jean-Claud Deschamps (1982, 91) reporting on multiple responses to the question, "Who am I?" noted that "women mentioned their sexual category membership more often than men, blacks referred more frequently to their ethnic affiliation than whites, Jews to their religious affiliation more often than Christians." He concluded, that "being placed in a position of minority or of being dominated produces in the individuals a heightened awareness of the social categories which determine their minority position" (Deschamps 1982, 91). Heightened awareness of distinctive identities presents personal crises with theological implications.

The Bible presents a two-fold possibility, both of which are less than God's intention and may be harmful to those who have become aware of their distinctive identities, as well as harmful to others. One possibility is pride and the other is self-hatred or lowered self-esteem. The human mind is so complex that it is possible to alternate between the two. Perhaps they are not that different. A third possibility, presented in the Bible, is to accept a "child of God" identity that relativizes all other identities.

On a more or less morally neutral level, it is possible to note that minorities often alternate between not wanting to be different and wanting to be different. These desires appear to be contradictory and sometimes become so in real feelings and in expression, but they are not contradictory if it is understood that in some respects a minority person wants to be different and in other respects wants to be the same as members of the majority group. If the deeper issue of the easy alteration between pride and self-hatred can be solved, then other ambivalent feelings can be dealt with in a healthy way. The subtlety and difficulty of the struggle over identity are indicated in the fact that the word "pride" (at least in the English language) can be used in both an evil and a good sense.

Just as the questions of domination and resistance to domination in human affairs need to be made subordinate to the issue of the domination of God and our resistance to that domination, so the question of our many identities, personal and social, needs to be subordinated to the more important identity given by God. This is a struggle in which majority and minority, dominant and subordinate, come to from different sides. Nevertheless, the Bible does indicate that there is a "preferential option." In the letter to the Corinthians (1:26-30) we read:

> Consider your call, brothers and sisters: not many of you were wise by human standards, not many were powerful, not many were of noble birth. But God chose what is foolish in the world to shame the wise; God chose what is weak in the world to shame the strong; God chose what is low and despised in the world, things that are not, to reduce to nothing things that are, so that no human being might boast in the presence of God. He is the source of your life in Christ Jesus, who became for us wisdom from God, and righteousness and sanctification and redemption, in order that, as it is written, "Let the one who boasts, boast in the Lord."

The Apostle is connecting the "low" position of the Cross with the low status of the Corinthians.

Those whose identities place them below others or in positions where others look down on them are in a position to welcome the Good News that they are important to God and that a new identity is available to them. That new identity, "child of God," is one in which the best gifts of God are available to them through Jesus Christ. On the other hand, to be in a position in which the identities of others appear to be inferior is to be in a dangerous position. The Good News will not sound like good news because there is no sense of need for lifting or for having a new identity that is granted by God through Jesus Christ. Some people (like the Apostle Paul) who have much to be proud of in their ethnic, national, professional, or religious identities (or a combination of all of them) may face a crisis in which they realize the great hollowness of these identities apart from a relationship with God that gives them a new identity. Sometimes groups of people face such a crisis. For still other people it is possible from an early age to know that whatever others may think of them or call them, they belong to God and anything else they are derives its value and fulfillment from their prior ownership by God who has claimed their lives through Jesus Christ.

If the identities by which we are known are accorded unusual respect and high status by people, then there is a danger that the most important identity, "child of God," will either be rejected or accorded a low priority. If, on the other hand, the identities by which we are known are not accorded much honor by others, then we are in a position (as Paul wrote to the Corinthian Christians) to hear the Good News of a new identity offered through Christ.

There is another danger which follows the acceptance of a new identity from God. That is the mixing of the new identity granted by God with a secondary identity. This has happened repeatedly in Christian history, when peculiarly national, ethnic, professional, or even gender identities became confused with the primary identity of belonging to God. The very condition that is conducive to the spread of Christianity, as of any religion (when a religion is perceived as contributing to the enhancing of a particular identity, often national or ethnic identity), then becomes the basis for false pride. Thus, what is favorable for the spread of the Gospel is also fraught with danger. The struggle over the mixing of identities is part of the salvation that is being worked out, not always with the necessary "fear and trembling."

The Sociology of the Knowledge of God

An underlying assumption of this book is that all knowledge is socially conditioned. It is God's humility that revelation is in human history and human language. Part of the humility required of us by God is the recognition that God deals with us through other human beings. Ideas themselves are part of the social conditioning that we all experience, but ideas should never be treated as though they are unaffected by social conditions. It is amazing how many people will discuss (argue over) ideas without any consideration of how their own social position may affect their thought. As to how our social condition may affect our thinking and our total lives, Jesus said, "How hard it will be for those who have wealth to enter the kingdom of God!" (Mark 10:23). I rest my case.

The approach of this book is against the intellectualist or mentalist interpretation of religion and history. Such an approach tends to abstract ideas from their social conditioning. The basic purpose has been to understand conducive conditions to the diffusion (and resistance to the diffusion) of religions. My theology is that God is working in history and through the conditions that affect us as individuals and as members of groups. I believe that we can speak of God as using conditions for our benefit, for both our salvation and our judgment. In fact, salvation and judgment are intertwined.

Some conditions are more dangerous than others. That is the way I understand the comment above from Mark 10:23. At the same time, all conditions contain inherent dangers. For example, I regard the Christian family as generally a favorable condition for the conveying of faith. I believe God uses families to convey a knowledge of the grace that has been extended to us through Jesus Christ. This has been my experience. However, in a Christian family, as in a Christian community, it is possible for the rising generation to lose a sense of gratitude for grace (unmerited favor) either because good conditions are taken for granted or bad conditions are attributed to faith.

There is no automatic result of conditions nor does God use conditions in a mechanical way. In fact, every condition contains opportunities for sin and salvation. Since I have been so interested in conducive conditions for receptivity to the Good News, it is important to note that such conducive conditions for faith contain within them the opportunity for sin. For example, as noted above, when an oppressed people learn that God loves them as much as anyone else and has even given them a special task of showing forth the power of God to redeem the lowly, then it becomes very easy to assume a "Manifest Destiny" and a privileged position in the world. Being special to God becomes the basis for feeling superior to others. The opportunity to have some valued aspect of our identity enhanced (a conducive condition for hearing the Gospel) easily becomes a basis for pride. Is there any deliverance from "this body of death?" (Romans 7:25). Yes! and that is our Message. But our knowledge of that Message will not come to us outside of our conditions of life, but in them and through them.

The Message and the Method

One of the values of using the social sciences as a tool in understanding human behavior is that we are forced back to basics as our pretenses are stripped away. The social sciences may seem to be (and in a sense actually are) "superficial" from a theological and a general humanities perspective, but the scientific method can also serve to expose the bases for our biases.

I noticed that Baker (1934, 303), in his early attempt at the application of the social sciences to understanding missions, returned to "the Christian Message." I hope that the analysis of this book of how Christianity and other religions spread will force those of us who are Christians to seek and to lift up that which is the basis for faith, as well as help others understand what we have been trying to say however imperfectly for the last 2000 years. In the end, what (who) we have to talk about is Jesus Christ.

The Christian Message is both a claim and a call epitomized by Jesus Christ before the Council. There he said in answer to the question "Are you the Messiah, the Son of the Blessed One?": "I am; and you will see the Son of Man seated at the right hand of the Power, and coming with the clouds of heaven." (Mark 14:61,62) A claim is made, but there is also in these words an invitation. For those who know the quotation from Daniel, "the Son of Man" refers to the people of God who are presented to God. Thus, at the trial, there is a double reference both to the Messiah and to redeemed humanity. Jesus wants his hearers to join him!

The New Testament is very clear in announcing the arrival of the last days. What has been hidden for ages has now finally been made clear. It is significant to me that this period of "the last days" accords very well with what we know of human history: that the last two thousand years come at the end of a very long period in which the world has been peopled. Jesus indicated that the time for gathering in had come (Mark 13:26,27; Luke 21:27,28; Matthew 24: 30,31). The early Christians came to understood that the coming of Jesus also meant their coming. A good example is the reference in Romans 8:19: "For the creation waits with eager longing for the revealing of the children of God."

When the Gentiles started believing in Jesus in large numbers, a meeting was held in Jerusalem to decide what to do. James, the leader of the Jerusalem church, interpreted the belief of the Gentiles reported by Peter and Paul as the fulfillment of the prophecy: "After this I will return, and I will rebuild the dwelling of David, which has fallen; from its ruins I will rebuild it, and I will set it up, so that all other peoples may seek the Lord - even all the Gentiles over whom my name has been called. Thus says the Lord, who has been making these things known from long ago" (Acts 15:16-18).

Eschatology is a controversial subject among Christians, but an honest reading of the New Testament shows that the Christian faith is an eschatological faith. When life is good, as it often is to establishment Christians, then we tend to forget this. We need the reminder of "the dominated ones" and the "ones of low status" to make clear that the old age must go and that a new age is dawning. The Message, called the Good News (Gospel), is that Jesus Christ came to lift humanity in himself to be reconciled to God and to be restored to the image of God, to become a new humanity. In Jesus we see both what God is like and what God wants us to be like, and by his death and resurrection we begin our participation in that life. It is through the Cross of Christ that we find acceptance with God and begin a life that is characterized by resurrection or newness. It starts now, but we can look forward to a final resurrection when God gathers up all things in Christ, things in heaven and things on earth (Ephesians 1: 10). Now, we live in the overlapping time between the old and the new ages.

This Message in all its forms and elaborations has been proclaimed and received very widely, as we have seen. It is important to look at this period (the last 2000 years) as a whole as we have attempted to do in this book. Our eschatological faith requires it. It will give us a "long term" perspective with an understanding that our long term is really a short term. Our missiological task is to make the Message clear so that it will be perceived by all people for what it is, not for what it is not. The latter is what often has been conveyed. This means that we have to take seriously the perceptions of people, which is what this book has attempted to do.

Discussion of strategies and tactics have their place in missiology and certainly by mission organizations and missionaries. This is not the place to attempt such a discussion. What I would like to contribute is at least some background concepts which are based on the analysis of the previous chapters.

Probably the most basic concept for influencing strategy that may be gleaned from the analysis is that the Gospel, to be perceived, needs to be presented "from below." According to the presentation of the four Gospels and of the Epistles (for example, in the first chapter of I Corinthians), the Cross of Jesus Christ is central to the Gospel. The power that is found through the Cross can only be perceived with great difficulty if the Gospel is presented in association with other forms of power. Similarly, if the Message is perceived as threatening rather than as lifting and enhancing, then it is not being perceived for what it is. If the Gospel is presented from a position of domination, then it is likely that no "good news" will be perceived, but only "bad news."

Walls' (1991, 147-149) and Martin's (1990, 275-277)) concept of the "periphery" is somewhat analogous to "from below." The Good News seems so often to have been heard most clearly at the periphery of societies and also to have moved from periphery to periphery, often converting peripheries to centers. The lifting power of the Gospel is perceived and experienced most by those who stand on the outside and, therefore, they appear best able to convey the Message of this power. There appears to be an echo here of Hebrews 13:12-14:

> Therefore Jesus also suffered outside the city gate in order to sanctify the people by his own blood.. Let us then go to him outside the camp and bear the abuse he endured. For here we have no lasting city, but we are looking for the city that is to come.

Since perception is so important, patience and deliberate work are required. The translation of the scriptures is clearly an important part of that patient work that accords honor and respect to those to whom the Message is being carried. Missionaries are important as bearers of the Message, but the number of missionaries is not so important as how the Message is perceived. The quick development of local organization and leadership is another way of emphasizing the power that is inherent in the Message as opposed to conveying the impression that power belongs only to those who come from the outside.

Probably the most important realization that creates humility in missionaries and the organizations that send them is the awareness of the historic failings of Christianity. There is disagreement about this because to many this seems to be unnecessarily self-effacing and negative. There are both dark and glorious streaks in Christian history. The realization of this mixture forces us not to point at Christianity, but at Christ. Those who hear and receive the Message need to make their own judgments about distinguishing Christ from Christianity, knowing that they also will fail. One purpose for being humble about Christian history is to help those who receive the Message to be humble about the history that they will develop.

Christianity will continue to be a missionary religion because it worships a missionary God, a God who wants to set people free and lift them. It believes in a Savior who was sent and who sent. Rejection is inevitable; it is even promised in scripture. The question is, however, how much do we create rejection based on needless misperception? Part of our arrogance is to believe that rejection is based on the sin of the hearers rather than our sin. I believe that the record of missions shows that rejection of the Message is based as much or more on the failings of the senders as on those of the receivers. The messenger is part of the Message, as much as we wish it were not true, and the messenger is not just an individual, just as the hearer is not just an individual. The bearer of the Message carries the baggage of the people he or she represents just as the hearer carries with him or her the experience of life in the receiving group.

Probably the most difficult task of the Church is really to believe the Gospel it proclaims, that the Gospel does not need our power, our techniques, and our strategies, only our presentation in a way that is consistent with the Author. "There's the rub."

The Gospel bears us more than we bear it. This means that a few missionaries may be more effective than many, that a few words may be better understood than many, that staying a long time in quiet work may be more effective than multi-faceted activity, that a single act of kindness, imprisonment, martyrdom, or other witness may be more effective than many words and actions, that paying attention to the humble and receptive may be more effective than gaining the approval of the powerful and resistant, that waiting for the hearers to organize may be better than imposing our organization, and that love and enjoyment of people may be more effective than our words. You may add your own list. None of these are rules or principles of strategy because any one of them (except for love) may be wrong. The question is, what is the strategy of those who come from below "not to be served but to serve" (Mark 10:44)?

One of the most sensitive areas of mission has to do with crossing the barriers of ancient hostility with Jews and with Muslims. The injuries inflicted by Christians (or people associated with Christians) in the past have been great. Christianity has been associated with direct threats and destruction to both Judaism and Islam. We cannot avoid the burden of this history, but in both cases we have only one word, "Look at Jesus and what he has done and we will try to do the same." They may tell us, "Show us the results first" and we will have no choice but to do so.

In the ancient societies of Asia, our message is also, "Look at Jesus Christ and what he has done," but in Asia there are many followers of Jesus to share in the presentation and more people wanting to hear what we followers have to say. There are even more followers in Africa, Oceana, and Latin America who are pointing at Jesus. These are on the periphery of the global order and therefore are to be increasingly important in the total world mission.

References

Abrams, Dominic and Michael A. Hogg, eds. 1990. *Social identity theory: constructive and critical advances.* New York: Springer-Verlag.

Arias, Mortimer. 1978. Contextual evangelization in Latin America: between accommodation and confrontation. *Occasional bulletin.* 2:19-28.

Aung, Maung Htim. 1967. *A history of Burma.* New York: Columbia University Press.

Babbie, Earl. 1986. *The practice of social research.* Belmont, CA:Wadworth Publishing Company.

Bainbridge, William Sims. 1992. The sociology of conversion. In *Handbook of religious conversion,* eds. H. Newton Malony and Samuel Southard. 178-91. Birmingham, AL: Religious Education Press.

Baker, Archibald G. 1934. *Christian missions and a world culture.* Chicago: Willett, Clark & Company.

Bakhash, Shaul. 1989. Historical setting. In *Iran, a country study,* ed. Helen Chapin Metz. 3-70. Washington, DC: Headquarters, Department of the Army.

Barker, John. 1993. "We are ekelesia": conversion in Uiaku, Papua, New Guinea. In *Conversion to Christianity,* ed. Robert W. Hefner. 199-230. Berkeley, CA: University of California Press.

Barnett, H. G. 1953. *Innovation, the basis of cultural change.* New York: McGraw-Hill Company, Inc.

Barrett, David, ed. 1982. *World Christian encyclopedia.* Nairobi, Kenya: Oxford University Press.

Bellah, Robert. 1969. Religious evolution. In *Sociology and religion*, eds. Norman Birnbaum and Gertrud Lenzer. 67-83. Englewood Cliffs, NJ: Prentice-Hall, Inc.

Benda, H. J. 1858. *The crescent and the rising sun*. The Hague: Bandung.

Bennett, Lerone, Jr. 1976. *Before the Mayflower, a history of the Negro in America 1619-1964*. Clinton, MA: The Colonial Press.

Benz, Ernst. 1976. Buddhism in the western world. In *The cultural, political, and religious significance of Buddhism in the modern world*, ed. Henrick Dumoulin. 305-322. New York: Macmillan.

Berger, Peter. 1969. *The sacred canopy*. Garden City, NY: Doubleday & Company.

Beyer, Peter. 1994. *Religion and globalization*. Thousand Oaks, CA: Sage Publications.

Boas, Franz. 1896. *The limitation of the comparative method of anthropology*. New York: Alfred A. Knopf.

Boskoff, Alvin. 1972. *The mosaic of sociological theory*. New York: Thomas Y. Crowell Company.

Brown, Ira Corinne. 1957. *The story of the American Negro*. New York: Friendship Press.

Burdick, Michael A. and Phillip E. Hammond. 1991. World order and mainline religions: the case of Protestant foreign missions. In *World order and religion,* ed. Wade Clark Roof. 193-213. Albany, NY: State University of New York Press.

Campbell, Robert A. and James E. Curtis. 1994. Religious involvement across societies: analysis for alternative measures in national surveys. In *Journal for the scientific study of religion*. 33:217-29.

Carmichael, Joel. 1967. *The shaping of the Arabs, a study of ethnic identity*. New York: Macmillan.

Ch'en, Kenneth Kuan Sheng. 1972. *Buddhism in China*. Princeton, NJ: Princeton University Press.

Cipriani, Roberto. ed. 1993. *"Religions sans frontieres?" present and future trends of migration, culture, and communication*. Rome: Presidenza Del Consiglio Dei Ministri, Dipartimento per L'Informatazione E L'Editoria.

Cohen, Paul A. 1963. *China and Christianity*. Cambridge, MA: Harvard University Press.

References

Cohn, Norman. 1961. *The Pursuit of the Millennium*. New York: Harper & Row.

Coleman, James. 1958. Relational analysis: the study of social organizations with survey methods. *Human organization*. 14:28-36.

Comaroff, Jean. 1985. *Body of power, spirit of resistance: the cultural history of a South African people*. Chicago: University of Chicago Press.

Conze, Edward. 1975. *Buddhism, its essence and development*. New York: Harper & Row.

Covell, Ralph. 1990. *Mission impossible, the unreached Nosu on China's frontier*. Pasadena, CA: Hope Publishing Company.

Cumings, Bruce. 1994. Historical setting. In *North Korea, a country study*, ed. Andrea Mattes Savada. 3-46. Washington, DC: Headquarters, Department of the Army.

Daniel-Rops, Henry. 1959. *The church in the dark ages*. Translated by Audrey Butler. London: JM Dent & Sons, Ltd.

Deanesly, M. 1950. *A history of the medieval church*. London: Methuen & Co., Ltd.

Demerath, N.J. III. 1994. The moth and the flame: religion and power in comparative blur. *Sociological analysis*. 55:105-17.

Deschamps, Jean-Claud. 1982. Social identity and relations of power between groups. In *Social identity and intergroup relations*, ed. Henri Tajfel. 85-98. Cambridge, U.K.: Cambridge University Press.

Dvornik, Francis. 1970. *Byzantine missions among the Slavs: SS Constantine --Cyril and Methodius*. New Brunswick, NJ: Rutgers University Press.

Edwards, Michael. 1961. *A history of India*. New York: Farrar, Straus, and Cudahy.

Erickson, Erik H. 1963. *Childhood and society*. New York: Norton.

Finney, Henry C. 1991. America's Zen's Japan connection. a critical case study of Zen Buddhism's diffusion to the west. *Sociological analysis*. 52:379-96.

Fliegel, Frederick C. and Joseph E. Kivlin. 1966. Attributes of innovations as factors in diffusion. *American journal of sociology*. 72:235-48.

Forman, Charles, W. 1983. The difficulty of understanding church growth in Madagascar. In *Exploring church growth*, ed. Wilbert R. Shenk. 3-11. Grand Rapids, MI: Eerdmans.

_____.1994. The study of Pacific Island Christianity: achievements, resources, needs. *International bulletin of missionary research.* 18:103-12

Frend, W.H.C. 1984. *The rise of Christianity.* Philadelphia, PA: Fortress Press.

Freston, Paul. 1994. Popular Protestants in Brazilian politics: a novel turn in sect-state relations. *Social Compass.* 41:537-70.

Giddens, Anthony. 1991. *Modernity and self-identity.* Stanford, CA: Stanford University Press.

Graebner, Fritz. 1911. *Methode der Ethnologie.* Heidelberg, Germany: Carl Winter.

Grayson, James H. 1985. *Early Buddhism and Christianity in Korea: a study in the emplantation of religion.* Leiden, Netherlands: Brill.

Grichting, Wolfgang L. 1971. *The value system of Taiwan.* Beckenried, Switzerland: Neue Zeitschrift fur Missionwissenschaft.

Gustafson, James M. 1961. *Treasures in earthen vessels.* New York: Harper & Brothers.

Hammond, Phillip E. 1988. Religion and the persistence of identity. *Journal for the scientific study of religion.* 27:1-11.

Harnack, Adof von. 1908. *The mission and expansion of Christianity in the first three centuries.* Vol. 2. New York: Putnam.

Harper, Susan Billington. 1995. Ironies of indigenization: some cultural repercussions of mission in South India. *International bulletin of missionary research.* 19:13-20.

Harrison, Brian. 1966. *South-east Asia, a short history.* London: Macmillan & Company, Ltd.

Hefner, Robert W. ed. 1993. *Conversion to Christianity.* Berkeley, CA: The University of California Press.

Heise, David R. 1967. Prefatory findings in the sociology of missions. *Journal for the scientific study of religion.* 23:278-91.

Hewitt, W.E. 1989. Origins and prospects of the option for the poor in Brazilian Catholicism. *Journal for the scientific study of religion.* 28:120-35.

Hogden, Margaret T. 1974. *Anthropology, history, and cultural change.* Tuscon, AZ: The University of Arizona Press.

Hoge, Dean R. and David A. Roozen. eds. 1979. *Understanding church growth and decline: 1950-1978.* New York: The Pilgrim Press.

References

Hogg, Michael A. and Dominic Abrams. 1988. *Social identifications*. London: and New York: Routledge.

_____. 1993. Towards a single-process uncertainty-reduction model of social motivation in groups. In *Group motivation, social psychological perspectives*, eds. Michael A. Hogg and Dominic Abrams. 173-90. New York: Harvester Wheatsheaf.

Hogg, Michael A., Deborah J. Terry, and Katherine M. White. 1995. A tale of two theories: a critical comparison of identity theory and social identity theory. *Social psychology quarterly*. 58:255-69

Horowitz, Donald L. 1985. *Ethnic groups in conflict*. Berkeley: CA: University of California Press.

Horton, Paul B. and Chester L. Hunt. 1976. *Sociology*. New York: McGraw-Hill Company, Inc.

Hunter, James D. 1991. *Culture wars: the struggle to define America*. New York: Basic Books.

Hutchinson, Paul and Winfred E. Garrison. 1959. *Twenty centuries of Christianity*. New York: Harcourt, Brace and Company.

James, William. 1928. *The varieties of religious experience*. London: Longmans, Green and Co.

Jenkins, Paul. 1986. The roots of African church history: some polemic thoughts. *International bulletin of missionary research*. 10:67-71.

Jongoneel, Jan A.B. 1995. *Philosophy, science, and theology of mission in the 19th and 20th centuries: a missiological encyclopedia, Part I, The philosophy and science of mission*. Berne, Switzerland: Peter Lang AG.

Kapleau, Philip. 1979. *Zen: dawn in the west*. Garden City, NY: Anchor Press/Doubleday.

Katz, Elihu. 1967. Comment on Prefatory findings in the sociology of missions. *Journal for the scientific study of religion*. 6:61-63.

Katz, Elihu, Martin L. Levin, and Herbert Hamilton. 1963. Traditions of research on the diffusion of innovation. *American sociological review*. 28:237-52.

Keyes, Charles F. 1993. Why are the Thai not Christians: Buddhist and Christian conversion in Thailand. In *Conversion to Christianity*, ed. Robert W. Hefner. 259-83. Berkeley, CA: University of California Press.

Koestler, Arthur. 1976. *The thirteenth tribe, the Khazar empire and its heritage*. New York: Random House.

Kroeber, Alfred. 1919. On the principle of order in civilization as exemplified by changes of fashion. *American anthropologist.* 21:235-63.

Kurtz, Lester. 1995. *Gods in the global village. the world's religions in sociological perspective.* Thousand Oaks, CA: Pine Forge Press.

Latourette, Kenneth Scott. 1937. *The history of the expansion of Christianity, the first five centuries.* Vol. 1. New York: Harper and Brothers Publishers.

———. 1938. *The history of the expansion of Christianity, the thousand years of uncertainty.* Vol. 2. New York: Harper and Brothers Publishers.

———. 1939. *The history of the expansion of Christianity, three centuries of advance AD 1500 to AD 1800.* Vol. 3. New York: Harper and Brothers Publishers.

———. 1943. *The history of the expansion of Christianity, the great century in northern Africa and Asia AD 1800 to AD 1914.* Vol. 4. New York: Harper and Brothers Publishers.

———. 1944. *The history of the expansion of Christianity, the great century in the Americas, Australasia, and Africa AD 1800 to AD 1400.* Vol. 5. New York: Harper and Brothers Publishers.

———. 1945. *Advance through storm, AD 1400 and after with concluding generalizations.* Vol. 6. New York: Harper and Brothers Publishers.

———. 1953. *A history of Christianity.* Harper and Brothers Publishers.

———. 1956. *The Chinese, their history and culture.* New York: The Macmillan Company.

Lauer, Robert. 1973. *The history of ethnological theory.* New York: Rinehart and Company.

Lee, Martha F. 1988. *The Nation of Islam, an American millenarian movement.* Lewiston, NY: Edwin Mellen Press.

Lee, Richard Wayne. 1992. Christianity and the other religions: interreligious relations in a shrinking world. *Sociological analysis.* 53:125-39.

Lewis, Bernard. 1993. *Islam in history.* Chicago: Open Court.

Lincoln, C. Eric. 1973. *The Black Muslims in America.* Boston: Beacon Press.

———. 1989. The Muslim mission in the context of American social history. In *African American religious studies, an interdisciplinary anthology*, ed. by Gayraud S. Wilmore. Durham, NC: Duke University Press.

Lincoln, C. Eric and Lawrence H. Mamiya. 1990. *The Black Church in the African American experience.* Durham, NC: Duke University Press.

References

Lowie, Robert. 1939. *The history of ethnological theory.* New York: Rinehart and Company.

Ludowyk, E. F. C. 1962. *The story of Ceylon.* New York: Roy Publishers.

MacInnis, Donald. 1988. Protestant and Catholic missions in south China: 1911-1986. *International bulletin of missionary research.* 12:6-11.

MacIver, Robert M. 1942. *Social causation.* Boston: Ginn.

_____. 1947. *The web of government.* New York: Macmillan Company.

MacMullen, Ramsay. 1984. *Christianizing the Roman empire (A.D. 100-400).* New Haven, CT: Yale University Press.

Malony, H. Newton and Samuel Southard. 1992. eds. *Handbook of religious conversion.* Birmingham, AL: Religious Education Press.

Mamiya, Lawrence H. 1982. From Black Muslim to Bilalian: the evolution of a movement. *Journal for the scientific study of religion.* 21:138-52.

Mannheim, Karl. 1940. *Man and society in an age of reconstruction.* New York: Harcourt Brace.

Martin, David. 1990. *Tongues of fire, the explosion of Protestantism in Latin America.* Oxford, U.K.: Basil Blackwell.

Mead, Margaret. 1975. *New lives for old.* New York: William Morrow and Company. Inc.

Merrill, William L. 1993. Conversion and colonialism in northern Mexico: the Tarahumara response to the Jesuit mission program, 1601-1767. In *Conversion to Christianity*, ed. Robert W. Hefner. 129-63. Berkeley, CA: University of California Press.

Merton, Robert K. 1968. *Social theory and social structures.* New York: The Free Press.

Miller, Jon. 1994. *The social control of religious zeal: a study of organizational contradictions.* New Brunswick, NJ: Rutgers University Press.

Missiology. an international review. Continuing *Practical anthropology.* Scottdale, PA: Quarterly publication of the American Society of Missiology.

Moffett, Samuel Hugh. 1992. *A history of Christianity in Asia, Beginnings to 1500.* Vol. 1, San Francisco, CA: Harper.

Mol, Hans J. 1976. *Identity and the sacred.* New York: The Free Press.

Montgomery, Robert L. 1984. Bias in interpreting social facts, is it a sin? *Journal for the scientific study of religion.* 23:278-91.

_____. 1986. Receptivity to an outside religion: light from interaction between sociology and missiology. *Missiology.* 14:287-99.

_____. 1991. The spread of religions and macrosocial relations. *Sociological analysis.* 52:37-53.

Morreale, Don. 1988. *Buddhist American centers, retreats, practices.* Santa Fe. NM: John Muir Publishers.

Newman, Bernard. 1945. *Balkan background.* New York: The Macmillan Company.

Niebuhr, H. Richard. 1951. *Christ and culture.* New York: Harper & Row.

Nisbet, Robert A. 1965. *Makers of modern social science: Emile Durkheim.* Englewood Cliffs, NJ: Prentice-Hall, Inc.

_____. 1969. *Social change and history.* New York: Oxford University Press.

Norman, Edward. 1981. *Christianity in the southern hemisphere.* Oxford, U.K.: Clarendon Press.

Noss, John B. 1949. *Man's religions.* New York: The Macmillan Company.

Nthamburi, Zablon. 1989. Toward indigenization of Christianity in Africa: a missiological task. *International bulletin of missionary research.* 13:112-18.

Nutting, Anthony. 1964. *The Arabs.* New York: The New American Library.

Odum, Howard. 1947. *Understanding society.* New York: Macmillan.

Ogburn, William F. [1922] 1966. *Social change.* New York: Dell Publishing Company.

Oliver, Douglas L. 1951. *The Pacific islands.* Garden City, NY: Doubleday & Company.

Park, Chris C. 1994. *Sacred worlds: an introduction to geography and religion.* London: Routledge.

Perry, Ronald W. 1992. Diffusion theories. In *Encyclopedia of sociology,* eds. Edgar F. Borgatta and Marie L. Borgatta. 487-92. New York: Macmillan Publishing Company.

Pollock, Donald K. 1993. Conversion and 'community' in Amazonia. In *Conversion to Christianity,* ed. Robert W. Hefner. 163-97. Berkeley, CA: University of California Press.

References

Rambo, Lewis R. 1992. The psychology of conversion. In *Handbook of religious conversion*, eds. H. Newton Malony and Samuel Southard. 159-77. Birmingham, AL: Religious Education Press.

Ranger, Terence. 1993. The local and the global in southern African religious history. In *Conversion to Christianity*, ed. Robert W. Hefner. 65-98. Berkeley, CA: University of California Press.

Redfield, Robert. 1957. *The primitive world and its transformation*. Ithaca, NY: Cornell University Press.

Reusch, Richard. 1961. *History of east Africa*. New York: Frederick Unger Publishing Company.

Rizvi, S.A.A. 1975. Islam in medieval India. In *A cultural history of India*, ed. A.L. Basham. 243-65. Delhi: Oxford University Press.

Robert, Henry M. [1876] 1981. *Robert's Rules of Order*. Eighth Edition. Glenview, IL: Scott, Foreman and Company.

Robertson, Roland. 1985. The sacred and the world system. In *Sacred in a secular age*, ed. Phillip E. Hammond. 347-58. Berkeley, CA: University of California Press.

_____. 1987. Church-state relations and the world system. In *Church-State, relations*, eds. Thomas Robbins and Roland Robertson. 39-51. New Brunswick, NJ: Transaction, Inc.

Robertson, Roland and J. Chirico. 1985. Humanity, globalization, and worldwide religious experience. *Sociological analysis*. 46: 219-42.

Robinson, Richard H. and Willard L. Johnson. 1982. *The Buddhist religion*. Belmont, CA: Wadworth Publishing Company.

Rogers, Everett M. 1962. *The diffusion of innovations*. New York: the Free Press.

_____. 1983. *The diffusion of innovations*. New York: The Free Press.

_____. 1995. *The diffusion of innovations*. New York: The Free Press.

Rogers, Everett M. and F. Floyd Shoemaker. 1971. *Communication of innovations: a cross-cultural approach*. New York: The Free Press.

Roof, Wade Clark. ed. 1991. *World order and religion*. New York: State University of New York Press.

Sanneh, Lamin. 1991a. *Translating the message*. Maryknoll, NY: Orbis Books.

_____. 1991b. The yogi and the commissar: Christian missions and the new world order in Africa. In *World order and religion,* ed. Wade Clark Roof. 173-92. New York: State University of New York Press.

Scott, William Henry. 1967. Celtic culture and the conversion of Ireland. *The international review of missions.* 56:193-204.

Seekins, Donald M. 1993. Historical setting. In *Philippines, a country study,* ed. Ronald E. Doland. 3-63. Washington, DC: Headquarters, Department of the Army.

_____. . Historical setting. In *Indonesia, a country study.* ed. Robert L. Worden. 3-67. Washington, D.C.: Headquarters, Department of the Army.

Shenk, Wilbert R. ed. 1983. *Exploring Church growth.* Grand Rapids, M.I.: William B. Eerdmans Publishing Company.

Shinn, Rinn-Sup and Robert L. Worden. 1988. Historical setting. In *China, a country study,* ed. Robert L. Worden. 3-58. Washington, D.C.: Headquarters, Department of the Army.

Sigelman, Lee. 1977. Review of the polls: multi-nation survey of religious beliefs. *Journal of Scientific Study of Religion. 16:289-94.*

Soloviev, A.V. 1967. Bogomils. In *The new Catholic encyclopedia,* ed. William J. McDonald. 633-34. Washington, D.C.: The Catholic University Press.

Spicer, Edward H. 1954. Spanish-American acculturation in the southwest. *American anthropologist.* 56:663-78.

_____. [1974] 1994. Anthropology in the society of the 1990s. *Human organization. 53:389-95.*

Stark, Rodney. 1995. Reconstructing the rise of Christianity: the role of women. *Sociology of Religion.* 56:229-44.

Starkloff, Carl F. 1985. Religious renewal in native North America: the contemporary call to mission. *Missiology.* 13:81-101.

Sztompka, Piotr. 1993. *The sociology of social change.* Oxford, U.K.: Blackwell.

Tajfel, Henri. 1972. Social categorization. English manuscript of La categorisation socials. In *Introduction a la psychologie sociale.* Vol. 1., ed. S. Moscovici. Paris: Larousse.

_____. 1974. Intergroup behavior, social comparison and social change. Unpublished Katz-Newcomb lectures at the University of Michigan, Ann Arbor.

_____. 1981. *Human groups and social categories*. London: Cambridge University Press.

_____. ed. 1982. *Social groups and intergroup relations*. Cambridge, U.K.: Cambridge University Press.

Tajfel, Henri and J.C. Turner. 1979. An integrative theory of intergroup conflict. In *The social psychology of intergroup relations*, eds. W.G. Austin and S. Worchel. Monterey, CA: Brooks-Cole.

Takayama, K. Peter. 1984. Review of William R. Shenk, Editor, Exploring church growth. Grand Rapids, Michigan: William B. Eerdmans Publishing Co., 1983, 312 pp., and Thomas Seetser, Successful parishes: how they meet the challenge. Minneapolis: Winston Press. 1983. 254pp. *Review of religious research*. 26:208-210.

Tarling, Nicholas. 1966. *A concise history of Southeast Asia*. New York: Frederick A. Praeger Publishers.

Taylor, D.M. and D.J. McKirnan. 1984. A five-stage model of intergroup relations. *British journal of social psychology*. 23:291-300.

Teggart, Frederick J. 1916. *Prolegomena to history*. Berkeley, CA: The University of California Press.

_____.1918. *The processes of history*. Berkeley, CA: The University of California Press.

_____. 1925. *Theory of history*. Berkeley, CA: The University of California Press.

_____. [1939] 1969. *Rome and China, a study of correlations in historical events*. Berkeley, CA: The University of California Press.

Taylor, D.M. and D.J. McKirnan. 1984. A five-stage model of intergroup relations. *British journal of social psychology*. 23:291-300.

Thapar, Romila. 1969. Asoka and Buddhism. In *Sociology and religion*, eds. Norman Birnbaum and Gertrud Lenzer. 43-51. Englewood Cliffs, NJ: Prentice-Hall, Inc.

Thomas, Norman E. 1987. Evangelization and church growth: the case of Africa. *International bulletin of missionary research*. 11:165-70.

Tippett Alan R. 1992. The cultural anthropology of conversion. In *Handbook of religious conversion*, eds. H. Newton Malony and Samuel Southard. 192-205. Birmingham, AL: Religious Education Press.

Turner, Harold W. 1973. Old and new religions among North American Indians: missiological impressions and reflections. *Missiology*. 1:47-66.

Tyler, Edward. 1865. *Early history of mankind and the development of civilization.* London: John Murray.

Vallentine, Charles A. 1970. Social status, political power, and native responses to European influence in Oceana. In *Cultures of the Pacific.* eds. Thomas G. Harding and Ben J. Wallace. 337-84. New York: The Free Press.

Van Leeuwen, Arend Th. 1964. *Christianity in world history.* New York: Charles Scribner's Sons.

Wagner, U. L., L. Lampen, and J. Syllwasschy. 1986. Intergroup inferiority, social identity and outgroup devaluation in a modified minimal group study. *British journal of social psychology.* 25:15-23.

Wallace, A. F. C. 1956. Revitalization movements. *American anthropologist.* 58:264-281.

_____. 1967. *Culture and personality.* New York: Random House.

Walls, A. F. 1991. World Christianity, the missionary movement and the ugly American. In *Religion and world order,* ed. Wade Clark Roof. 147-72. Albany, NY: State University of New York Press.

Weber, Max. 1958. *From Max Weber: essays in sociology,* eds. H.H. Gerth and C. Wright Mills. New York: Oxford University Press.

_____. 1964. *Religion of China.* New York: The Free Press.

Wieb, Donald. 1994. On theology and religious studies: a response to Francis Shussler Fiorenza. *Bulletin of the council of societies for the study of religion.* 23:3-6.

Wiedner, Donald L. 1962. *A history of Africa.* New York: Random House.

Williams, Rhys H. 1991. World order and religion: a match made in heaven or a marriage of convenience? In *World order and religion,* ed. Wade Clark Roof. 297-311. New York: State University of New York Press.

Woo, Jean, compiler. 1992. *China News Update.* China Program of the Global Mission Unit, Presbyterian Church (USA). September, 11.

_____. 1993. *China News Update.* China Program of the Global Mission Unit, Presbyterian Church (USA). May, 11.

Wuthnow, Robert. 1987. *Meaning and moral order.* Berkeley, CA: University of California Press.

———. 1991. International realities: bringing the global picture into focus. In *World order and religion*, ed. Wade Clark Roof. 19-37. New York: State University of New York Press.

Yengoyam, Aram A. 1993. Religion, morality, and prophetic traditions: conversion among the Pitjantjatjara of Central Australia. In *Conversion to Christianity*, ed. Robert W. Hefner. 233-57. Berkeley, CA: University of California Press.

Zainu'ddin, Ailsa. 1970. *A short history of Indonesia*. New York: Prawger Publishers.

Zurcher, E. 1959. *The Buddhist conquest of China*. Leiden, Netherlands: Brill.

Name Index

Abrams, Dominc, 26, 27, 28, 29, 30
Abul Abbas, 85
Aglipay, 109, 110
Aguinaldo, 109
al-Amin, 85
Alfonso, Bishop, 127
Altan Khan, 46
Arias, Mortimer, 138
Asoka, 37, 38
Aung, Maung Htin, 39, 40

Babbie, Earl, xix
Bainbridge, William Sims, xx
Baker, Archibald G., xx, 21, 189
Bakhash, Shaul, 83
Barker, John, 161
Barnett, H. G., 10, 58
Barrett, David, xviii, xx, 35, 103, 104, 105, 106, 107, 108, 110, 115, 116, 117, 124, 125, 130, 131, 132, 133, 134, 137, 138, 139, 141, 142,
Bellah, Robert, 164
Benda, H. J., 90
Bennett, Lerone, Jr., 126
Benz, Ernst, 47
Bertha, Queen, 64

Berger, Peter, 154
Beyer, Peter, xvi
Boas, Franz, 2
Bogomile, Jeremiah, 67, 70
Boris, King 67
Boskoff, Alvin, 6, 21, 24, 26, 29, 154
Brown, Ina Corinne, 142
Burdick, Michael A., xvi
Buddha, Gautama, 37, 48

Campbell, Robert A., xvii, 34
Candragupta, 37
Carmichael, Joel, 82
Castro, Fidel, 182
Ch'en, Kenneth Kuan Sheng, 42, 44, 47, 49
Ch'ien Lung, Emperor, 111
Chirico, J., xvi
Cipriani, Roberto, xvii
Clotilda, Queen, 63, 64
Clovis, 63
Cohen, Paul, 112
Cohn, Norman, 71
Coleman, James, 9
Comaroff, Jean, 145
Constantine (Cyril), the missionary, 67, 68

Constantine, Emperor, 61, 179
Conze, Edward, 47, 48
Cook, Captain, 125
Covell, Ralph, 113, 118
Cromwell, Oliver, 182
Cumings, Bruce, 45
Curtis, James E., xvii, 34

Daniel-Rops, Henry, 63, 64, 65, 67
Deanesly, M., 59, 64, 70
Demerath, N. J., III, xvii, 35
Dennis, James S., xx
Deschamps, Jean-Claud, 185
Dingaan, 128
Drew, Timothy, 92
Durkheim, Emile, 165
Dvornik, Francis, 66

Edwardes, Michael, 89, 101
Edwin of Northumbria, 65
Eliot, John, 140
Erickson, Erik H., 31
Ethelbert, King, 64

Farrakhan, Louis, 93
Finney, Henry C., 13, 151
Fliegel, Frederick C., 7
Forman, Charles W., 21, 22, 122, 125
Frend, W. H. C., 63
Freston, Paul, 139

Garrison, Winfred E., 64
Genghis Khan, 72
Giddens, Anthony, 171
Graebner, Fritz, 1
Grayson, James H., 9
Grichting, Wolfgang L., 114
Gustafson, James, 162

Haarfager, Harold, 66
Hamilton, Herbert, xvi, 6, 8, 9

Hammond, Phillip E., xvi, 166, 168
Harnack, Adof von, 59
Horoun, 85
Harper, Susan Billington, 103, 104, 120
Harris, William Wade, 132
Harrison, Brian, 90
Hefner, Robert W., xvii, 10, 12, 23, 152, 154, 155, 160, 161, 163
Heise, David, xv, 11
Herodotus, 1
Hewitt, W. E., 182
Hideyoshi, 115
Hogden, Margaret T., 1, 2, 3, 4
Hoge, Dean R., xvii
Hogg, Michael, 26, 27, 28, 29, 30
Horowitz, Donald L., 143
Horton, Paul B., 1
Hunt, Chester L., 1
Hunter, James D., 165, 167
Hus, John, 70
Hutchinson, Paul, 64

Inge, son of Stenkil, 66
Iyeyasu, 115

James, William, xxi
Jenkins, Paul, 127
Jesus Christ, 177, 182, 183, 186, 187, 188, 189, 190, 191, 192, 193
Johnson, Willard L., 40, 41, 46, 51
Jongoneel, Jan A. B., xx

K'ang Hsi, Emperor, 111
Kabir, 89
Kadfiz, 42
Kanishka I, 42
Kapleau, Philip, 47
Katz, Elihu, xvi, 6, 7, 8, 9, 11
Keyes, Charles F., 161, 163

Name Index

Kimbangu, Prophet Simon, 132
Kivlin, Joseph E., 7
Koestler, Arthur, 69
Kroeber, Alfred, 2
Kublai, Khan, 72
Kurtz, Lester, xvii, 24, 41, 47, 95

Lampen, L., 26
Las Casas, Bartolome de, 136
Latourette, Kenneth Scott, xix,
    14, 59, 60, 61, 62, 63, 64, 65,
    66, 67, 68, 69, 70, 72, 73, 88,
    101, 102, 103, 104, 105, 106,
    108, 109, 110, 111, 112, 113,
    116, 122, 123, 124, 125, 127,
    131, 132, 136, 137, 138, 140
Lauer, Robert, 3
Lee, Martha F., 93
Lee, Richard Wayne, xvii
Levin, Martin L., xvi, 6, 8, 9
Lewis, Bernard, 86, 87, 89, 95
Lincoln, C. Erik, 92, 93, 146
Lowie, Robert, 2
Ludowyk, E.F.C., 39

MacInnis, Donald, 113
MacIver, Robert, 6, 24, 29, 155
MacMullen, Ramsey, 61
Malony, H. Newton, xx
Mamiya, Lawrence H. 93, 146
Mannheim, Karl, 6
Mao, Tse-tung, 117, 180
Marcion, 60
Martin, David, xviii, 22, 23, 24,
    26, 32, 115, 116, 117, 145,
    154, 159, 182, 183, 191
McKirnan, D.J., 28
Mead, Margaret, xviii, 8, 181
Merrill, William L., 161
Merton, Robert, 7
Methodius, 67
Miller, Jon, xvi
Moffett, Samuel H., 59, 61, 71,
    72, 73,

Mohammed, 79, 80, 84, 85,
Mol, Hans J., 30, 31, 32, 155
Montgomery, Robert L. xiv, xv
Moon, Sun-myung, 120
Morreale, Don, 47
Mutimir, 67
Muhammed, Elijah, 93
Muhammed, Wallace, 93

Nanak, 89
Nathan, the Prophet, 182
Newman, Bernard, 68, 88
Niebuhr, H. Richard, 181
Nisbet, Robert A., 4, 165
Nobunaga, 115
Norman, Edward, 146
Noss, John B., 38, 41, 42, 47, 48,
    83, 89
Nthamburi, Zablon, 145
Nutting, Anthony, 80, 82, 83,
    84, 85, 86, 87

Odum, Howard, 6
Ofrid von Werssenburg, 66
Ogburn, William F., 8
Oliver, Douglas L., 121, 124, 125,
    126
Omar, 85
Otto I, 68

Park, Chris C., 11
Patrick, Saint, 64, 151
Paul, the Apostle, 186
Perry, Ronald W., xvi, 1, 2, 3, 5,
    7, 8, 11, 14, 19, 20, 21, 29,
    51, 152, 153
Perry, W. J., 1
Philip II, 109
Pollock, Donald K., 161
Pomare, 122
Pomare II, 122

Radama, King, 134
Rambo, Lewis, R., xx

Ranavalona I, Queen, 134
Ranavalona II, Queen, 134
Ranger, Terrence, 133, 161
Ratana, 124
Ratislav, 67
Redfield, Robert, 24, 41, 48, 78, 95
Reusch, Richard, 92
Ricci, Matteo, 111
Rizal, 109
Rizvi, S.A.A., 89
Robert, Henry M., 183
Robertson, Roland, xvi
Robinson, Richard H., 40, 41, 46, 51
Rogers, Everett M., xvi, 1, 3, 6, 7, 8, 9, 11, 171
Roof, Wade Clark, xvi
Roozen, David A., xvi

Saladin, 87
Samuel, the Prophet, 182
Sanneh, Lamin, xvi, xviii, xx, 59, 60, 66, 71, 76, 81, 85, 86, 134, 135, 185
Scott, William Henry, 25
Seekins, Donald M., 109, 110, 111
Shenk, Wilbert R., xxi
Shinn, Rinn-Sup, 113
Shoemaker, F. Floyd, xvi, 6, 7, 8, 11, 171
Shotoku Taishi, 46
Sigelman, Lee, 34
Smith, G. E., 1
Soloviev, A. V., 68
Songzen Gampo, 46
Southard, Samuel, xxi
Spicer, Edward, 10, 27
Stark, Rodney, xvii, 59, 154
Starkloff, Carl F., 141
Suzuki, Dr. 47
Sverker, 66
Syllwasschy, J., 26

Sztompka, Piotr, 2, 3

Tajfel, Henri, 23, 26, 27, 28, 29, 31, 154
Takayama, K. Peter, xxi
Tarling, Nicholas, 90, 105
Taylor, D.M., 28
Teggart, Frederick, xix, 3, 4, 149
Terry, Deborah J., 28
Tertullian, 61
Thakombau, 123
Thapar, Romila, 37, 38
Thomas, Apostle, 72
Thomas, Norman E., 126
Thomas, W. I., 6
Timurlane, 88
Tippett, Alan R., xx, 168
Turner, Harold W., 146
Turner, J.C., 28
Tyler, Edward, 1

Ulfilas, 63

Vaca, Cabeza de, 137
Vallentine, Charles A., 123, 124
Van Leeuwen, Arend Th., 62, 82, 100, 163
Vitoria, Francisco de, 136

Wagner, U.L., 26
Wallace, A. F. C., 23, 24, 26, 32, 141, 154
Walls, A.F., xvi, 191
Weber, Max, xix, 49, 78, 161, 162, 163, 175
White, Katherine M., 28
Wiebe, Donald, xiii
Wiedner, Donald L., 91, 92, 127, 128, 129, 131
Williams, Rhys H., 171
Williams, Roger, 140
Woo, Jean, 113
Worden, Robert L., 113

Wuthnow, Robert, 21, 23, 154
Wycliffe, John, 70

Xavier, Francis, 101, 111

Yengoyan, Aram A., 161

Zainu'ddin, Ailsa, 90
Znanieki, F., 6
Zurcher, E., 43, 44

Subject Index

Aboriginals, ix, 114, 115, 125, 184
Acculturation, 4, 10
Adopter characteristics, 6, 9, 16, 21, 22, 26, 51, 59
Advanced and backward peoples, 143
Animistic, 41, 105, 108, 112, 113
Anti-foreign, 75, 112, 115
Arab, Abbasids, 85, 87, 94
  dissolution of power, 85, 94
  flowering of civilization, 85
  language of, 85, 93
  liberation by, 82
  Omayyads, 81, 84, 85, 86, 87, 95
  spirituality in, 85
  tolerance by, 84, 85, 87, 94
Arianism, 60, 63, 156
Asian Pattern, 114, 117
Attitudes, study of, 169, 170
Authority, relativization of, 164, 170
  types of, 162

Borrowing, 2, 4, 5
Bogimils, 67, 70, 88, 95
Brahmanism, 38
Buddhism, Amidism or Pure Land School, 48
  Ch'an or Zen, 47, 49
  Dhamma, 38
  diffusion to the West, 13, 46-47, 151
  compassion in, 47, 155
  Hinayana, 39, 42, 49, 53
  Kwan-yin, 48
  lay leadership in, 49, 156
  Mahayanna, 39, 41, 42, 43, 48, 49, 53, 107, 155, 156
  monks, 41, 45, 46, 48, 80, 83
  Nirvana, 41
  persecution of, 44
  rise of, 37-39
  teachers in, 39, 40, 43
  scriptures in, 43
  Theravada, 39, 40, 41, 42, 49, 107, 155, 156, 164
  Zen boom, 47

Calvinists, 183
Cargo cults, 122, 123
Case studies vs explanatory studies, 33, 172
Caste, 29, 38, 75, 86, 90, 101-105, 143
Christianity, ancient nationalities in, 60
  christo-paganism in, 137, 138

eschatological emphasis in, 71, 190
first kingdom in, 60
hopes for Mongols, 73
iconoclastic movement in, 62
importance of women in, xvi, 58, 154
message of, 189-193
negative effect of Constantine conversion, 61, 72, 179
persecution of, 72, 73
purifying movements in, 61, 62, 69, 79
rise of, 58, 59
Collective behavior, 3, 10, 11
Comparative religion, xvii
Compartmentalization under pressure, 9
Compassion, 20, 48, 54, 76, 81, 155
Confucianism, 13, 14, 33
Conquest, 2, 52, 64, 82, 84, 85, 87, 93, 96, 97
Conversion, xv, 10, 11, 12
Culture, adaptive and material, 8
contact, 4, 11, 49, 155
Cultural argument, 159, 160
compatibility, 5, 153, 159

Demarcation, xiii-xv, 173-175
Diffusion, acceptance of, 4, 5, 7, 8, 13, 15, 16
agents of, 6
concept of, xvi, 1-5, 10, 15, 16
contagious, 11
cultural, five claims, 9
cultural facilitation of, 5
decision process, 8
early adopters, 5
early schools of thought, 1,
expansion, 11

facetious argument, 157
from below or above, 52, 54, 59, 74, 77, 78, 94, 97, 122, 148, 152, 153, 191
from periphery, 57, 58, 191
hierarchical, 11
migration, 4, 11, 12.13
motivational patterns in, 6
of innovations, 3, 7, 11, 15
of religions, 6, 7, 10, 11, 12, 13, 15
receptivity of ascendant groups, 39, 95, 156
relocation, 11
research traditions in, 3, 6, 7, 8, 9, 10, 11, 16
target public of, 5
through culture contact, 11, 49, 155
upward and downward, 8, 35
Dissemination, 5
Double affiliation, 140
Dynamic Assessment, 5, 24, 154

Egalitarianism, 20, 76
Emplantation, 8
Evolutionism, 2, 3
Exogenous and endogenous forces, 4
Experimental approach, 34, 150

Faddism, 5

Globalization, xvi, 171, 172
Great tradition and little tradition, 24, 41, 48, 79, 96

Hellenism, 62, 100
Heresy, 63, 69, 95, 147
Hinduism, 13, 33, 39, 40, 41, 50, 52, 54, 55, 108, 109, 121
History, xix, 2-5, 15

Subject Index

Humanitarian approach, 137
Humanities, xiii

Identity, and globalization, 172
   and moral community, 154, 163
   and sacred order, 31
   as child of God, 184, 185, 187
   awareness of, 185
   defense of, 31
   enhancement of, 155, 159, 185
   from primary or secondary groups, 168
   limited definition of, 27
   neglected in anthropology, 27
Indigenization, 66, 104, 105, 132, 144, 145, 147
Indigenous church, 117, 133
   theologies, 159
Individualism, 12, 13
Intellectuals, 10
Islam, as counter movement, 100
   civilization of, 86, 87
   emphasis on compassion in, 81
   heresy in, 95
   human equality in, 93, 94
   liberation by, 84
   reform movements in, 91, 92, 96
   Shi'a, 39, 84, 87, 88, 89, 90, 95
   Sufism, 89, 96, 98
   Sunni, 82, 87, 88, 89, 90
   tolerance in, 94, 95
   unitary view in, 80, 81

Jesuits, 111, 137, 183
Judaism, 12, 13, 70, 72, 85, 194
   conversion of Khazars to, 69
Just war, 180

Lag theory, 8
Liberation theology, 183
Loyal opposition, 164, 183

Macro or micro levels, 12, 13, 17, 23, 24, 25, 26, 32, 120, 151, 154, 155
Mainline denominations, 167
Manichaeism, 13, 14, 33, 45, 61, 68, 71
Marxism, 14, 33, 117, 120, 158, 180
Measurements, difficulties of, 35
Mentalist approach, 12, 152, 160, 161, 162, 188
Minimal groups, 26
Minorities, 73, 87, 95, 100, 114, 115, 118, 132, 143, 148, 149, 160, 166, 187
Missiology, xvii-xix, xx, 173-193
Moral order, 24, 25, 26, 30, 31, 32, 39, 101, 119, 120, 126, 142, 155, 177
Motivation, 6, 29, 30
Movements, contained, 162
   independent church, 124, 131, 132, 145
   magic in, 129, 130
   mass, 103, 104, 131, 134
   millenarian, 71
   nationalistic, 34, 43, 69, 76, 78, 96, 102, 110, 116, 117, 120, 130
   purifying, 60, 61, 68, 70, 79, 81, 95, 97, 156
   revitalization, 141, 154
Multiculturalism, xv

Nestorianism, 44, 45, 60, 72, 73, 74
Normative view or approach, ix,

xiii, xiv, 5, 10, 53, 153, 167, 175
Ontocratic pattern, 163, 164
Oppositional ideology, 23, 24, 53, 75, 88, 89, 95, 96, 97, 154, 158

Perigrini, 65
Persecution, 44, 45, 47, 49, 62, 72, 74, 83, 85, 106, 107, 112, 116, 131, 133, 135
Pluralism, xvii, 148, 167
Positivism, xiii, xxii
Preliterate, 22, 39, 100, 127
Primitive, 143
Proselytism, xviii, 11
Puritan Revolution, 181, 184

Raw empiricism, 160
Rites controversy, 112
Religion, and domination, 161-166
  and human yearning, 175-177
  and identity formation, 166-168
  as political bodies, 162
  compassion in, 20.
  egalitarianism in, 20
  differentiation in, 164
  missionary goal of, 20
  traditional or folk, 14, 15, 29, 30, 32, 58, 67, 109, 119, 126, 129, 133, 139, 145, 146, 147, 148, 157, 159, 162, 164
  world, xix, 10, 13, 20, 144, 159, 161, 163
Resistance tradition, Biblical 179

Scripture translation, 43, 64, 66, 67, 68, 76, 102, 135
Sikh movement, 89
Sin, 177, 178, 182
Slaves, 11, 12, 58, 93, 127, 128, 136, 137, 138, 142, 143
Social identity, and intergroup relations, 28
  and moral order, 31
  and motivation, 30
  and religious identity, 31
  and social change, 29
  and social mobility, 6
  contribution of approach, 28
  definition of, 27
  perspective, 27, 168
  theory compared, 28
Social scientific model, xviii-xix
  and hypothesis testing, xix, 150
Sociology of knowledge, xiv, 187
Sociology of missions, xv, xvii-xx, 11
Subversive bricolages, 146

Taipings, 14, 112, 120
Theology, open to all, 174
Traders or trading, 41, 46, 80, 91, 94, 95, 108, 109, 122, 127, 128, 140
Trail of tears, 141
Tribe or tribal, 25, 41, 93, 105, 107, 112, 113, 119, 120, 142, 145, 160, 179
  resistant, 114

Uncertainty reduction, 30
Units of analysis, 9, 12
Untouchables, 12

Variables, background, 151
  circularity of, 170

dependent, 4, 5, 8, 13, 14
independent, 19, 31
intervening, 23
measuring, 35
modification of received religion, 171

Zoroastrianism, 43, 45, 54, 62, 83, 94, 95